National Currencies and Globalization

Globalization and money – two concepts inextricably linked. In many ways the speed with which financial resources traverse the globe, the opportunities which this provides for the efficient allocation of resources, the possibilities which this creates for financial crises, and the traders who act as agents removed from the concerns of national citizens have come to symbolize the phenomenon, hopes and fears of "globalization."

However, inextricably linked they may be, but well understood they are not. In the case of national currencies, a wide variety of predictions and analyses can be found. For some, national currencies represent barriers to a seamless global economy. Others argue that national currencies will disappear due to the power of international financial markets which will force national governments to adopt more credible currencies and abandon their own. In contrast, others see imperialism or regionalism as the main challenges.

Paul Bowles provides an innovative and systematic analysis of the implications of theories of globalization for national currencies. He critically examines whether, as a result, the world is heading for fewer currencies. He argues that the main "force of globalization" which is endangering national currencies is that of globalization as "neoliberal globalism." However, there is no single neoliberal position on money and so the "contingent" nature of neoliberalism explains why this particular force of globalization operates more strongly in some countries than others. This is demonstrated in case studies of four systemically significant currencies, namely, those of Australia, Canada, Mexico, and Norway.

National Currencies and Globalization will be of interest to researchers and students of International Political Economy, Politics, Economics, and Finance.

Paul Bowles is Professor of Economics and International Studies at the University of Northern British Columbia, Canada.

This series, published in association with the *Review of International Political Economy*, provides a forum for current debates in international political economy. The series aims to cover all the central topics in IPE and to present innovative analyses of emerging topics. The titles in the series seek to transcend a state-centred discourse and focus on three broad themes:

- the nature of the forces driving globalization forward
- resistance to globalization
- the transformation of the world order.

The series comprises two strands:
The *RIPE Series in Global Political Economy* aims to address the needs of students and teachers, and the titles will be published in hardback and paperback. Titles include:

Political Economy of a Plural World
Critical reflections on power, morals and civilizations
Robert Cox with Michael Schechter

A Critical Rewriting of Global Political Economy
Integrating reproductive, productive and virtual economies
V. Spike Peterson

Contesting Globalization
Space and place in the world economy
André C. Drainville

Global Institutions and Development
Framing the world?
Edited by Morten Bøås and Desmond McNeill

Global Institutions, Marginalization, and Development
Craig N. Murphy

Critical Theories, International Relations and 'the Anti-Globalisation Movement'
The politics of global resistance
Edited by Catherine Eschle and Bice Maiguashca

Globalization, Governmentality, and Global Politics
Regulation for the rest of us?
Ronnie D. Lipschutz, with James K. Rowe

Critical Perspectives on Global Governance
Rights and regulation in governing regimes
Jean Grugel and Nicola Piper

Routledge/RIPE Studies in Global Political Economy is a forum for innovative new research intended for a high-level specialist readership, and the titles will be available in hardback only. Titles include:

1. **Globalization and Governance ***
   Edited by Aseem Prakash and Jeffrey A. Hart

2. **Nation-States and Money**
   The past, present and future of national currencies
   Edited by Emily Gilbert and Eric Helleiner

3. **The Global Political Economy of Intellectual Property Rights**
   The new enclosures?
   Christopher May

4. **Integrating Central Europe**
   EU expansion and Poland, Hungary and the Czech Republic
   Otto Holman

5. **Capitalist Restructuring, Globalisation and the Third Way**
   Lessons from the Swedish model
   J. Magnus Ryner

6. **Transnational Capitalism and the Struggle over European Integration**
   Bastiaan van Apeldoorn

7. **World Financial Orders**
   An historical international political economy
   Paul Langley

8. **The Changing Politics of Finance in Korea and Thailand**
   From deregulation to debacle
   Xiaoke Zhang

9. **Anti-Immigrantism in Western Democracies**
   Statecraft, desire and the politics of exclusion
   Roxanne Lynn Doty

10. **The Political Economy of European Employment**
    European integration and the transnationalization of the (un)employment question
    Edited by Henk Overbeek

National Currencies and Globalization

Endangered specie?

Paul Bowles

Routledge
Taylor & Francis Group

LONDON AND NEW YORK

First published 2008
by Routledge
2 Park Square, Milton Park, Abingdon, Oxon OX14 4RN

Simultaneously published in the USA and Canada
by Routledge
270 Madison Ave, New York, NY 10016

Routledge is an imprint of the Taylor & Francis Group, an informa business

Typeset in Times by
HWA Text and Data Management, Tunbridge Wells
Printed and bound in Great Britain by
MPG Books Ltd, Bodmin

British Library Cataloguing in Publication Data
A catalogue record for this book is available from the British Library

Library of Congress Cataloging-in-Publication Data
A catalog record for this book has been requested

ISBN10: 0–415–77427–6 (hbk)
ISBN10: 0–203–93337–0 (ebk)

ISBN13: 978–0–415–77427–7 (hbk)
ISBN13: 978–0–203–93337–4 (ebk)

For Liam, Rowan, and Corin

Contents

Figures

Tables

Series preface

Money will always have a future, but understanding the contemporary foundations of that future is not an easy achievement to realize. Paul Bowles recognizes the puzzle of money and offers an intriguing way of thinking about it. For him, as for many others, the relationship between money and globalization is both self-evident and puzzling. It is self-evident insofar as an increasingly integrated and globalized world should almost of its own accord move towards a single global currency. It is puzzling that we should not be doing so; even stranger, national currencies today remain mostly robust and healthy in a highly competitive world. To understand why this is the case, Paul Bowles applies systematic logic and sound principles of political economy to analyse what he considers to be four "systematically significant" currencies, and concludes that they will remain part of the world of national currencies for some time yet.

A crucial contribution of Bowles' argument is to recast the debate about money and globalization to more accurately reflect what he identifies as the most significant "driver" of globalization: globalism, or more properly, a neoliberal globalism that is itself historically situated and contingent. The forces supporting globalization, when viewed through the empirics of currencies, are highly diverse and always engaged in contested ideological practices which do not allow sweeping, homogeneous claims to be made about them. And indeed, by looking closely at the case studies of Australian, Canadian, Mexican and Norwegian currency developments, Bowles demonstrates the deep institutional and historical foundations of their respective political economies. In this way Bowles practices a deeply historical form of international political economy, one which is able to fuse political, economic and social currents into an integrated analytical whole. Such an approach to IPE situates this manuscript very nicely in the tradition of the Series, alongside recent volumes edited by Brett Bowden and Leonard Seabrooke, Andreas Bieler and Adam David Morton, and Dieter Plehwe, Bernhard Walpen and Gisela Neunhöffer.

The Routledge/RIPE Series in Global Political Economy seeks to publish innovative and cutting edge scholarship that pushes forward our understanding of how the world is organized, why it is developing in particular directions, and how globalizing tendencies across a range of social relations are reinforcing or undermining these changes. This volume fits in with this mandate precisely because it subjects a key foundational element of our world – money – to sustained critical analysis. And it does this by undertaking a careful and systematic examination of globalization within the context of four well-developed case studies. This work will be read by those who value clear thinking, lucid writing and sustained analysis at the intersection of developments that are at once political, economic, social and ideological; and this is a wide readership indeed.

Louise Amoore
University of Newcastle upon Tyne, UK

Randall Germain
Carleton University, Canada

Rorden Wilkinson
University of Manchester, UK

Acknowledgments

In writing this book, I have benefited from the generosity and intellectual input of many people. Brian MacLean and Osvaldo Croci were co-authors on two early papers in this line of research, and I learned much from them. Jerry Cohen provided excellent critical comments on many of the chapters. I also benefited from comments from the three series editors and from three anonymous referees who reviewed the entire manuscript. In presenting parts of the argument of this book at various conferences and workshops over the last few years, I have learned much from the comments of experts in the field. Particular appreciation in this regard is extended to Mark Beeson, James Dean, Eric Helleiner, Richard Pomfret, Tom Willett, and Amy Verdun.

The book arises from my participation in a Social Sciences and Humanities Research Council of Canada Major Collaborative Research Initiative. The research team, known as *The Globalism Project*, was headed by Gordon Laxer, and I am grateful to him for inviting me to join the team and for encouraging me to write this book. Being part of the project gave me the opportunity to visit all four countries included as case studies here and to interview researchers in their central banks and other experts. In the course of interviewing Juan Carlos Moreno-Brid in Mexico and Ådne Cappelen in Norway, it became clear that we saw the world in similar ways and had similar intellectual interests. On the basis of these conversations, joint authorship of these two country chapters was discussed and agreed. I am grateful to both for contributing to this volume. Research on Australia was greatly enhanced by spending a sabbatical at the University of Adelaide. My thanks to Ray Broomhill for inviting me there and for filling me in on Australia's political economy.

Parts of this book, in earlier versions of the argument, have appeared in print previously, and I am grateful to the publishers for permission to reprint material here. Some of the material in Chapter 2 appeared in Bowles, P. (2005). A section of Chapter 3 draws upon Bowles, P., Croci. O. and MacLean, B. (2003). Some of the material in the country case studies draws on Bowles, P. (2004) and (2006) and Bowles, P., Croci, O. and MacLean, B. (2004).

To my partner, Fiona, I extend my love and thanks for her continued support. This book is dedicated to our three children, Liam, Rowan, and Corin, who among other things, prevented the writing of this book from becoming too much of an obsession.

1   Introduction

The questions

Globalization and money—two concepts inextricably linked. In many ways, the speed with which vast financial resources traverse the globe, the opportunities that this provides for the efficient allocation of resources, the possibilities that this creates for financial crises, and the bankers and foreign exchange traders who act as agents removed from the concerns of national citizens have come to symbolize the phenomenon, hopes, and fears of "globalization."

And yet, inextricably linked they may be, but well understood they are not. Globalization, a concept that, according to McGrew (2001: 293), has "colonized the intellectual imagination of the social sciences," remains deeply contested as to its meaning and its ability to accurately capture the dynamics of the contemporary phase of capitalism. There is no agreement as to what constitute the "forces of globalization." As a result, the implications of globalization for understanding the world of money remain complex. In the case of national currencies, a wide variety of predictions and analyses can be found.

For some, national currencies represent barriers to the free movement of goods and capital, the stitching that needs to be removed before the seamless global economy is complete. According to Rose and van Wincoop (2001), for example, national currencies represent a "barrier to international trade," the removal of which would provide significant economic benefits. "Globalization" requires, and is likely to lead to, the disappearance of national currencies. Others argue that national currencies will disappear because the power of global financial markets has become so great that national governments will find themselves forced to adopt more credible currencies and abandon their own. In such an environment, according to Taylor (2000), "only monies of the highest quality are likely to survive." Globalization as global financialization dictates this outcome.

For others, the spread of "dollarization" and "euroization" reflects imperial structures—the real structures of globalization. Here it is the "hegemony of the dollar" that acts as a symbol of U.S. imperial ambition and helps to explain the form that it takes. Thus, for Wade (2003), the role of the dollar in the global economy represents a part of "the invisible hand of the American empire," a part of the "paradox of economic globalization" (2003: 87) that appears as agentless process and yet reinforces the power of the United States.

In contrast, the birth of the euro represents an event of epochal significance to others, a significance that points to the emergence of regional, rather than global, currencies. For some, such as Beddoes (1999), "regional currencies" represent the future. Others still, the "globalization skeptics," see no epochal change, only neoliberal ideology at work—as globalism—as the force for removing monetary autonomy, and perhaps independent currencies, from national governments. For Fligstein (2001: 211), it is "the politics of domestic constituencies" that hold the key to understanding currency crises; globalization imposes no binding constraints on governments, and it is to domestic politics that we must look.

How can these competing interpretations and claims be assessed? If national currencies are an endangered specie, what are the "forces of globalization" causing this? Do they emanate from the processes of global economic integration? From imperial ambition? From the power of global financial markets? From regionalism? From neoliberal globalism? Globalization has been conceived in many different ways. To analyze in which guises and to what extent globalization threatens the landscape of national currencies that characterizes the contemporary world is the central concern of this book.

The originality of this book, and the first contribution I claim for it, is precisely that it interrogates the concept of globalization closely and, by doing so, teases out the implications explicitly for national monies. It does not assume at the outset "what globalization is" or assume that the dynamics of the contemporary period are self-evident. Rather, the contentious concept of globalization is critically analyzed itself, its various meanings are explored, and their implications for national monies are distilled. This enables us to tease out how *exactly* globalization is allegedly changing the currency landscape, which specific *forces* have been invoked, and which specific *actors* are involved. Globalization is such an open-ended term, its extent, measurement, and meaning so contested, that an analysis of its impacts requires that the scene setting be carried out carefully and in detail before the plot unfolds.

It is by taking this approach the book is able to make its second contribution, namely, identifying that the main "force of globalization" which is endangering national currencies is globalization as neoliberal globalism. Other versions of globalization, which specify different mechanisms, have some analytical purchase too, but the main driving force in the case studies presented here is that of globalism. However, its force has been felt unevenly and with different implications in the four countries analyzed; it is not just states' positions within the global political economy and their currencies' place within what Cohen (1998) has termed *the currency pyramid* that is important here, but states' domestic histories, institutional structures, and policy stances that determine whether, and how, neoliberal globalism endangers their currencies.

The thesis

Based on detailed case studies of four "systemically significant currencies" (SSCs), namely, those used by Australia, Canada, Mexico, and Norway, I argue that the main threat to the continued viability of these SSCs comes from globalization as neoliberal globalism. Certainly, economic integration, regional initiatives, and imperial ambitions have some explanatory power as well, but the main "force of globalization" that impinges on the future viability of the system of national currencies that we see in the world today is globalism. For all the attention paid to "global forces" in many contemporary debates, in the context of these systemically significant national currencies at least, it is the political economy of domestic debate that is critical.

However, there is a twist. Neoliberalism has no single position on money. In fact, there are many positions. So, whereas neoliberalism may have clearly identifiable and predictable implications for some policy areas, this is not the case for monetary governance. There may be a common neoliberal belief in "sound money," but the best of way of achieving it is a matter of debate. For this reason, I propose the concept of "contingent neoliberalism"—the idea that the content of neoliberal prescriptions depends on the context in which they are to be applied—as best explaining currency debates in the four countries studies here.

The "contingent" nature of neoliberalism explains why this particular force of globalization operates more strongly in some countries than others. It explains why the debates over national currencies were more vigorous in Canada and Mexico than they were in Australia and Norway. It also explains, for example, why the currency debate was quite different in Australia and Canada, two countries that otherwise share similar political and economic characteristics. And it explains why the currency issue was much more muted in Norway, where neoliberalism has not taken such a strong ideological hold. More contentiously, it also helps to explain, along with country-specific factors, why the vigorous currency debates that took place between roughly 1998 and 2003 in Canada and Mexico have disappeared from the political and economic radar screens as the influence of neoliberal globalism has waned.

The background

That the implications of globalization for the continued existence of national currencies should be a prominent feature of debate is not surprising. Historically speaking, the association of nation-states with national currencies has been a relatively recent one (Cohen, 1998; Helleiner, 2003). The question remains whether it will be a fleeting association as the forces of globalization undermine the nation-state and lead to a world of a few, or even one, supranational currencies.

In many countries, money initially came from many sources. Coins from numerous countries circulated within any particular set of national borders. It was only in the relatively recent past that it can unambiguously be said that nation-states have been dominant in the control of money. According to Helleiner

(2003: 243), "territorial currencies have had a relatively short life." Zevin (1992: 46) dates this life as the period 1870–1970. That is, it was only in the late nineteenth and twentieth centuries that money became truly national in character. The institutional accompaniment of this trend was the rise of national currency-issuing central banks.

Even in this period, there were numerous examples of countries either sharing or subordinating their monetary sovereignty, to use Cohen's terms (1998). He provides many examples—Panama, Liechtenstein, San Marino, Monaco, Andorra, Liberia, Lesotho, Namibia, Bhutan—of jurisdictions where the currency of another country has been used in lieu of a "national" currency and where monetary sovereignty has therefore been subordinated (1998: 48–9). Furthermore, sharing monetary sovereignty also has a nineteenth- and twentieth-century history, as the examples of the Latin Monetary Union, the Scandinavian Monetary Union, the Belgium-Luxembourg Economic Union, and the CFA Franc zone, among others, demonstrate (1998: 69–74).

These examples notwithstanding, Zevin's argument is essentially correct. Since around the 1970s, however, it has been argued that national currencies no longer exhibit a one-to-one correspondence with nation-states. For example, Scholte (2000: 52) argues that "the 'American' dollar, the 'Japanese' yen, and the 'German' mark and other 'national' currencies have undergone a significant degree of deterritorialization. They circulate globally, being used anywhere on earth at the same time and moving (electronically and via air transport) anywhere on earth in effectively no time … Money has become considerably (though of course not completely) detached from territorial space."

This deterritorialization of money is also supported by Cohen (1998: 17), who argues that "the notion of simple territorial currencies … is at best a convenient fiction. The organization of currency space, no less than political space, has become to some extent deterritorialized."

Evidence for this deterritorialization can also be found in the rapid expansion of financial markets—global financial markets. To give just one example, the daily turnover in foreign exchange markets increased from $100 billion in 1979 to more than $1.9 trillion in 2004 (Scholte, 2000: 86; BIS, 2005). Further evidence can be found in changing monetary arrangements around the world. New forms of "monetary governance" have emerged, most obviously in Europe where the long process of integration now includes a new common currency for thirteen of the EU member states and a European central bank.[1] The EU accession states in Central and Eastern Europe will also become part of the euro zone. In Asia, the response to the financial crises of 1997 has resulted in a new "monetary regionalism" emerging (Dieter, 2000) and the idea of an Asian currency unit has been floated (ADB, 2004). In both West and East Africa, currency union is on the agenda, with both regions planning to launch regional currencies in 2009; the Gulf Cooperation Council has announced it will do so a year later. In the Americas, El Salvador and Ecuador have unilaterally dollarized, and debates about dollarization have been evident in much of the continent, most notably in Argentina before its financial crisis in 2001, but the issue also received considerable attention from politicians and business groups alike in both Canada and Mexico. Although these debates and initiatives all involve governments, in many parts of the world citizens are increasingly adopting the U.S. dollar or other "safe" currencies in lieu of their own national currencies.

These issues have been analyzed by others, and there is already a significant body of literature. Among this, the recent contributions of Cohen (2004), Helleiner (2003), and Porter (2005) stand out as exemplars.[2] The latter analyzes the globalizing world of finance since the 1960s, arguing that it is quantitatively and qualitatively different from past episodes of "globalization." Porter distinguishes between money and finance and concentrates on the latter with relatively little analysis of money, and its national character, as such. His analysis is useful as a demonstration of the extent to which global markets have grown and, more especially, the range of actors that is now involved in, and the "institutional complexity" (2005: 13) of, the regulation and coordination of global finance. Porter's contribution is also useful in setting out some of the frameworks (market-based, state-centric, Marxist, and institutional) within which globalization is viewed and the contestations that surround this concept. The focus of these frameworks, however, is global finance rather than national currencies. For explicit analyses of the latter, we need to look elsewhere.

Helleiner (2003) adopts a historical approach, and he investigates the reasons for the emergence of national currencies. Here, he identifies two preconditions—the emergence of nation-states and the technology to produce money—and three primary motives, namely, "the desire to construct national markets, the various macroeconomic and fiscal goals, and the objective of strengthening national identities" (2003: 15). Helleiner also considers the "widespread nature of challenges to territorial currencies" (ibid.: 219) in the contemporary period. In this task, he finds the historical analysis illuminating in pointing to ways in which the challenges take both old and new forms. For him, the desire to construct global markets, the waning of belief in the efficacy of activist macroeconomic policy, and the emergence of new identities (both subnational and supranational) point to the forms that new challenges take. Thus, the contemporary era of globalization has led to challenges for territorial currencies. Nevertheless, he concludes that predictions of the demise of national currencies should be treated "very cautiously" (ibid.: 244).

Cohen (2004) opens with the question, "What is the future of money in an increasingly globalized world economy?" a question similar to that posed here. His answer: that the world will not see a dramatic reduction in the number of currencies. He argues that what he terms the "contraction contention"—the proposition that the number of currencies will significantly contract—is exaggerated, a conclusion also similar to that reached here.[3] What differs between our accounts is the reason for reaching this conclusion. Cohen takes as his starting point the increasing competition between currencies as sufficient proof that globalization, implicitly equated with an increase in cross-border flows, can be assumed and that the task is to analyze its implications, an analysis that considers the policy choices facing states at various levels of the currency pyramid. He concludes that those choices are unlikely to lead to many states giving up their currencies.

This volume may start with the question of how globalization affects national currencies, and it may conclude that they are endangered only to a limited degree, as other authors have also argued, but the claim made for this volume is that it explores more precisely globalization's effects and provides a unique explanation for reaching a common conclusion.

This conclusion is reached here on the basis of four detailed case studies. The aim is not to provide an exhaustive account of the possibilities for all currencies. Both Cohen (2004) and, to a lesser extent, Helleiner (2003) have provided this type of analysis. Here I focus in detail on four examples of currencies that, as I explain further below, can be seen as critical to an understanding of whether the *system* of national currencies is likely to continue in its current form.

In writing this book, I am able to claim a temporal advantage over other authors. Not only I have been able to benefit from their insights, but the challenges to national currencies are less "widespread" now than, say, five years ago when dollarization or currency unions (or both) were more prominently on the policy agenda. In one way, this makes my task easier in that the continuance of national currencies is probably a much less controversial conclusion than it was in the early 2000s, notwithstanding influential commentators, such as Wolf (2004) advocating a single global currency. However, it also opens up new intellectual questions for consideration, such as why the debates over national currencies seemed to peak in the early part of the decade and have disappeared in many countries since. What are the conjunctural factors that have led to this disappearance? What does this tell us about the "forces of globalization" that have been invoked to predict a move to fewer national currencies? In particular, I argue that the disappearance of the "national currency question" is, in part, a reflection of the broader waning of influence of neoliberal globalism, as suggested, for example, by Saul (2005) and Bello (2006).

The approach: identifying the "forces of globalization"

Assessing the impact of the forces of globalization on national currencies is not a straightforward empirical exercise; we need a theoretical framework within which the data can be interpreted. As noted above, the approach taken here differs from other discussions of currency issues by explicitly analyzing the implications of different theories of globalization for national currencies. The theoretical debates over the nature of globalization need to be reflected in the analysis of currency issues; the implications of globalization for national currencies depend on which approach to globalization is adopted. Different approaches posit different mechanisms and actors, and these need to be identified and examined if we are to get a better understanding of which of the forces of globalization are the most relevant in this context.

To obtain an analytical handle on the implications of globalization for national currencies, therefore, the first step is providing a guide to the vast literature on globalization itself. I therefore present a taxonomy of theories of globalization and, on the basis of this taxonomy, examine the implications of these theories of globalization for national currencies. This is set out in Part I of the book.

In Chapter 2, theories of globalization are differentiated on the basis of the changing relationship that they ascribe to states and markets. Four distinct categories are proposed in this taxonomy. The categories used are:

- *globalization*, according to which a technologically driven process is seen as strengthening markets and weakening nation-states;
- *globalism*, according to which the extent of global integration is seen as exaggerated and in which nation-states remain actually or potentially strong; the popularity of globalization is ascribed to its ideological use as a support for neoliberalism rather than its objective features. For this reason, this position can also be described as *neoliberal globalism*;
- *imperialism*, according to which globalization is seen as process that strengthens the states and firms of imperial powers but in which peripheral states and firms are weakened;
- *regionalism*, according to which new regional structures, economic or political (or both), are seen as the most accurate description of contemporary changes. Regionalism can be interpreted as being either complementary to, or as competing with, globalization.

Focusing on the relationship between states and markets as the central taxonomic device for analyzing national monies is an attractive one. Currencies have developed with nation-states over recent history. One of the questions arising from the alleged development of a "global market" is precisely the implications for nation-state-based currencies. It is useful, therefore, given that the topic under investigation concerns a nation-state institution and the global market, to differentiate between theories of globalization by how they posit the relationship between states and markets.

A similar approach is taken by Cohen (1998: 23), who argues that money can be best analyzed as having an "authoritative domain," a concept that "captures the critical role of not just one but both major influences on the geography on money, markets and governments." Differentiating between theories of globalization on the basis of their view of the relationship between state and market (as the two influences on the authoritative domain of money) arises from a similar judgment about what is important when analyzing money. The focus on the relationship between states and markets also permits us to place boundaries on what parts of the vast literature on globalization are most relevant here. "Globalization" has many dimensions: environmental, social, cultural, economic, and political. Here limits are necessarily placed on the discussion of globalization; in analyzing money, it is the economic and political dimensions that are given primacy.

Within each category of the taxonomy, money holds a special place as the questions identified in the opening section indicated. In Chapter 3, the implications of the four categories of theories of globalization for national currencies are examined in detail. Each category suggests a different future for national currencies. They also suggest different interpretations of the recent past as well. As we will see, each of the categories provides different perspectives on the operations of national and international monetary arrangements.

In examining the implications of theories of globalization for national currencies, both the politics and economics of monetary institutions and arrangements will require exploration. That is, we will need to consider both the *power theoretic* framework adopted by political scientists and the *choice theoretic* framework that characterizes the terrain usually inhabited by economists. For political scientists, money requires an analysis of power (see Andrews, 2006). Thus, monetary arrangements are seen as a reflection of, and as contributing toward, domestic and international power relations. For this reason, analysis of the Gold Standard era, the Bretton Woods era, and the post-Bretton Woods period all involve assessments of power relations in the international system. These assessments imply particular roles for the currencies of the most powerful states, most particularly the British pound, the U.S. dollar, the German mark, the Japanese yen, and now the euro. The prospects for national currencies will therefore require, in part, an examination of the politics of the international monetary system.

"Internal" or "domestic" politics also matters. The future of national currencies depends on the choice of the exchange-rate regime; national currencies will disappear if countries opt for the choice at one end of the spectrum—and this choice is not simply a technocratic one but reflects wider political pressures and constellations of interests (see Frieden, 1994). Different agencies within government may have interests in the adoption of certain policies, for example. The central bank and the Ministry of Finance would be obvious examples here. More broadly, firms in different sectors of the economy, firms with different trade exposures, labor organizations, and the general public may have preferences for types of exchange-rate regime. How globalization affects internal power relations and interests—that is, affects actors—also needs to be examined for its implications for exchange-rate choices.

Within the economics literature, choice theoretic considerations dominate, with states' choice of exchange rate and currency regime depending on rational calculations of welfare-maximizing agents. However, policy choice in this area is complicated by the fact that there are numerous examples of "exchange rate puzzles," instances of economic theory failing to match empirical reality. For example, Chen and Rogoff (2002: 6), have summarized the state of the literature as follows: "The connection between economic fundamentals and exchange rate behaviour has been one of the most controversial issues in international finance, manifesting itself in various major empirical puzzles such as the Meese–Rogoff (1983) puzzle and the purchasing power parity (PPP) puzzle." These two puzzles refer to the inability of economic theory to explain why exchange rates are so volatile and why national price levels respond so slowly to changes in the exchange rate; in other words, why there is so little "connection between economic fundamentals and exchange rate behaviour" (ibid.; see also Obstfeld and Rogoff, 2000).

This points to a wider characteristic of the economics literature on exchange rates: it is a field with few empirical certainties, and this has contributed to its being prone to fads. Exchange rate policy becomes prone to policy cycles or swings of the "pendulum."[4] Sometimes fixed exchange rates are the flavor of the month; other times hard fixes, such as currency boards and dollarization; intermediate regimes (such as crawling pegs) went out of fashion in the 1990s but have subsequently made something of a comeback, whereas floating rates have always had their supporters. Thus, though there have been several high-profile conferences, such as that sponsored by the IMF (2000) entitled "One World, One Currency: Destination or Delusion?" suggesting that the emergence of a "global economy" might lead to a parallel emergence of a "global currency," it is nevertheless necessary to ask whether this represents a trend or an eye-catching fad whose time has passed.

Combining the power theoretic and the choice theoretic frameworks will enable us to use a broad political-economy approach to examine the implications of different theories of globalization for the continued viability of national currencies. In Part I of the book, the scope of the discussion will be global and will draw on examples and trends from around the world.

The approach: analyzing four "systemically significant currencies" (SSCs)

In Part II of the book, covering Chapters 4–7, the focus moves to case studies of specific countries and their currencies. The chapters on Australia, Canada, Mexico (co-authored with Juan Carlos Moreno-Brid), and Norway (co-authored with Ådne Cappelen) provide the finer grain, the texture that enables us to feel the contours of the contemporary debate over globalization and its implications for national currencies.

Exercises in what might be called *currency accounting* can be useful. There are several measures that could be used to gauge the relative importance of different currencies. For example, currencies could be ranked in terms of their use in foreign exchange trading, in the cross-border liabilities of banks, in the composition of official foreign exchange reserves, or in the issue of debt instruments.[5] Here, I present one such measure—the use of currencies in foreign exchange transactions—to provide an admittedly approximate but nevertheless indicative guide to the relative importance of various national currencies. This measure reveals that the U.S. dollar is used in nearly one-half of all currency transactions, with the euro, the yen, and the pound sterling lagging behind, as shown in Table 1.1 These four major currencies are then followed by a "long tail" as the use of another 22 currencies in the world's foreign exchange markets slowly falls. The remainder of the world's currencies—approximately 120 of them—constitutes only 3 per cent of daily foreign exchange turnover. This ranking, and the percentages accounted for by the various currencies, have remained fairly stable since the early 1990s.

In the field of global economic governance, the economic hierarchy is reflected in various groupings of countries. The G7 represent the leading Western

Table 1.1 Currency distribution of reported foreign exchange market turnover, 1992–2004 (selected years, percentage shares of average daily turnover in April)

	1992	1995	1998	2001	2004
US dollar	82.0	83.3	87.3	90.3	88.7
Euro	~	~	~	37.6	375
Deutsche mark[2]	39.6	36.1	30.1	~	~
French franc	3.8	7.9	5.1	~	~
ECU and other EMS currencies	11.8	15.7	17.3	~	~
Japanese yen	23.4	24.1	20.2	22.7	20.3
Pound sterling	13.6	9.4	11.0	13.2	18.9
Swiss franc	8.4	7.3	7.1	6.1	6.1
Australian dollar	2.5	2.7	3.1	45	5.5
Canadian dollar	3.3	3.4	3.6	4.5	4.2
Swedish krona[3]	1.3	0.6	0.4	2.6	2.3
Hong Kong dollar[3]	1.1	0.9	1.3	2.3	1.9
Norwegian krone[3]	0.3	0.5	0.4	1.5	1.4
Korean won[3]	...	...	0.2	0.8	1.2
Mexican peso[3]	...	...	0.6	0.9	1.1
New Zealand dollar	0.2	0.5	0.3	0.6	1.0
Singapore dollar[3]	0.3	0.3	1.2	1.1	1.0
Danish krone[3]	0.5	0.6	0.4	1.2	0.9
South African rand[3]	0.3	0.2	0.5	1.0	0.8
Russian rouble[3]	...	...	0.3	0.4	0.7
Polish zloty[3]	...	....	0.1	0.5	0.4
Taiwan dollar[3]	...	...	0.1	0.3	0.4
Indian rupee[3]	...	...	0.1	0.5	0.3
Brazilian real[3]	...	...	0.4	0.4	0.2
Czech koruna[3]	...	...	0.3	0.2	0.2
Thai baht[2]	...	...	0.2	0.2	0.2
Hungarian forint[3]	...	...	0.0	0.0	0.2
Chilean peso[3]	...	...	0.1	0.2	0.1
Malaysian ringgit[3]	...	...	0.0	0.1	0.1
Other currencies	7.7	7.1	8.2	6.5	6.1
All currencies	200.0	200.0	200.0	200.0	200.0

Source BIS, www.bis.org (2005: 9)

Notes
1   Because two currencies are involved in each transaction, the sum of the percentage shares for individual currencies totals 200% instead of 100%. The figures relate to reported "net–net" turnover, i.e., they are adjusted for local and cross-border double-counting.
2   Data for April 1998 exclude domestic trading involving the Deutsche mark in Germany.
3   For 1992–8, the data cover home currency only.

economies, with Russia often tagging along to make it the G8. In 1999, a new body was formed, the G20, which expanded the group to include "systemically important economies," economies that though not of the top tier are nevertheless important for the stability of the global economic system.

The world of currencies can be viewed in an analogous way. Using the data provided in Table 1.1, we can classify the dollar, euro, yen, and pound as the G4 of the currency world. Next come thirteen currencies, from the Swiss franc to the Russian ruble, which are used in trading to an extent that they are significant members of the currency system as it now operates. If the *system* of predominantly national currencies—the euro being the exception—that now operates is to change in a major way, it will have to involve these G17 currencies; in this sense, they are SSCs.[6] The creation of the euro has already led to change; indeed, it is for this reason that some commentators have regarded the change as "epochal" as signaling a new currency order no longer based on national currencies. However, whether this is indeed the case or whether it is instead an example of "European exceptionalism" depends on the forces operating on other SSCs. The SSCs may not be the first national currencies to disappear but, if we wish to analyze whether the system of national currencies is undergoing fundamental change, it is on the SSCs that we must focus.

The "system" of national currencies can be defined in terms of simply the number of currencies in existence. That is, the rough correspondence of the number of separate currencies with the number of nation-states could be seen as defining the system. And yet, within this system, some currencies are clearly more important than others in terms of the extent of their circulation and their importance in international exchange and, consequently, the significance of their potential disappearance. If some countries form a currency union—such as those currently being proposed in West Africa or in the Gulf—this undoubtedly has important implications for them. However, the quantitative significance of their currencies in international exchange is minimal, and their adoption of a common currency will have little impact on the overall picture presented in Table 1.1; certainly the euro is a much more significant development in these terms. It is to the quantitatively more important currencies that we must look to spot the most potentially significant changes to the currency system.

The currencies of Australia, Canada, Norway, and Mexico were ranked sixth, seventh, tenth, and twelfth, respectively, in 2004 in currency transactions (see Table 1.1). They fall in the G17 group of currencies but outside of the G4. Combined, they account for more than 6 percent of the international foreign exchange dealings, more than twice the turnover of the 120 or so currencies that make up the "long tail" beyond the G17. If the world's currency mapping is to be changed, it is here that change will have to occur. If a few currencies in the lower reaches of the long currency tail disappear, the wider implications of this are limited; if one or more systemically significant currencies disappear, the implications for our understanding of the currency mapping may fundamentally change. If Mexico dollarizes, if Canada and the United States form a currency union, if Norway joins the euro, if Australia joins an "Asian currency bloc," this is important not only for the countries involved but also for how the wider currency system is configured.

If we are looking to see whether significant changes are taking place (or will), if we want to know whether national currencies are an endangered specie, the SSCs are the crucial ones to consider. As McCallum (2000: 7), then chief economist at the Royal Bank of Canada, noted, "[I]n a world that would otherwise have only three currencies, it is unlikely that the Canadian dollar would constitute the fourth." If we are moving to a world of fewer currencies and a different system of national currencies, we must look at the Canadian dollar and currencies of similar significance to understand which forces are leading to this outcome. By providing an analysis of four SSCs, the extent of the changes underway and their causes can be more clearly seen.

The four countries whose currencies provide the case studies all occupy a middle position within the international political economy, a position that is reflected in the usage of their currencies in the foreign exchange markets. All of these countries have long been much more open to international pressures and stimuli than core countries. All four are closely integrated into the United States and Western-centered global order as junior partners. They were all exposed to forms of global integration early in their political histories. A history they share in varying degrees is that, as countries long subjected to the influences of powerful core countries, they developed state-centered policies aimed at overcoming market disadvantage, and achieving more autonomy, diversified development, and redistribution of incomes. Even though expressions of domestic autonomy were always conditioned by external constraints, their policies diverged significantly from the classical liberal models of Britain and the United States. Social class configurations were affected by the nature of these economies' insertion into global production and trade. Analyzing country experiences permits a more detailed discussion of how class and sectoral interests support particular exchange rate regimes. All of the countries have sought throughout their histories, albeit to varying extents and with varying degrees of success, to first define and then to defend "national identities and institutions" in the face of imperial and globalizing forces.

In these more qualitative respects, all of the four countries can be seen as belonging to a group of middle countries. Their histories have perhaps peculiarly been shaped by the twin forces of external imperatives emanating from world markets and world powers on the one hand and the internal pressures for national autonomy on the other. As such, the four countries offer a rich analytical terrain on which to examine the implications of globalization for national currencies; they are countries where the "global" and the "national" have long contested dominance.

All four countries have retained their national currencies. However, in each there have been contemporary debates and analyses about whether they should switch to a different form of monetary arrangement. In Mexico, this has taken the form of a debate over dollarization with the United States, a debate that has also occurred in Canada, although there a monetary union with the United States has been prominently advocated. In Norway, the relationship with and impact of the euro has been the focus of attention, and in Australia there has been discussion of an ANZAC dollar, although most of the impetus for this has come from the New Zealand side of the Tasman Sea. Each country can also claim some uniqueness in its exchange rate and currency affairs. Canada has stood out in the period since the Second World War as one of the few countries that has favored flexible exchange rates over most of the period. Australia, in contrast, adhered to fixed exchange rates from 1901 until 1983. Norway was the first non-EU country to peg its currency against the ECU. Mexico has the dubious privilege of being the country that experienced in 1994 what some have called the first exchange rate crisis of a new global period.

The context and the debates over national currencies have therefore been quite distinct in each of the four countries, even though the countries are comparably positioned in the international political economy and their currencies are of similar significance as national currencies. In examining these four country case studies, therefore, we will analyze which forces of globalization best explain the course of the debates in them, drawing on the four categories of globalization theories set out in Part I. In other words, we will ask how approaches to globalization help to understand the currency debates occurring in these countries and whether one particular approach is able to shed more light than the others in understanding the disparate experiences of countries holding similar positions within the international political economy.

Each country study assesses the explanatory power of theories of globalization. As such, the book is a contribution to both the specialized field of studies in money and to the broader field of globalization studies. In this way, it is hoped that both the "money specialists" and "globalization generalists" will find the book's arguments of interest.

In Chapter 8, the concluding chapter, the case studies are reviewed comparatively, and the case for the "contingent neoliberalism" explanation providing the most insight into the debates in the four countries is summarized. I also discuss why the debate has disappeared and link this to arguments that posit the waning of "globalism" more generally.

Part I

Globalization and national currencies

2 The economic and political dynamics of globalization

Four interpretations

Introduction

The phenomenon popularly referred to as globalization has been interpreted in many ways. Classifying these interpretations in a way that attempts to bring some categorization to a large and disparate literature so that analytical clarity can be brought to bear on aspects of globalization is no easy task. My task is made easier, however, as I know what I want to use my classification for: to shed light on the relationship between globalization and national currencies. As I argued in Chapter 1, for the purposes of analyzing the impacts of globalization on national currencies, the most useful classification is one that distinguishes between theories of globalization based on the ways in which they view the relationship between states and markets, the two agencies influencing what Cohen (1998) referred to as the "authoritative domain" of money. This purpose also provides the rationale for paying primary attention to the economic and political dimensions of globalization in constructing a taxonomy.[1]

From this starting point, it is possible to identify four main categories of theories. These can be briefly stated:

1 *Globalization* as a primarily technologically driven process that strengthens markets and market actors while weakening and requiring adaptation by nation-states. This interpretation argues therefore that globalization weakens the nation-state.
2 *Globalization* as a "myth" that has not significantly weakened the national basis of economic activity or the dominance of nation-states. The popularity of "globalization" has more to do with its neoliberal ideological agenda than as an objective description of contemporary capitalism; that is, it is an ideology of *globalism*. The globalism interpretation regards states as still (actually or potentially) powerful.
3 *Globalization* as *imperialism*. Some states are weakened by globalization while other states and their market actors (corporations) are strengthened. The process of globalization is a strategy designed to enhance the interests of imperial powers by opening up the markets of weaker countries. In this

interpretation, some states—imperial states—are still powerful and possibly becoming more so.

4   *Globalization* as inadequate as a descriptor of the processes underway; the contemporary period is better described as one of regionalization or *regionalism* (or both). Nation-states may be weakened, but emerging governance structures are regional in nature (at both the macro- and micro-regional levels) rather than global. The contention in this interpretation is that regionalism is more important.

Each interpretation, therefore, posits a different relationship between the nation-state and "the market" in the contemporary period. Within each category, however, a range of theories can be found that explain this particular state-market relationship. In some cases, this range is rather small. For example, authors who view globalization as a form of imperialism are largely (although even here not exclusively) influenced by Marxist writings. Other categories contain a more heterogeneous collection of writings. This is particularly the case for the first interpretation that views globalization as weakening nation-states. Theories are assigned to each of these categories by their analyses of state–market relations but this, of course, allows for diversity among them on the causes and desirability of the processes that they analyze. That is, theories are classified on the basis of the relationship that they posit between state and market; they may, and often do, differ in other important respects.

The categorization of theories used here finds resonance with classifications made by other commentators. Held et al. (1999: 10), for example, distinguish between hyperglobalists, skeptics and transformationalists as a device for distinguishing between theories analyzing the politics, economics, and culture of globalization. The hyperglobalist position is closely related to that of (1) in the list above, whereas the skeptic's position overlaps with that found in (2), and possibly (4), above. As another example, Hobson and Ramesh (2002: 5) write that "much, although certainly not all, of the literature on globalization is cast in terms of two main propositions: either a 'strong globalization/decline of the state' or 'weak globalization/strong state' thesis." The former category corresponds to (1) above, whereas the second category corresponds to (2) and possibly elements of (4) above. The taxonomy presented here, therefore, is broadly consistent with that provided by others. I prefer the fourfold classification as it allows for a wider range of state–market relationships to be specified and analyzed. This provides for a richer set of possibilities in examining the implications of views of globalization for national currencies, the topic of the next chapter.

The remainder of this chapter sets out in more detail the arguments that have been used in support of each the four interpretations of globalization identified above. The aim is not to be exhaustive in presenting summaries of the four positions but rather to be illustrative, to provide the reader with sufficient information to move on to the implications of these positions for national currencies but not to be overburdened by the scale of the literature surveyed. In providing these summaries, a broad brush approach is therefore taken but it should be noted that each of the categories outlined here have also undergone some internal change over the last two decades of debate, and some of the language has also departed from its original meaning. For example, the globalism view is, as indicated above, associated with a "skeptical" view of globalization, although the term *globalization skeptic* has itself expanded from its meaning used here— to signify those who are skeptical of the existence of globalization—to now also include those who are skeptical of the benefits of globalization (and may therefore fall within my first category). Imperialism was until relatively recently a term confined to Marxist circles but has now again become more broadly academically acceptable. The "regions" that underpin regional analyses placed greater emphasis on Japan in the 1980s but much less so in the 1990s and 2000s as Japan slumped and China reemerged. The categories presented here, therefore, constitute a snapshot, but it should be remembered that it is taken of a literature that is itself evolving.

Globalization as weakening the nation-state

This is probably the most well known of the four views and finds support across the political spectrum. According to this view, the beginning of the twenty-first century is marked by an inexorable and inevitable process of globalization driven by technological change. The basis of this is the information, computing, and telecommunications (ICT) revolution that allows the possession, processing, and transmission of huge quantities of information at very low cost and at very high speed. In general, this view sees globalization as a technologically driven process with the current period (dated variously as from the 1970s onward) characterized by the scope and intensity of technological change, a factor that differentiates the contemporary era from both the immediate prior period and from other episodes of "globalization" that have occurred in the past. On this reading, globalization is also "inevitable."

Technology is identified as a critical (although not necessarily the only) causal factor. For example, the World Bank (2002: 325) answers its rhetorical question, "What is globalization?" as follows: "In broad terms it reflects the growing links between people, communities, and economies around the world. These links are complex—the result of lower communications and transport costs and greater flows of ideas and capital between high- and low-income countries."

On the basis of this definition, the Bank (2002: 326) continues by distinguishing between three waves of globalization, each of which is defined in technological terms.

> The first wave of global integration, between 1870 and 1914, was led by improvements in transport technology (from sailing ships to steamships) and by lower tariff barriers. Exports nearly doubled to about 8 percent of world trade. The second wave from 1945 to 1980, was also characterized by lower trade barriers and transport costs. Sea freight charges fell by a third between 1950 and 1970. And trade regained the ground it lost during the Great

Depression. Spurring the third wave of integration has been further progress in transport (containerization and airfreight) and communications technology (falling telecommunications costs associated with satellites, fiber-optic cable, cell phones, and the Internet). And along with declining tariffs on manufactured goods in high-income countries, many developing countries lowered barriers to foreign investment and improved their investment climates.

Globalization in this and other periods is, therefore, seen as being driven by scientific advance coupled with policy responses that lower barriers to economic flows. Such a starting point is not confined to international institutions. For example, the Global Policy Forum (GFP), an NGO with consultative status at the UN, also appeals to the technological basis of globalization:

> Human societies across the globe have established progressively closer contacts over many centuries, but recently the pace has dramatically increased. Jet airplanes, cheap telephone service, email, computers, huge oceangoing vessels, instant capital flows, all these have made the world more interdependent than ever. Multinational corporations manufacture products in many countries and sell to consumers around the world. Money, technology and raw materials move ever more swiftly across national borders.[2]

The GFP collates various measures of this global "connectivity" arising from technological and other trends. For example, the percentage of the world's population that are Internet users has risen from 0.73 percent in 1996 to 9.57 percent in 2002. The radio took thirty-eight years from invention to 50 million users; the World Wide Web took only four years.[3]

Other analyses posit a key role to technology although they also rely on other interrelated and codependent causal factors to explain the onset of globalization. Scholte (2000: 99), for example, argues that "globalization patently could not have occurred in the absence of extensive innovations in respect of transport, communications and data processing" although he adds rationalism, capitalism, and political regulation as other causes.[4]

The argument advanced is that these technological changes are leading to (or have led to) a global economy as evidenced by the trends in production, trade, and finance. With respect to production, it is argued that there has been a dramatic change in the way in which businesses operate and that they have "gone global." The period prior to 1980 looked more like the linking of national economies, whereas now we see genuine global production and markets.

Scholte (2000), in one of the most popular textbooks on globalization, uses the term *supraterritorial* to describe the way in which firms have had their relationship with territorial space changed by globalization. He argues (2000: 125) that:

> thousands of firms have in the context of globalization given their organization a substantial supraterritorial dimension, either by establishing affiliates in two or more countries or by forging strategic alliances with enterprises

based in other countries. Some of these global company networks are huge. For example, as of the mid-1990s the Unilever corporation encompassed more than 500 subsidiaries in over 90 countries. ... Global companies have acquired a very prominent place in contemporary capitalism. For example, the collective annual sales of the 50 largest unitary global enterprises rose from $540 billion in 1975 to $2,100 billion in 1990, equivalent to around 10 percent of recorded world product.

For this reason, Scholte prefers the term *transborder companies* to multinational corporation.

An integrating world economy can be seen from the data that between 1990 and 2002, the percentage of trade in goods to world GDP increased from 32.5 percent to 40.3 percent; gross private capital flows increased from 10.1 percent of world GDP to 20.8 percent; and gross direct foreign investment from 2.7 percent to 6.0 percent of world GDP (see World Bank, 2004: 308). The turnover in foreign exchange markets is approximately $2 trillion a day, more than forty times the daily volume of world trade.

All of this has led more populist writers, such as Ohmae (1990), to point, in a provocative but brilliantly encapsulating phrase, to the "borderless world" and underlies Friedman's claim (2005) that the "world is flat," with corporations, as a result of the ICT revolution, being able to roam anywhere on the global plains. For Friedman, the latest phase of globalization dates from 2000 based on the personal computer, fiber-optic cable, and "work flow software" (2005: 10).

It should be noted, however, that while this view of the world can readily be found in business-oriented publications, in the documents of the Bretton Woods institutions and in the NGO movement, it can also be found in the work of those who adopt Marxist approaches. For example, Teeple (2000) argues that the 1970s witnessed the start of a "revolution in the means of production" with this revolution being "grounded in the development of computers" (2000: 13). Furthermore, "these changes were revolutionary because of the qualitative turn they brought to the pursuit of knowledge, the objectification of science, the transmission of information and the production process" (2000: 13). The result of this revolution was that "national structures of accumulation" were no longer compatible with the new technologically driven global accumulation strategies of firms. As a result, Teeple argues that the role of nation-state has changed and been weakened. As he colorfully puts it, "[I]f the 'first' bourgeois revolutions represented the political consolidation of capitalism by creating the nation-state, then this 'second' bourgeois revolution is the globalization of national regimes of accumulation. It represents a shift from the mitigated framework for capital, the Keynesian Welfare State, liberal democracy, and so on, into a more or less unmitigated framework, supranational agencies for capital alone" (2000: 14). These supranational agencies (such as the IMF, the World Bank, the WTO, and the BIS) oversee a corporate-dominated globalization in which there is a "decline of national political powers" (2000: 17). Indeed, Teeple argues that globalization represents "the end of national history" (2000: 22).[5]

For Desai (2004), globalization represents "Marx's revenge." Revenge, that is, against twentieth-century attempts to construct state socialism under his name. Desai invokes Marx's belief that capitalism would come to an end only after it had become global and had played fully its historic role of developing the productive forces. Capitalism was playing this role until it was sidetracked by the First World War. For the next seventy years, state socialist and capitalist countries, although in their different ways, deglobalized the world as the state took center stage in economic management. However, it is "the underdevelopment of capitalism that allows and supports substantial market intervention. As capitalism develops, it sheds rather than strengthens such restrictions" (2004: 214).

When capitalism underwent a process of "reglobalization" in the 1980s, therefore, the state as economic manager was weakened. Capitalism became more like Marx's vision of a "self-organizing organic process" (2004: 222) with a more limited role for the state. The reglobalized economy has placed severe restrictions on the ability of states to manage their economic affairs. As Desai argues, "the state has to adapt and adjust to forces which it cannot control but must respond to" (2004: 300). And it is applicable to all states: "For the first time in two hundred years, the cradle of capitalism—the metropolis, the core—has as much to fear from the rapidity of change as does the periphery" (2004: 305). As with Friedman (2005), the world is now flat and all countries face the same pressures from a technologically driven globalization.

This is a conclusion that finds wide agreement. Scholte (2000: 102) for example argues that globalization has "put even regulators from the most powerful states under great pressure to facilitate the rise of supraterritoriality." For Susan Strange (1997), globalization has marked the "retreat of the state" as a result of the "diffusion of power" in the world economy among non-state actors.

The conclusion that a primarily technologically driven globalization has weakened the nation-state is therefore a common proposition. The point is that in all these accounts, the integration of markets, the increased mobility of capital, and increases in connectedness have reduced the efficacy of state regulatory regimes. As they all share this same position, I group all of these theories together here for the purposes of my taxonomy. Obviously, they differ in other ways, including what mechanisms they specify to lead them to this common conclusion. There is also a sharp divide between them on the desirability of this dynamic and the appropriate policy responses to it.

For the proponents of globalization, the reduced role for the state is a desirable outcome. Or, put in a different way, neoliberalism is the rational policy response to globalization. It is not so much the cause of globalization as the policy response necessary to ensure that globalization achieves its potential. For advocates, the new global economy offers the prospect of rising living standards for all, through increased trade and the international diffusion of technology, and of the consolidation of democratic institutions. An open global economy offers the developing countries, for example, the opportunity to "catch up" with the core countries. The vehicle for this "catch-up" is the access to technology embodied in traded goods and from the technology that open borders can bring with the global corporation. The policy implications of this are that national governments should maximize the flow of technology, the basis for the new global economy, into their countries through a package of trade and investment liberalization measures; security of property rights, including intellectual property rights; low taxes on profits to encourage firms to operate in one particular jurisdiction rather than another; a stable monetary order; and a ready, disciplined, and low-taxed supply of highly trained workers. Any state able to refashion itself in this way would be well placed in the new global economy.

The implication of this is that it is firms—mobile capital—that have new power as the much-sought-after providers of success in the global economy. International agreements, such as free trade agreements, world trade liberalization, and multinational investment agreements, are seen as providing the international architecture necessary to encourage the greatest spread of the benefits of global firms. These types of agreements tie the hands of national governments in many ways, ways that are viewed as beneficial by the supporters of globalization because they prevent interventionist politicians from interfering with the course of market progress. Thus, with capital-friendly national governments and capital-friendly international agreements, globalization is seen as delivering greater economic efficiency and higher levels of material well-being to all who participate. As a result, governments are not only becoming more limited in scope but state policies are converging toward a common set of "market-friendly" policies as policy makers are increasingly exposed to the inexorable logic of the global economy.

It is important to note that supporters of globalization not only claim that all can prosper by participation in the global economy but that poor countries will benefit more than others; as a result, global income inequality can be expected to decline, and economic convergence will occur. In the language of economists, this is referred to as "conditional convergence" (i.e., convergence is conditional on the right—read neoliberal—policies being adopted).

If the conditions are right, a utopia is possible. Consider, for example, the views of prominent Chicago economist Robert Lucas (2000):

> Ideas can be imitated and resources can and do flow to places where they earn the highest returns. Until perhaps 200 years ago, these forces sufficed to maintain a rough equality of incomes across societies (not, of course, within societies) around the world. The industrial revolution overrode these forces for equality for an amazing two centuries: That is why we call it a "revolution." But they [the forces of equality] have reasserted themselves in the last half of the 20th century, and I think the restoration of inter-society income equality will be one of the major economic events of the century to come.

Globalization, by facilitating the flow of ideas and resources, leads Lucas to predict that by 2100 all states could be "equally rich and growing."

The same contours of globalization are analyzed very differently by the opponents of globalization. For them, globalization, applied within a neoliberal framework, presents us with a new catastrophe, economically, socially, politically, culturally, and environmentally. The rise of corporate power and the increasing inability of nation-states to control their activities as corporations become "stateless" present opponents with a scenario of an undemocratic, intensified capitalism. States are forced to comply with the demands of global corporations in the latter's pursuit of profits. The drive for profits by global corporations opens up more and more areas of life to corporate or market control; new areas are commodified and others, such as health and education, are re-commodified. States themselves are commodified and seek to "brand" themselves, as van Ham (2001) puts it. According to him, "Singapore and Ireland are no longer merely countries one finds in an atlas. They have become "brand states," with geographical and political settings that seem trivial compared to their emotional resonance among an increasingly global audience of consumers. A brand is best described as a customer's idea about a product; the brand state comprises the outside world's ideas about a particular country" (van Ham, 2001: 2). In the competitive struggle to attract foreign investment and maintain political influence, states seek to develop a good "brand image."

As technology leads corporations to dominate the world and as the ability of states to regulate them and protect citizens declines, the expected outcome is increased inequality and economic insecurity. The economic insecurity arising from the "global turbulence" caused by global financial markets is also a prominent feature of this new stage of capitalism.

According to this interpretation, the desirable policy response is to develop new forms of (non-neoliberal) governance that enable the benefits of globalization to be realized. That is, because globalization is a result of technological change and as such can provide beneficial outcomes, the task becomes to fashion the (non-neoliberal) governance structures and policies that lead to the realization of these outcomes. Consider, for example, the World Commission on the Social Dimensions of Globalization (2004), which reports that "the potentials of globalization, in terms of growing connectivity and productive capacity, are immense. However, current systems of governance of globalization at national and international levels have not realized such potentials for most of the world's people – and in many instances have made matters worse." They continue, "we judge that the problems that we have identified are not due to globalization as such but to deficiencies in its governance" (2004: xi). What is required, therefore, are new forms of global and national governance to make good the potential benefits of an irreversible and technologically-driven globalization.

Globalism as ideology with nation-states still powerful

A second set of theories starts from the premise that the argument set out above about the relative decline of nation-states greatly exaggerates the extent of "globalization." As an empirical matter, it is argued that the vast majority of production and investment—around 90 percent—remains national in character. For example, Lipsey et al. (1995: 60–1) write that "given all the attention that 'globalization' has received from scholars, international organizations, and the press, [our data] are a reminder of how large a proportion of economic activity is confined to single geographical locations and home country ownership. Internationalization of production is clearly growing in importance, but the vast majority of production is still carried out by national producers within their own borders."

This "home country bias," meaning that firms and consumers are much more likely to trade with and purchase from fellow nationals than across borders with foreigners, has been supported by numerous studies. For example, Helliwell (1998: 118), after reviewing the data on flows of goods, capital, and people, concludes that "the striking size and pervasiveness of border effects reveal that the global economy of the 1990s is really a patchwork of national economies, stitched together by threads of trade and investment that are much weaker than the economic fabric of nations."

The long-standing Feldstein-Horioka (1980) result that domestic savings and investment rates are highly correlated suggests that international capital markets remain limited as devices for redistributing the world's capital.[6] Zevin (1992) also argues that international financial markets are now only reaching the levels of integration that they attained in the late nineteenth century. In fact, he argues that "while financial markets have certainly tended toward greater openness since the end of the Second World War, they have reached a degree of integration that is neither dramatic nor unprecedented in the larger historical context of several centuries" (1992: 43). As Bairoch (1996: 173) has written, "[W]hat many regard as a new phenomenon is not necessarily so." What globalization there is, therefore, is hardly new.

The rise of the "global firm" is also cast into doubt. Veseth (1998: 49–50; italics in original), for example, argues that a global firm signifies

> a business form that both produces and sells in global pools—that it exhibits both demand-side and supply-side globalization. There is a qualitative difference between a global firm, as defined here, and a firm that produces in one place and sells everywhere or has international production processes but essentially sells in distinct local markets (with distinct local character and competition). The former type of firm is multilocal and the latter is transnational. These are important and growing types of business arrangements, but they are not *global* in a meaningful sense. ... The definition of a globalized business is not easy to satisfy. There are not many truly global firms, but some do exist.[7]

As Vertora (2006: 6) notes, for the skeptics "TNCs are seen as national companies with international operations, but subject to national controls."

Furthermore, the role of the state in the economy as measured by the share of government spending in the national incomes of the core capitalist economies shows no sign of being reduced (despite the best efforts of neoliberal governments to achieve this outcome). For example, Navarro *et al.* (2004: 133) argue that the welfare states of most developed capitalist countries have not converged during the globalization period towards a reduced welfare state. On the contrary, over the globalization period, whether measured as a share of GDP or by public employment, welfare states have grown across the large majority of the world's richest economies. Also, during this period, welfare states have continued to be different, retaining their individual characteristics, shaped primarily by the dominant political tradition that governed each country during the pre-globalization period.

This line of reasoning is supported by a plethora of studies pointing to the continued importance of national systems. Summarizing this literature, Radice (2000: 721) writes that

> many writers argue that both the extent and the consequences of globalization have been greatly exaggerated: recent monograph contributions along these lines ... as well as a raft of shorter contributions ... indicate the wide support for this "sceptical" view of globalization. Equally, although some "comparativists" have charted the erosion of "Rhenish" and/or East Asian models by both external and internal pressures for change ... many have maintained that national differences are not being significantly eroded, and this is probably the majority view among students of comparative political economy.

To draw on just one example from this literature, consider the conclusion of Fligstein (2001: 189) who argues that

> there is no evidence that the world is converging on a single form of state-finance sector-industrial corporation relations. Families, managers, and states alternate in their domination of ownership in various societies. There is also little evidence that relations between firms are converging toward markets, hierarchies, networks, or strategic alliances as the dominant form of governance, and stable situations with different configurations abound across various societies. Large firms in different societies also differ in their product mix and integration. Finally, the types and degree of state involvement in markets vary widely within and across regions. The total effect is still one of national capitalisms.[8]

According to these interpretations, therefore, national economies (or national capitalisms) are still the basic economic units of the global economy, and economic activity remains deeply embedded in national structures and states remain powerful economic actors. As *The Economist* (1995: 15) and Weiss (1998) popularly put it, the powerless state is a "myth." Or, to use Wade's words (1996: 60), "reports of the death of the national economy are greatly exaggerated." Jacques (2004) has gone even further and, after reviewing the evidence from East Asia, has concluded that "the era we have now entered would be more appropriately described as the moment of the nation-state."

However, if "globalization" is in fact "globaloney," to use another word that has gained wide usage amongst the globalization skeptics,[9] how can the widespread presence of arguments for its existence and inevitability be explained? One explanation is that it is simply an intellectual fad, a catchphrase that has caught the popular and academic imagination but is likely to become redundant when the next fad comes along. Other fads—the leisure society, the peace dividend—can be given as other examples that have failed to stand the test of time. A more sophisticated explanation suggests that though the case for globalization may not be compelling empirically, its real purpose is to serve as an ideological weapon of the neoliberal agenda. That is, what is occurring is not so much globalization but globalism, an ideology.

This ideology—"a set of ideas that reflect a point of view" (Fligstein, 2001: 221)—of neoliberalism is based on the view that markets and firms *should* play the dominant role in the organization of capitalist economies and that states *should* play limited roles.[10] The purpose of this ideology has been to get citizens to accept that "there is no alternative" and to promote what McQuaig (1998) has called a "cult of impotence." Governments could be more powerful if they wished, but the ideological onslaught of neoliberalism has found in globalization a powerful and convenient argument that posits that capital must be allowed to have more power and that states must adjust to the imperatives of the global economy. It is for this reason, as an ideological tool to make citizens accept a restructuring of their working lives and a restructuring of public services, that globalization has found such resonance among global elites. In other words, as Veseth (1998: 133) argues, "globalization is a lever that special interests can use to pry open certain public policy doors that would otherwise be tightly shut." He therefore concludes (1998: 2) that "globalization is really a delivery system, not a final product." What is being delivered is neoliberalism in the form of the "inevitability" of globalization and a restructuring of the state to that of a "competition state" (Cerny, 2000).

And though state elites, especially of the neoliberal persuasion, and corporations have been successful in persuading the doubters of the "inevitability" of globalization, they have also been actively dismantling the power of the state by liberalizing markets to give credence to that very "inevitability." That is, much of the impetus for the globalization of trade, finance, and production has come from states themselves. Globalization has, to a significant extent, been state-led rather the state's being the passive adaptor to an exogenously determined technologically driven globalization. Thus, Bienefeld (1996: 420) argues that "the claim that the nation-state's decline is an irreversible result of exogenous, technological changes is as ubiquitous as it is implausible. ... The primary driving force behind the liberalization of the world's financial markets is political, not technological." The "big bang" of the 1980s in world financial markets can be read as an attempt by a number of core states, the United Kingdom and the United States especially, to secure a larger portion of the financial services industry for themselves (see

Helleiner, 1994). Free trade agreements, such as the NAFTA, were similarly not driven by technological necessity but by an ideological preference for free trade and greater power for capital over labor. The purpose was to deliberately limit state capacity.

Thus, globalization is really a myth designed to support the neoliberal agenda with its political redistribution of power to corporate and financial elites. To the extent that states have ceded power to markets, it is because they have chosen to do so for ideological reasons rather than being compelled to do so by the juggernaut of technological change. Globalization is neither inevitable nor irreversible. Saul (2005) has argued that where states were once willing to cede power to markets, they are now moving to reassert national control in light of globalization's failure to deliver rising living standards. That is, for all the alleged "inevitability" of globalization, it is in fact reversible in significant respects.

Imperialism with some states still powerful

A third interpretation of globalization is that while it has weakened some states, it has enhanced the power of others and deliberately so. It is argued that the most powerful core capitalist countries, particularly the United States, have used globalization as a way of expanding their global power and the profitability of their corporations. Globalization—or the global spread of capitalism—is a project being carried out by core capitalist states in support of the expansion of the capitalist system as a whole and their multinational corporations in particular. The world, far from being flat, has become more hierarchical.

Unlike the globalism interpretation, theories in the imperialism category do not dispute that globalization is occurring; what is disputed is how it should be understood and interpreted. As McQueen (2001: 210) argues, "[O]ne of the few certainties about globalization is that it is most often Americanisation. Its logic does not require the United States to be borderless, only everybody else." This is the key point in this interpretation of globalization. It is a process that weakens only some states—the weakest—by either forcing on them, or by having their comprador leaders willingly embrace, market liberalization measures and privatization that give greater reign to foreign capital.

Meanwhile, the core states' positions are enhanced by the continued opening of more areas of economic activity in other countries to their firms. Globalization is therefore characterized by advanced capitalist states, finance capital, and multinational corporations acting in concert to open up foreign markets. These characteristics recall late nineteenth-century imperialism. "Free trade" is again the banner under which imperial powers seek to open up the economies of others (see Gallagher and Robinson, 1953). Just as imperialism in the late nineteenth century encompassed not only the economic and political spheres but the domination of the colonies' cultures and values by those of the imperial powers, so too does imperialism at the beginning of the twenty-first century. And, of course, the willingness of imperial powers to use military force to ensure this domination is also common to both periods.

Thus, globalization appears, not as an objective description of what must "inevitably" happen but as imperialism. For McQueen (2001: 197), the term *globalization* is seen as a "public-relations gloss." The purpose of this gloss is to present "monopolising capitals as the outcomes of ineluctable forces of nature, rather than of contestable social practices, [which] helps corporations to elude the hostility sparked by the word 'imperialism'" (ibid.).

A similar conclusion is reached by Petras and Veltmeyer (2001: 62), who argue that "to the extent that globalization rhetoric persists, it has become an ideological mask disguising the emerging power of U.S. corporations to exploit and enrich themselves and their chief executive officers to an unprecedented degree. Globalization can be seen as a code word for the ascendancy of U.S. imperialism."

This argument, that there has been a reemergence of imperialism, is one that has recently flourished (see, for example, Harvey, 2003; Kiernan, 2005; Petras et al., 2006). Indeed, the term *imperialism* might be said to have undergone something of a resurrection owing in no small measure to the unilateralist stance adopted by the Bush administration, especially in the wake of September 11. Here, for space reasons, I do not enter into the nuances and differences between these works but will take Petras and Veltmeyer (2001) as illustrative and representative of this body of work.

For Petras and Veltmeyer (2001), the argument that globalization is "inevitable" and the result of the types of technological developments discussed in the view outlined above—that "globalization weakens the nation-state"—is fundamentally misleading. Though accepting that technological change has taken place, they reject the claims that it is of such a large nature that it has of necessity revolutionized production methods. Indeed, the empirical evidence that they present points to the absence of any great technological breakthrough in productivity over the last few decades. In short, if globalization is being driven by a qualitative—indeed a revolutionary—leap in technology why, they ask, is productivity growth on a global scale still lower than that achieved in the "pre-global" period of the 1950s and 1960s?

They argue that "globalization" is a ruling-class and imperial project aimed at restoring profitability in response to the "crisis of capitalism" from the 1970s onward. They argue that globalization exhibits a cyclical pattern under capitalism, with its latest manifestation being structurally similar to other previous phases. Capitalism has had periods when accumulation has been focused on the national market and others when international market expansion has been in the ascendancy. The determinants of these phases include the strength of the export class, the strength of labor, and the political composition of the state. In the period 1930–70, they argue, national economies were the basis of capitalist expansion as a result first of the international crisis of the 1930s and then of the postwar power of labor and its influence over the state. However, the crisis of profitability that arose from these constraints led to a capitalist class counterrevolution that launched the globalization project aimed at weakening labor, reorientating the state, and forcing the creation of a world market open for capitalist exploitation.

"The origins of globalization as an economic strategy were thus the consequences of an ideological project backed by state power and not the 'natural unfolding' of the market" (Petras and Veltmeyer, 2001: 43), a project that was first piloted in Chile and then adopted elsewhere in the Reagan–Thatcher era. For the imperial powers, globalization is therefore a project aimed at weakening the power of labor domestically and advocating and requiring the opening up of markets abroad. Neoliberalism has been used as the policy thrust to achieve these objectives.

This latest phase, therefore, represents a "cyclical process which is still deeply implicated in national economies and highly dependent on the nation-state for its projections abroad" (ibid., 2001: 36). Thus, they argue that contemporary globalization differs from previous cycles in quantitative terms but not in terms of the "structures and units of analysis that define the process" (ibid., 2001: 41): that is, the imperial states and large capitalist firms. To suggest that this process represents a weakening of the core states is to miss the point. In fact, "never has the nation-state played a more decisive role or intervened with more vigor and consequence in shaping economic exchanges and investment at the local, national and international levels. It is impossible to conceive of the expansion and deepening involvement of multinational banks and corporations without the prior political, military and economic intervention of the nation-state" (ibid., 2001: 54).

In this process, they argue, the main actors are the capitalist class through its control of the world's 37,000 multinational corporations; imperial states' governments that have become a servant to the interests of the capitalist class and have promoted the latest incarnation of a "world market" through domestic deregulation (particularly of finance); and, through their influence in the IMF and the World Bank, the rest of the world through structural adjustment, "market-friendly" policies, and privatization. The Trilateral Commission and the World Economic Forum are added to the international financial institutions as agents representing and serving the interests of the new international capitalist class.

They prefer the term *imperialism* to globalization as the descriptor of the current phase of capitalism on a number of grounds. First, it clearly identifies the main actors and agents in the creation of the world market rather than relying on the fetish of attributing to abstract "market forces" human qualities, needs, and "imperatives." Second, it highlights the power relationships operating in the world political economy rather than implying an interdependent, mutually reliant "global economy." Third, it highlights the key role played by imperial states and the country-based nature of multinational corporations' operations rather than globalization's characterization of the world as one inhabited by stateless global corporations and weakened states. Fourth, the term *imperialism* indicates that the methods of enforcement in the "global economy" are not simply "markets." Instead, "Washington is prepared to defend its newly regained economic ascendancy by all means necessary: by free trade if possible, by military force if necessary" (ibid., 2001: 65). And for the latter to be realized, "the political-economic role of the state is accompanied by the deep penetration of the police, military and intelligence agencies of dominated nations by the U.S." (ibid., 2001: 54–5). Imperialism is not simply an economic system. Fifth, in terms of distributional outcomes, the dynamics of increasing world income and wealth inequalities, the enrichment of the few and the impoverishment of the many, are better captured by the concept of imperialism with its structures of dominance than globalization that suggests a mutual interdependence and offers, at least to its proponents, the prospects of a generalized rise in living standards. On this reading, globalization has been an economic failure but has been politically very successful in supporting structures of domination.

Petras and Veltmeyer argue that the imperial powers are the United States and "Europe," though it is unclear whether this means imperial nations within Europe or an "imperial Europe" as a whole. Panitch and Gindin (2004), however, argue that because of the pattern of corporate alliances and U.S. investment in Europe, European capital is in fact tied to, and dependent on, U.S. capital with the result that the site of imperialism shrinks more unambiguously to that of the United States. For them, inter-imperialist rivalries are not as prevalent as in previous imperial eras.

Though these writings are derived from Marxist analysis, historians who do not subscribe to this framework have nevertheless agreed that globalization cannot be understood without reference to empire.[11] Ferguson (2001: 6–7), for example, argues

> that empires did not (and do not) matter in globalization seems implausible. ... The history of the integration of international commodity markets in the seventeenth and eighteenth centuries is inseparable from the process of imperial competition between Portugal, Spain, Holland, France and Britain. The spread of free trade and the internationalization of capital markets in the nineteenth century are both inseparable from the expansion of British imperial, and especially naval, power.

For Ferguson, therefore, "globalization" must be seen as an historical process "inseparable" from imperialism, a conclusion in keeping with the analysis of Petras and Veltmeyer. However, though Petras and Veltmeyer view imperialism as a force for inequality and oppression, Ferguson (2001: 7) prefers to argue that

> the British Empire in the nineteenth century, for example, can be understood in part as an agency for imposing free trade and the rule of law directly on a quarter of the world's land surface and indirectly on a great many other places, to say nothing of the world's oceans. If we believe that economic openness is good then, by extension, one might have expected some global benefit to result from this immense undertaking.

The globalization as imperialism interpretation shares some similarities with the globalism interpretation in that it points to the continued importance of nation-states and stresses the importance of neoliberalism as the ideological underpinnings of globalization. However, the two interpretations differ in the extent to which they believe states have maintained autonomy. The globalism position argues that nation-states are still viable decision-making structures, especially the core states, and that national projects are still possible. The imperialism view, in contrast, stresses the power relations that condition and constrain national possibilities for all but the imperial states. Though the globalism position is likely to ascribe some autonomy to national elites, the imperialism interpretation, especially in its Marxist variant, is more likely to stress the role of those elites as compradors with imperialism.

Regionalism as more important

The final set of writings examined here argues that state and corporate structures and activities are changing but that regionalism (as a state-led integration process) or regionalization (as a market-led integration process) or a combination is a more accurate description of the changes underway than is globalization. This interpretation—the "Regional World" in Storper's (2005) words—comes in various forms with one difference between them being the extent to which they view regionalism and globalization as competing or complementary processes. Almost as much has been written on regionalism, with distinctions between "old" and "new" regionalisms, as on globalization, and so our review here will necessarily be brief.

The major (macro) regional blocs are, of course, Europe, the Americas, and East Asia, although the leadership of the latter bloc, firmly seen as belonging to Japan in the late 1980s–early 1990s, is now more ambiguously defined as a result of Japan's post-bubble slump and the rise of China.[12] The view that contemporary capitalism is best described as regional rather than global rests on the strong regional biases to trade and investment flows and on the regional supranational political structures that have been put in place. In terms of the former, though world trade and investment have expanded rapidly over the last two decades, there is a strong regional bias in these flows. In trade terms, gravity models have been used to examine the extent to which trade flows are determined by "distance" (a negative relationship) and a common border (a positive relationship) in addition to other economic determinants, such as size of the economy and GNP per capita. Regional biases in trade are typically measured by the size and statistical significance of the coefficients on the "distance" and "common border" variables. An examination of the data led Chortareas and Pelagides (2004: 253), for example, to conclude that "trade integration is more of a 'regional' phenomenon than a 'global' one."

Added to this are regional biases in foreign direct investment (FDI). That is, there are investment clusters with each member of the dominant "Triad" in the world economy—the U.S., Japan, and the EU—having its own set of countries with which it is tied in terms of FDI flows.[13] The World Investment Report in 1999 (UNCTC, 1999) concluded that "the overwhelming focus of TNCs is on the Triad countries of North America, Western Europe and Japan. The concentration of FDI assets in the Triad has risen from 61 percent in 1988 to 63 percent in

1997." The 2006 Report again details the dominance of the Triad countries as sources of FDI outflows and inflows, though Japan's role as a source of outflows has fallen sharply since the early 1990s. The Report also points out the increasing intraregional flows of FDI in West Asia (UNCTC, 2006: 62) and South, East, and Southeast Asia (UNCTC, 2006: 54).[14]

On the basis of reviewing the evidence in the late 1980s and early 1990s, Hirst and Thompson (1996: 95) conclude that "MNCs still rely on their 'home base' as the centre for their economic activities, despite all the speculation about globalization. From these results we are confident that, in the aggregate, international companies are still predominantly MNCs and not TNCs. ...There are two aspects of the home centredness. One is the role of the 'home country' and the other that of the 'home region'."

This conclusion is also supported by Rugman (2000), who argues that globalization is a "myth." For him, there are clearly evident triadic patterns in trade, FDI, production networks, and corporate strategies. From a business perspective, he argues that the most successful corporations will be those that adapt to the regionally based world economy rather than those that seek to "go global." The leading MNCs, he argues, are already pursuing this strategy.

Both of these trends in regional trade and investment flows have been reflected in, and furthered by, economic integration agreements. Almost all countries are signatories to at least one such agreement, with the number of agreements worldwide increasing dramatically over the last couple of decades and with eighty-seven alone signed in the 1990s (see Schiff and Winters, 2003: 1). The large majority of these agreements are between countries in the same region.

To this evidence of regional economic integration must be added the political dimensions most evident in Europe with the European Union and the European Parliament. There are no comparable bodies in other regions. The North American Free Trade Agreement of 1994 between the United States, Canada, and Mexico and the proposed Free Trade Agreement of the Americas do point to the existence of a regional project but its supranational political structure is currently limited (though NAFTA has been discussed as a "constitution"; see Clarkson, 2002). In Asia, the ten members of the Association of South East Asian Nations (ASEAN), which was formed in 1967, created a free trade area in 1992 and have now negotiated an agreement with China. In the wake of the 1997 financial crisis, the ASEAN countries have also joined with China, Japan, and South Korea, in an ASEAN+3 framework, to put in place mechanisms for financial cooperation and represents for some an emerging regionalism (see Bowles, 2002; Das, 2004; Zhang, 2005).

Thus, macro-regional economic and political integration is taking place, though one aspect on which all commentators agree is the degree to which regionalism, especially the political dimension, differs around the world. For some, this indicates that regions are at different stages of integration on a linear path that all might be expected to follow. For others, it represents fundamental differences in the nature of the regional projects. This opens up the possibility for some regional projects to be neoliberal in orientation (such as that in the Americas) whereas others might be less so or not so at all (as, for example, in the claims for a "Social Europe"). The key is that regionalism is not a homogenous process, and regional differences are evident. Indeed, there may be alternative forms of regionalism taking place within the same region; the newly formed Bolivarian Alternative for the Americas (ALBA), a trade pact between Cuba, Bolivia, and Venezuela—led by the "Pirates of the Caribbean" in the words of Ali (2006)—providing an ideological alternative to the neoliberal FTAA project sponsored by the United States.

Thus, Mittelman (2000: 41), for example, argues that "it would be fruitless to seek to define a single pattern of regional integration, especially a Eurocentric model emphasizing legal principles, formal declarations, routinized bureaucracies, and institutionalized exchange." The distinctiveness of regionalism in Asia has also been emphasized by writers such as Stubbs (1995), who has argued for a distinctive form of Asian capitalism based on the networking activities of Japanese multinationals and the Chinese diaspora, and by He (2004), who has analyzed the nationalism(s) underlying Asian regional initiatives. Each region, therefore, has its own political dynamic, and regionalism can be used for a variety of political purposes. For Katzenstein (2005), too, regionalism differs between Asia and Europe, though he argues that one commonality is the role of the United States in their constructions.

Though many commentators agree on the importance of regional differences, there is much less agreement about the relationship between regionalism and globalization (i.e., whether they are competing or complementary processes). In general, the economics literature tends to view regional and global processes as competitors. The methodology relies on the collection and interpretation of primarily trade data and examines the extent to which "regional bias" is occurring. Evidence of regional bias is typically taken as a rejection of globalization. Given the focus on the nature of the statistical trends, the reasons why regionalism is occurring have often been left underexplored, with regions often being viewed as being "natural" and, as such, determined without reference to human political institutions, such as nation-states (see Frankel, 1998). As such, the literature addresses regionalization—to be determined through statistical data—rather than regionalism that has an explicit political content. Where the driving forces for regionalization are identified, they are typically based on regional production networks and regional FDI patterns. The power structures—which have characterized much of the literature seeking to explain and justify the term *imperialism*—are largely absent.

Where the economics literature has addressed the nature of regionalism, it has primarily been in the context of assessing the extent to which it poses a threat to an open international trading system (see Krueger, 1999; Krishna, 2005): that is, whether regional blocs are "stumbling blocs" or "building blocs" for the global economy. The fear of those who interpret regional arrangements as stumbling blocs is that we will witness a return to the insularity of the 1930s, wherein imperial trading blocs were formed in an attempt to avoid the transmission of volatility from other regions. This fear finds expression in the description of the EU or the NAFTA as creating "Fortress Europe" or "Fortress America." For others, however, the "new regionalism" of the 1990s is characterized by its "openness" and its potential to spur greater global integration (Frankel and Wei, 1998). On this reading, regionalism can be a part of the process of creating the global economy.

Political scientists have tended to focus more on regionalism as a process in which the policies of states must be explicitly analyzed, and here the links between regionalism and globalization have been seen as being largely complementary processes. Mittelman (2000: 34), for example, argues that globalization should be seen as a global division of labor and power that "involves a restructuring among world regions, including their constituent units, notably states, cities, and the networks linking them." Within this restructuring,

> there is no single wave of globalization washing over or flattening diverse divisions of labour both in regions and in industrial branches. Varied regional divisions of labour are emerging, tethered in different ways to global structures, each one engaged in unequal transactions with world centres of production and finance and presented with distinctive development possibilities. Within each region, subglobal hierarchies have formed, with poles of economic growth, managerial and technological centres, and security systems.
>
> ((Mittelman, 2000: 41)

Thus, to quote again from Mittelman (2000: 4), "globalization proceeds through macroregionalism sponsored by states and economic forces seeking to open larger markets as a means toward greater competitiveness." Regionalism may be a distinctive process, therefore, but it is part of a broader process supportive of globalization; hence the term *global regions*. The concept of a global region emphasizes the fact that contemporary regions are not "fortresses" but linked together, in much the same way as is the concept of "open regionalism" that is used more extensively in the economics literature. This concept also finds resonance with others who have referred to the process of "continental globalization" in the context of North America, indicating that regionalism is the vehicle through which globalization is delivered. Regionalism and globalization are not, therefore, seen as incompatible on this reading, but the regional trends are seen as being as critical as, or more so than, the global trends. Post-September 11 concerns with border security have tended to reinforce the importance of regions and regional mechanisms for meeting security objectives.

Another approach, common in the early 1990s but less so now, stressing the importance of regionalism, is that emanating from the international relations literature and concerns, whether a tri-polar world is emerging within which the post-1945 hegemonic power of the United States is disappearing. The agenda this raised was of how to forge cooperation and contain rivalries in this new period between the newly emerging regions. Basically, the world is perceived as three regional blocs centered around the Triad, the question being the extent to which the "minilateralism" (Yarborough and Yarborough, 1994; Bergsten, 2000) and coordination practiced between the three Triad members would be successful in maintaining an open international trading system, and stable exchange-rate system, in the same way that the post-1945 multilateral system had done. This set of questions derived from hegemonic stability theory that posits that a hegemon is necessary to create and enforce the rules of an international order; without this hegemonic role, stability cannot be ensured. With the perceived decline of the United States as a hegemonic power and the transition to a (regionally based) multi-polar world, the stability of the international order is therefore open to question. In the early 1990s, this was framed in terms of a multi-polar world, with the United States, Japan, and Europe as the poles; in the mid-2000s, this question is more likely to be framed with the United States, China, and Europe as the poles. A further variant sees the emergence of a number of "mega-states" (Brazil, Russia, India, and China—the BRICs) competing with existing blocs in Europe and North America (Goldman Sachs, 2003). With the combined GDP of the BRICs predicted to exceed the combined GDP of the G-6 sometime before mid-twenty-first century, a new multi-polar world system is envisaged (ibid).[15] This new system of BRICs and blocs again differs from the vision of a seamless, borderless, global economy.

Though much of the literature surveyed here under the heading of "regionalism" has been framed in terms of macroregions, other contributions have analyzed the emergence of microregions at the subnational level (as in the case of Italian industrial districts, for example; see Newhouse, 1997) or cross-subnational level (as in the case of the growth triangle in southeast Asia, for example; see Yue, 1997). In Africa, regionalism has been interpreted as fragmentation again at the subnational level (Bach, 2005). Key issues have been how globalization affects these processes and the links between regionalisms at both the sub- and supranational levels (see Scott, 2005; Storper, 2005).

Conclusion

The taxonomy presented here has highlighted the different ways in which the relationship between nation-states and markets has been interpreted as a result of globalization. Within each group, there are considerable variations to be found in the methodology used and assessment of the desirability of the changes in the relationship between state and market that are ascribed to globalization. There have also been variations over time within each category; the imperialism view has become much more to the fore following the Bush policy of unilateralism since the early 2000s, whereas China's rise has led to some rejigging of the contours of the regional dynamics at play in the regionalism category. Nevertheless, cutting across these variations are the fundamental differences in the way in which state–market relations are perceived in the "era of globalization" and which provide us with our taxonomy. The four categories are summarized in Table 2.1 together with some representative theories and authors surveyed in the chapter.

This review generates important questions for the study of the impacts of globalization on national currencies. If we are to examine the implications of globalization, we must first have a clear understanding of what constitutes global-ization. However, as we have seen, there is no single theory of globalization; in

Table 2.1 A taxonomy of theories of globalization: summary

Globalization	Globalism	Imperialism	Regionalism
Trade and investment integration leading to the "borderless world" (Ohmae)	"Home bias" in trade and capital flows (Helliwell)	Globalization as a "public relations gloss" (McQueen)	World economy organized around the EU, U.S., Japan (and possibly China?) triadic relationships (Hirst and Thompson, Rugman)
Emergence of the "global" corporation (Scholte)	No global capital pool (Feldstein–Horrioka puzzle)	Globalization as a "mask" (Petras and Veltmeyer)	Emerging new "regions" (Goldman Sachs, Scott)
The result of the ICT revolution (Friedman, Teeple, Global Policy Forum)	Most companies still multinational not global (Veseth)	Opening up of markets designed by powerful states, implemented by the international institutions they control, for the benefit of elites and corporations of imperial powers (Petras and Veltmeyer, Harvey, Panitch and Gindin)	Regional FDI clusters (UNCTC)
The state is weakened by the increased mobility and power of corporations (Scholte, Strange, Desai, Friedman)	Contemporary globalization is neither new nor exceptional (Zevin, Bairoch)	Advanced by "free trade" is possible but military force if necessary (Petras and Veltmeyer)	Gravity models and the regionalization of trade (Frankel)
Viewed as desirable by some (Lucas) and requiring new forms of global governance by others (World Commission on the Social Dimensions of Globalization)	National systems remain dominant (Fligstein, Radice, Wade)	Historically, globalization and imperialism have gone together (Ferguson)	Regional groupings as building blocs or stumbling blocs to globalization (Krueger, Krishna, Frankel and Wei)
	Globalization as a "myth" (Weiss)		"Global regions" as part of the dynamic of globalization (Mittelman)
	National powers ceded by the state not taken away and therefore reversible (Bienefeld, Saul)		Distinctiveness of regional processes (Mittelman, Stubbs)
	"Globalism" as neoliberal ideology the driving force (Veseth, McQuaig)		Sub-national economic and political regionalisms (Yue, Bach, Storper)

fact, there are many. To get an analytical handle on this vast literature, a fourfold taxonomy has been developed in this chapter that enables us to divide and classify theories on the basis of the relationship that they posit between states and markets. The questions that arise from this classification can be summarized:

1   If globalization is a technologically driven process weakening all states, are the national currencies that constitute part of the state structure threatened? If so, which actors would be important in bringing about a change? What would be their rationale?
2   If globalism is correct and it is neoliberal ideology that is underpinning "globalization," what does neoliberalism have to say about monetary governance in general and national currencies in particular?
3   If imperialism best captures the dynamics of the contemporary period, what role does money play in imperial structures? What are the implications of this for the currencies of non-imperial states?
4   If regionalism is more important, does this imply that regional currencies are a likely accompaniment?

These questions guide the analysis of the next chapter.

3 The implications of the four interpretations of globalization for national currencies

The four interpretations of globalization set out in Chapter 2 have widely different implications for how the relationship between states and markets should be analyzed in the contemporary period. For some, nation-states are withering away as capital has "gone global'; for others, the fabric of the nation-state remains tightly woven. For yet others, the contemporary period is best analyzed as one of U.S. (and European) imperialism, and others are struck by the regional nature of present economic and political structures. All four interpretations point to different futures for things "national." In this chapter, I explore the implications for national currencies—an institution located at the intersection of market and state.

In setting out the four interpretations in Chapter 2, it was stressed that within each interpretation a number of different theories could be found, theories that were grouped together because they shared a similar view of state–market relations even though they differed in important respects in other ways. This is also case for the analysis in this chapter; each interpretation includes a variety of theories. As such, the aim again will be not to provide an exhaustive review of all contributions but rather to highlight some important contributions and arguments that might be regarded as representative.

Globalization with weakened nation-states: toward a global currency?

> It appears likely that the number of currencies in the world, having proliferated along with the number of countries over the past 50 years will decline sharply over the next two decades.
>
> (Rogoff, 2001: 243)

According to this interpretation, the contemporary period is best characterized as one wherein integration through trade and capital flows and the rise of global corporations, all a result of technological advances, have weakened nation-states. These phenomena have been invoked in the analysis of national currencies.

The view that globalization is a primarily technologically process that has enhanced the power of markets and weakened the nation-state is consistent with a prediction that the world will move to fewer currencies or even one currency.

National currencies will be replaced by supranational currencies reflecting the spatial reorganization of production from the national to the global level. "Currency convergence" is the monetary version of the general process of homogenization and institutional convergence that occurs under the dictates of the global market. However, this is not the only possible outcome; for others, a technologically driven globalization may lead to the continuation of national currencies, though states may have less control over their management.

Let us start with the arguments that point to a reduction in the number of national currencies as suggested above by Rogoff. There a number of mechanisms postulated by which such a reduction might occur.

The first set of arguments supportive of this general proposition can be grouped together under the heading of *efficiency*. For example, the integration of national economies through increased trade and investment flows, one of the primary indicators of economic globalization, means that the use of different currencies incurs unnecessary transactions costs and that use of a single currency would result in increased microeconomic efficiency. Mundell (2003: 40), for example, asks, "If everyone used the same currency, wouldn't that make a great improvement in the way prices are compared, transactions are effected, and payments are made? There would be no currency crises, and the 2 trillion dollars' worth of cross-border transactions that exist only because of uncertainty over exchange rates would disappear."

The actors pushing for such a "great improvement" in efficiency can come from a number of sources. Using the power-theoretic framework of political science, it can be argued that increasing cross-border trade and investment flows will lead to a powerful constituency among exporters and global firms that would benefit from the use of a single currency. In an era of globalization, therefore, political pressures for the adoption of fewer currencies might be expected from business interests, particularly from the larger and more globally oriented firms.

The choice-theoretic framework more typically employed by economists would more likely identify rational, welfare-enhancing governments as the agents of change here. The microeconomic benefits of the use of a single currency have, in fact, long been realized by the optimal currency area (OCA) literature that Mundell (1961) pioneered and, as such, predates the latest period of globalization. OCA theory essentially enunciates the conditions under which the microeconomic efficiency benefits of using a single currency outweigh the macroeconomic benefits of using multiple currencies—and flexible exchange rates—to allow economies to adjust differently to common external shocks. As Willett (2003) notes, the criteria used to determine which currency areas are "optimal" have expanded over time and have proved difficult to both quantify and weigh. Willett (2003: 159–60), summarizing Tavlas (1994), lists nine characteristics for economies that are important for assessing whether they might form an optimal currency area, namely "similarity of inflation rates, the degree of factor mobility, the openness and size of the economy, the degree of commodity diversification, price and wage flexibility, the degree of goods market integration, fiscal integration, real exchange rate variability, and political factors."

The OCA literature has been long used to argue that optimal currency areas do not necessarily coincide with national borders. OCA theory therefore raises the question of whether there are economic benefits from using multiple currencies within one country or from more than one country using a single currency. It is the latter question that has typically been the greater focus of attention. From the perspective of this book, the critical question is whether globalization has expanded the geographical range over which optimal currencies might operate. In other words, has globalization changed the OCA calculus of the rational policy maker toward greater use of a common or a single currency? Certainly, this can be inferred from Mundell since, as Willett (2003: 166 n.1) observes, "Mundell's thinking has evolved considerably since his original contribution and he now sometimes argues that the whole world is an OCA." In which case, the whole world would benefit from the use of a world currency.

Globalization might make the "whole world an OCA" if economic integration makes countries more similar in their responses to external shocks. This is exactly the finding of Frankel and Rose (1998: 1009), who report "a strong and striking empirical finding: countries with closer trade links tend to have more tightly correlated business cycles." Increasing trade flows, one dimension of globalization, may therefore lead to the conditions for optimal currency areas being more easily met (see also Bordo and Helbling, 2003).

Furthermore, as Frankel and Rose point out, as closer trade links are also the *result* of the adoption of a common currency, the criteria for optimal currency areas are endogenous. Rose (2000) argues that the use of a common currency boosts trade by a significant factor. Using a gravity model to estimate the effects of currency unions on international trade and with a data set covering more than 185 countries, he finds a large positive effect of a currency union on international trade. His estimates (2000: 7) "imply that two countries sharing the same currency trade three times as much as they would with different currencies. Currency unions like the European EMU may thus lead to a large increase in international trade, with all that that entails." For Rose, therefore, the benefits of globalization—in this case the increase in allocative efficiency that accompanies a more extensive international division of labor and volume of international trade—are better realized by the use of common currencies. National currencies are a "barrier to trade" (Rose and van Wincoop, 2001).Welfare-enhancing government policy should therefore include the possible adoption of a common currency to remove this barrier.

The economic-efficiency arguments outlined above are, in general, ambiguous as to whether they point to the emergence of a few supraterritorial currencies or just one global currency; the arguments are consistent with both propositions depending on the exact conditions specified. Or, the road to "one world, one currency" (IMF, 2000) might be a sequential one involving progressively fewer currencies as the world becomes more and more integrated.

There is also an imprecision in much of the literature around exactly what constitutes "supraterritoriality," to use the term favored by Scholte (2000), and "deterritorialized," as used by others (including Scholte). That is, when referring to currencies, a distinction needs to be made, though often is not, between propositions that currencies are becoming supraterritorial—in the sense that their use and authority derives from macro-state formations or supranational bodies (such as the euro and the EU) and therefore beyond the control of any one nation-state—and "deterritorialized" in the sense that a currency is so widely used and traded beyond the borders of the issuing nation-state that its usage can be said to be beyond the control of the state. The efficiency arguments surveyed so far point to the emergence of supraterritorial currencies.

The economic-efficiency arguments are also, in general, ambiguous about how such supraterritorial currencies should be governed; that is, whether they should be new supranational currencies provided on the basis of shared sovereignty or whether a few currencies or one existing currency should be used with other countries delegating sovereignty to the most widely used currencies in return for compensation payments for loss of seniorage revenues. (See Cohen, 2004; Hawkins and Masson, 2003 Appendix A for lists of countries in these categories.) Perhaps an exception to this is the case of the dependencies and micro-states that use the currencies of other countries. In these cases, they are small countries (or dependencies) that have small populations and for which separate currencies might make little economic sense. They are extremely open economies for whom the costs of exchanging currencies would be an unwarranted additional cost of trade. From a practical point of view, it would be a waste of scarce human resources to operate a central bank or monetary authority charged with administering an independent currency, and such states, in any case, have limited objectives. These micro-states, in fact, make up the sizeable majority of the countries considered in Rose's (2000) study. For them, there are efficiency gains from using the currency of another country even without seigniorage sharing.

If we consider countries other than what I have termed here "micro-states," however, efficiency arguments are ambiguous with respect to the choice of which currency to use. That is, the economic efficiency arguments suggest that the adoption of a single currency is mutually beneficial for all countries in an optimal currency area. Thus, states might be expected to join in a common currency arrangement by a pooling or sharing of monetary sovereignty in anticipation of the enhanced efficiency and growth that such a pooling offers. Theoretically, there is no particular significance to the choice of common currency. It could be an entirely new currency or it might be an existing one. If the latter, the most widely used national currency would be the obvious choice as this would minimize the costs of changing monetary regimes. In this case, the seigniorage gains from currency issue (i.e., the real resources that the government receives in return for the supplying currency) would all accrue to one country though mechanisms could easily be devised, at least in theory, for the redistribution of this seigniorage to other member countries. However, monetary union in this form would also require representation of states officially adopting another country's currency on the latter's central bank governing board and the extension of lender of last resort facilities to all participating countries.

At its limit (and, some might say, at its most utopian), this type of argument leads to the creation of a global central bank, issuing a global currency and representing the interests of all of its member countries: a global pooling of monetary sovereignty. Proposals for a world central bank are not, however, new (see, for example, Cohen, 1977). Indeed, as Walter (1991: 63) notes, "the idea of a world central bank ... has been a reasonably common one in the twentieth century." The basis for this idea has not generally relied on arguments which are simply translatable as "globalization." More common have been arguments that have relied on the problems of international coordination between nation-states in monetary affairs. As Walter (1991: 63), states, "the case for a [world central bank] is usually founded upon the notion that as in domestic monetary systems, there is some kind of inexorable historical tendency towards increasing levels of centralization in international monetary organization. The emergence of a hierarchy in national monetary systems, as in the British case, is seen as a logical and necessary extension to the global level." As such, the case for a world central bank and world currency has predated the latest phase of globalization and has appealed to an "inexorable historical tendency" derived from extensions of the historical experience of nation-states. Appeals are still made to the desirability of a global currency and global central bank by both neoliberal (see Mundell, 2003) and neo-Keynesian (see Frankman, 2002; Arestis and Basu, 2003) economists, but what is perhaps surprising in the current era of globalization is how little a role this history of proposals for a world central bank has played in contemporary arguments for global currencies; for the most part, proposals for sharing monetary sovereignty have typically relied on appeal to other examples.[1]

The most popular example of shared monetary sovereignty is, of course, the euro and the establishment of the European Central Bank. This model implies a high degree of shared sovereignty, and the European case would seem to require some minimal level of equality between states entering into the arrangement; though countries differ in their motives, it can be seen as falling within a "shared sovereignty among equals" framework. Another example of currency arrangements that fit this framework is provided by the Eastern Caribbean Currency Union and by prospective currency unions involving the fourteen members of the Economic Community of West African States (ECOWAS) and the Gulf Cooperation Council. For some, this constitutes part of a global trend.[2]

The argument that globalization will lead, for efficiency reasons, to a reduction in the number of currencies and to the disappearance of some (many?) national currencies draws primarily on the globalization of trade and production for its argument. As such, pressures from globalization for supraterritorial currencies can be experienced by countries at any level of development and might be expected to be strongest among countries with the highest levels of trade integration.

However, the globalization of international financial markets provides an additional set of arguments. One argument here is that the power of global financial markets and their capacity to generate instability unconnected with "economic fundamentals" might lead industrial countries to move to a common currency. Thus, Cooper (2000) argues that "in the long run the major industrialized nations—the core of the international monetary system—may find it advantageous to adopt a common currency" to avoid the disruptions caused to the real sector by instability generated by volatile (and often irrational) international financial markets (see also Cooper, 2006).

A second set of arguments start from the premise that in a world of expanded international financial markets, countries face the risk of being punished by (basically rational) international capital markets for policy failures. Faced with such a risk, countries require ways to establish their *credibility* in the face of powerful financial markets. Such credibility can be gained by abandoning the national currency.

The "credibility" of money, as a store of value, has long been viewed as dependent on institutional design. History provides many examples where political institutions have failed to provide this credibility and where hyperinflation has resulted in currencies being replaced, typically by barter temporarily and eventually by new national currencies. In a world of free capital movements and in the absence of exchange controls, however, when national currencies lose their credibility, private agents can spontaneously elect to use the currency of another country. That is, countries whose domestic institutions fail in providing credibility to their currencies will experience "currency substitution," also known as "unofficial or de facto dollarization."

The extent of currency substitution is documented by Balino et al. (1999). They provide as a measure of unofficial dollarization the ratio of foreign currency deposits to broad money. They calculate this ratio for a number of "highly dollarized countries," typically developing or transition economies, such as Argentina, 43.5 percent; Azerbaijan, 50.3 percent; Bolivia, 82.3 percent; Cambodia, 56.4 percent; Croatia, 57.4 percent; Nicaragua, 54.5 percent; Peru, 64.0 percent; Turkey, 46.1 percent; and Uruguay, 76.1 percent (all figures for 1995). These countries' integration into the global economy, facilitated by IMF programs, has led to their citizens and firms substituting more credible currencies for their own national varieties. This forms half of what can be called the "deterritorialization" story; currencies of other countries circulate where they are seen as more credible stores of value than the national currency, posing challenges for monetary policy in highly dollarized countries (Balino, 1999). The other half of the story is that the credible currencies become deterritorialized with respect to the issuing government; for example, it is estimated (Fiege et al., 2003) that between 40 and 60 percent of all U.S. dollars circulate outside of the United States (though the extent to which this "extra-territorial dollarization" restricts the Federal Reserve in its control of domestic monetary policy is limited).

This aspect of the "deterritorialization' argument suggests that national governments' policy choices are constrained by the extent to which the technology of international financial markets makes eliminating competing currencies from domestic circulation an impossibility. As governments' currencies now face competition, their policy autonomy is reduced, and they are disciplined by this competition in their monetary policy. This is the implication of Cohen's description (1998, 2004) of national governments no longer holding a monopoly on currency issue but being more akin to oligopolists; they still possess substantial power, but it is now challenged by a small number of other currencies, a challenge that benefits private agents by providing alternative currency vehicles. This is true for the currencies of all governments, though the degree to which they are affected and the manner in which they are affected differ between countries at different levels of the currency hierarchy. Nevertheless, for Cohen, the same general message is applicable to all, namely, that "in relations between states and society, it is plainly the latter that are favoured by deterritorialization. Governments are privileged less, some elements of the private sector more" (1998: 129–30).

The fact that private actors (both firms and individuals) now have greater choices between currencies and are not bound by national boundaries in their use of currencies leads to greater currency competition in Cohen's view. However, this deterritorialization of money might weaken state control over money, but it does not necessarily imply, as Cohen is quick to point out, that this will lead to a reduction in the number of national currencies. For others, a greater role for markets is likely, because of the "network externalities" (Fiege et al., 2003) associated with the use of money as a medium of exchange, to result in the use of many fewer currencies than a state monopoly outcome; to the extent that the state's monopoly is broken and private actors' is strengthened, a reduction in the number of currencies might be expected.

The credibility argument may also lead to a reduction in the number of national currencies if unofficial currency substitution contributes to pressures for official or de jure dollarization (though official dollarization may also be considered by countries that are not experiencing unofficial dolllarization). The lack of credibility that leads to currency substitution by domestic agents may also lead to currency flight by foreign investors and currency crises. On the assumption that some states have shown themselves to be incapable of sound monetary governance, these states are encouraged to replace their institutions with those of countries who have shown themselves to be more reliable. On this reading, countries are viewed as having institutional "endowments," and countries with poor institutional endowments should import better institutions from abroad; institutions simply become one more tradable service. If a country does not have a comparative advantage in the institutions of monetary governance, it should import such institutions from abroad by adopting a foreign currency.

States may fail to exercise good "monetary governance" because of seigniorage; as Ball (1999: 1821) argues, "there is a near universal temptation for governments to pursue monetary policies that are too expansionary and lead to excessive inflation." This temptation requires an institutional remedy that curbs the desires of governments to use, or rather abuse, monetary policy for their own ends (such as stimulating the economy prior to elections or as an easy solution to otherwise difficult distributional conflicts).

A number of institutional remedies suggest themselves here. One is "central bank independence." It has become something of a "stylized fact" within much of the economics literature that more independent central banks result in lower inflationary outcomes, though the empirical evidence in support of this claim is weak (see Forder, 2000). The widespread acceptance of the stylized fact is shown, however, by the number of countries that now adhere to this institutional arrangement. Independent central banks can be seen as institutional attempts to provide credibility to international financial markets, to provide international investors with reassurances about the conduct of monetary policy.

Another institutional remedy can be found through the exchange rate, and it is through this mechanism that the implications arise for the viability of national currencies. It has long been argued that policy discipline can be imposed through fixed exchange-rate regimes, most obviously through the "automatic" discipline of the Gold Standard. Added to this, in countries with a record of poor monetary management, there is a "fear of floating," as Calvo and Reinhart (2002) have put it. The poor monetary governance record results in lenders being unwilling to lend in domestic currency over longer-term contracts with the result that domestic currency-denominated credit and housing markets are thin and lending and borrowing contracts are made in other, more confidence-inducing currencies. The result of this is that countries have a fear of floating exchange rates because any depreciation will increase the costs of all borrowers in long-term markets, thereby risking political and financial instability. For these countries, some kind of fixed exchange rate is needed.

Under contemporary globalization, it is various forms of "hard fixes" such as currency boards and official dollarization that have been advocated as mechanisms to impose discipline on domestic policy making and thereby to avoid the threat of currency crises, crises that national governments are largely powerless to control given the relative size and power of international financial markets. Furthermore, the currency crises of the 1980s and 1990s were argued to be qualitatively different from those of earlier periods, with the difference the result of the new globalized financial markets (see Saxena, 2004 for review).

Currency boards and official dollarization have been advocated widely for many developing and transition countries and were particularly popular in the 1990s. The so-called bipolar view of exchange-rate regimes held sway with the implication that countries were faced with the choice between fully flexible exchange rates and a "hard fix"; here the strengthening of markets takes the form of reducing the exchange-rate regime choices available to national governments. Intermediate regimes, such as crawling pegs, were unsustainable, it was argued, in the face of international financial market pressures and would invite speculation. As Eichengreen (2001: 1) colorfully put it, operating intermediate exchange-rate regimes "is tantamount to painting a bull's eye on the forehead of the central bank governor and telling speculators to 'shoot here.'" The speculative attacks against the pound, the lira, and the Swedish krona in 1992 provide evidence of the problems with one particular type of intermediate regime, the European Exchange Rate Mechanism (ERM). Britain, Italy, and Sweden were forced out of the ERM. Mexico provided another example in 1994. Even traditional fixed exchange-rate regimes, that is, currencies pegged to the dollar or another currency, were not immune. The Asian crisis in 1997 affected countries with dollar pegs that proved unsustainable in the face of attacks by international financial markets.

International financial markets therefore either force governments to abandon control over the international value of their national currencies if they keep them or to adopt "hard fixes," such as a currency board or official dollarization, if they wish to maintain some influence over currency stability. Currency boards involve the setting of a fixed exchange rate and backing domestic currency with 100 percent reserves in a safe currency. This is the route followed by Hong Kong, Argentina (between 1991 and 2001), and some of the newly independent countries of Eastern and central Europe. However, even this arrangement may not be sufficient to provide confidence in the monetary regime, as Argentina painfully discovered in 2001. In this case, the extreme case of currency adoption or dollarization becomes relevant. That is, countries simply adopt the currency of another country and thereby import the monetary credibility of that country.

This option implies an admission of institutional failure but one that, it is argued, may be necessary to restore confidence and prevent further economic malaise. An example that is argued to fit this case is the situation in which policy makers in Ecuador found themselves in 2000; they chose to unilaterally adopt the U.S. dollar as a last-ditch effort to restore some semblance of economic order to its economy. The unilateral adoption of the U.S. dollar (or any other currency, such as the euro) presupposes that one currency is definitively more advantageous than another: in the Ecuadorian case, that the U.S. dollar brings with it the credibility that its own currency lacks. There is no question, therefore, of a shared sovereignty or a new currency; the rationale is to replace a failed currency, and its supporting governing institutions, with that of a successful currency and its institutions. Sound money replaces bad money, and monetary sovereignty is delegated to more credible foreign institutions.

Though there are not many examples of official dollarization occurring in practice, its supporters have advocated a wide implementation; as Dean (2000) notes, "several prominent economists have begun to argue that essentially all developing countries should dollarize." This view is shared by Taylor (2000), who argues that "only monies of the highest quality are likely to survive" and that "only some central banks (maybe only one or two?) have a 'comparative advantage' in producing [money services]." This resonates with Cohen's (1998) "Darwinian struggle" in which only the fittest currencies—perhaps one or two on Taylor's reckoning—will survive in a world of globalization.

Advocates of dollarization further argue that it not only provides monetary credibility but stimulates growth in the adopting country. With the use of the U.S. dollar, for example, exchange-rate risk is removed, and international borrowing is possible with lower interest rates and thereby boosts investment. This case perhaps explains the decision of El Salvador's policy makers to unilaterally officially dollarize in 2001.

The role of increasingly powerful global financial markets and the implications for national currency management has also been analyzed using a Marxian framework. For example, Bryan and Rafferty (1999) argue that globalization means the global accumulation of capital. For them, international financial flows are the "pivotal dimension of globalization" (1999; 180). Studying the Australian case, they argue (1999: 197) that,

> in the past two decades most companies have become systematically exposed to exchange rate volatility, either because they used imported inputs, export some of their output, are investors abroad, or are themselves subsidiaries of international firms. As a result, companies are now required to maintain some degree of exchange rate trading to hedge against currency volatility. This means that the international price of the Australian dollar (the exchange rate) is being determined, at least for corporations, largely in global derivatives markets.

The growth of derivative and swap markets has meant that the Australian dollar has become "denationalized" (1999: 194), "being used as a currency for denominating part of global capital-raising which may or may not have any relation to the national source of the funding, where the funds will be invested, or even the eventual counterparty to a swap contract" (ibid.). Thus, accumulation on a global scale has resulted in the emergence of global currencies, nominally national but in important respects "denationalized" or deterritorialized using the preferred term of the literature summarized above. On the basis of this, Bryan and Rafferty argue that as at least some currencies have become "global," their values cannot be managed effectively by national governments. Though the literature discussed above stressed the problems of monetary policy in highly dollarized economies, Bryan and Rafferty stress the exchange-rate policy problems for countries whose currencies have become deterritorialized global currencies.

The implication, they argue, is that for these countries, floating exchange rates are inevitable. Presumably, however, exporting and international firms have interests in the development of a single global currency to avoid the cost of hedging, although Bryan and Rafferty do not take this step as a logical counterpart to facilitating "global accumulation." Instead, they point to a number of currencies becoming "global" rather than "national" currencies, with the implication that for the issuers of those currencies, such as Australia, exchange-rate regime choice is completely taken away and there is only the unipolar world of flexible exchange rates. The solution to the problems of global accumulation in a world of national currencies is found in the rapidly expanding international derivates markets that "bridge the discontinuities in the international monetary system that arise from different national currencies being 'generated' and 'sustained' in different national localities" (Bryan, 2002: 7).

There are, therefore, some differences between this Marxian approach and other approaches to the question of the impact of globalization on national currencies, but also some important similarities are seen in that trade and production across national borders lead some currencies to become deterritorialized and thereby limit national policy autonomy.

To conclude this section, it is worth drawing attention to one more argument with respect to the impact of globalization on currencies. This argument arises from the suggestion that globalization, and economic integration in particular, may lead to a redrawing, or fragmentation, of states themselves. That is, economic integration at the macro-regional level weakens the political case for large nation-states and leads to the viability of smaller political units. Alesina and Barro (2001: 384) have argued that

> if countries are linked more by trade and common currency, then the benefits from having a larger political union (i.e. a larger size country) diminish. Thus, if a country joins a monetary union, it may be easier for one of its regions to secede. The reason is that the benefits from free trade and common currency are no longer linked to the political union. ... Together with the progress of economic integration and monetary unification, regionalism and the demand for regional political autonomy have shown renewed vigour.

In this particular argument, globalization weakens one specific type of state: large ones. More broadly, by delinking the economic and political boundaries of the state, globalization opens up new spaces for political expression and autonomy. As examples of the applicability of this type of argument in practice applied to currencies, consider the cases of East Timor, which adopted the U.S. dollar as its official currency on January 24, 2000, and the adoption of the Deutschmark (and now the euro) by Kosovo.[3] In both cases, it could be argued that the adoption of a credible external currency paved the way for the exercise of other forms of political autonomy. More states may use the currencies of others because there are more (small) states.

This review has indicated the variety of theories that have been used to trace the implications of a view of globalization as a process of strengthening markets and weakening states for national currencies. Some of the arguments point straightforwardly to pressures for a reduction in the number of currencies as a result of trade and production integration (the efficiency argument) or the power of international financial markets (the credibility argument). Other arguments, however, based more on the deterritorialization of money suggest otherwise. The strengthening of markets does pose new challenges to states, as they are no longer territorial monetary monopolists, and imposes limits on their autonomy, but this is more likely to be experienced in ways other than giving up national currencies, such as the necessity to abandon exchange-rate intervention.

Globalism: national monies viable but "contingent neoliberalism" dominates

> Almost all of the recent [currency] crises are the result of intended or unintended governmental policy that was framed around the politics of domestic constituencies. While currency markets may have punished currencies, the penalty usually came after long time lags and extensive policy errors.
>
> (Fligstein, 2001: 211)

The argument that the disappearance of national political economies, or their convergence, under the forces of globalization has been greatly exaggerated implies that national monies, a central part of those political economies for the last century or more, are not inevitably going to disappear. As economies are primarily national in orientation, the pressures for supraterritorial currencies emanating from multinational firms or from welfare-enhancing policy makers can be regarded as limited; international trade, production, and capital markets simply are not that integrated to change the present viability of, or even preference for, national currencies. Nation-states remain viable but may be threatened by neoliberalism; the same argument can be extended to national currencies.

The viability and longevity of national currencies find support on a number of grounds. On empirical grounds, it has been argued that there is no historical trend toward supraterritorial currencies. There are also strong and weak versions of the argument that national monetary authorities have not lost power to global financial markets. The strong version argues that global financial markets have not imposed additional discipline (and may, if fact, have loosened it) on national governments and that the activities of the latter are still the primary determinants of a currency's value. The weaker version argues that nation-states have not so much lost power to global financial markets as ceded it to them, power that, in theory at least, could be reclaimed if desired.

As an example of the empirically based arguments, consider Pomfret (2002), who examines the forces of monetary *disunification*. He points out that, the euro notwithstanding, there are more currencies in Europe today than there were in 1991. This is because of the process of monetary disunification that has gone on in the former ruble zone. Though the political process of monetary unification in the European Union has received widespread attention, the political process of monetary disunification in the former Soviet Union is equally relevant and suggests that globalization imposes no inexorable logic in favor of monetary union. The economic benefits of monetary union in terms of increased trade have also come under sustained empirical investigation (see Rose and Stanley, 2005 for review and a defense).

On theoretical grounds, if the power of the nation-state is retained and the extent of its erosion by global markets is exaggerated, the traditional arguments in favor of national currencies retain their force as they have done for the last century and a half. These arguments, as summarized by Cohen (2004: 17), are "first, a potential reduction of domestic transaction costs to promote economic growth; second, a powerful instrument to manage the macroeconomic performance of the economy; third, a possible source of revenue to underwrite public expenditures; fourth, a potent political symbol to promote a sense of national identity; and finally, a practical means to insulate the nation from foreign influence or constraint."

Globalization might challenge a number of these benefits. We have already seen the argument that, given the increase in international transactions, it is international transaction costs that now need to be reduced through a common currency. We have also seen that the globalism position rejects the argument of increased international integration as exaggerated. New forms of transnational political identity might be promoted as in Europe, with the euro playing an important symbolic role; this will be discussed further in the regionalism section. Perhaps the most significant challenge to these benefits of national currencies comes from the alleged demise of the power of macroeconomic management.

With respect to macroeconomic management, a number of arguments have been advanced, of varying strengths, by those adhering to a globalism position to refute the claim that national authorities have lost the capacity to manage their currencies as part of macroeconomic policy as a result of the growth of international financial markets. In short, they argue that the power of international financial markets in particular, and globalization in general, has been exaggerated. Fligstein (2001), for example, argues that the growth of world financial markets has served the interests of governments and that the latter have benefited from being able to borrow extensively on these markets and have also benefited from the exchange-rate stabilizing activities of currency speculators. He accepts (2001: 213) that "world financial markets have grown in size and complexity." However, he continues that "it is difficult to ascertain if government dependence on these markets has increased to the point of limiting fiscal and monetary policy."

Currency crises might be taken as examples illustrating exactly these limits, but Fligstein argues that they are not indicators of the inexorable rise of the power of international financial markets and the weakness of governments. Rather, he views currency crises as the result of government policies that are eventually punished by international markets. In the case of the Mexican peso crisis in 1994, for example, he argues (2001: 212) that "this case shows that, yes, world financial markets eventually punished the peso. But it also shows that the Mexican and American governments, for basically political reasons, propped it up in the first place. ... This is a complex story that implicates markets, governments, and economic elites. It also fails to make international currency traders the obvious scapegoats." His analysis of the Asian financial crisis of 1997 (2001: 213) is similar in that "world currency markets and lenders who were not careful in their loan activities played a role in these crises. But the financial crises were caused at least as much by the policies pushed by international organizations and put into action by willing governments."

He further notes that world financial markets are limited to currencies and government bonds (and there are no world markets for equities or corporate control), that this expansion has served government interests, that the growth of these markets has not necessarily limited the role for independent monetary and fiscal policy, and that currency crises reveal at least as much about the folly of politically driven national governments (and international bureaucrats) as they do about the power of international financial markets.

A strong version of the argument can therefore be read as casting doubt on the extent to which globalization has changed the traditional role of monetary policy as an effective macroeconomic tool. Indeed, Fligstein (2001: 213) argues that international financial markets may have allowed governments to borrow to run deficits more cheaply than they might have otherwise; international financial markets have *increased* policy discretion. Thus, economic convergence has not occurred to the extent that countries need to give up their own macroeconomic policy autonomy and adopt common currencies.

Economies remain national and, therefore, the use of a national currency allows the monetary authorities to choose the appropriate exchange-rate regime and monetary policy to best suit the country's interests. That is, if the authorities believe that a flexible exchange rate is necessary to enable the domestic economy to respond to external shocks, this policy can be followed. Alternatively, if they wish to set a fixed exchange rate and retain control of interest rates to influence the level of domestic economic activity, this is also a viable policy option. Furthermore, the once-unfashionable intermediate exchange-rate regimes (for inviting speculative attack) have now come back into contention as plausible policy options.[4]

A weaker version of the argument suggests that globalization has threatened national policy autonomy but that this has been the result of the deregulation of international financial markets. That is, it has been the result of a deregulation which was not "technologically inevitable" but a deliberate policy choice and, as such, one that is reversible through political processes. This can be done at the national level through the reintroduction of capital controls, as both Malaysia and Chile have done in the recent past, or their continued maintenance, as in the case of China. At the international level, proposals such as the "Tobin tax" that seek to "put sand in the wheels of international finance" are possible. The argument that, to use Blecker's words (1999), global capital markets need to be "tamed," is typically derived from a Keynes-inspired framework that still regards economies as essentially national in character and monetary policy as still a nationally based policy tool. There is no historical inevitability to the erosion of the nation-state and national monies but instead a politically contestable and reversible decision to give more power to international financial markets at the expense of the nation-state. The state can and should reclaim this power; in some cases, this is seen as a return to the Bretton Woods era wherein capital controls gave policy makers more policy autonomy.

This raises the wider issue that though policy choices may be different today, fundamentally the need for policy choice has not changed. That is, policy makers everywhere are confronted with the so-called trilemma or "unholy trinity" (Cohen, 1993), namely, that they cannot simultaneously have control of interest rates and the exchange rate and allow free capital mobility. One of these has to be forfeited. Under the Bretton Woods system, it was free capital mobility that was forfeited; under the post-Bretton Woods arrangements, it is the exchange rate or interest rates. The trilemma has always existed, however; this is not new to globalization.[5] The post-Bretton Woods period differs in the variables over which policy choice is exercised but not in the necessity of choice. New international institutional arrangements could be envisaged that lead to different policy choices.

If national economies remain the basic units of the international economy and if international financial markets are not (or need not be) stronger than nation-states, the question remains why there has been so much discussion of dollarization and of national impotence in the face of international financial markets. The answer to this links to the wider interpretation of globalization, not as an exogenously determined technological imperative but as globalism, an ideology. This is the ideology of neoliberalism, the conscious decision to empower markets at the expense of states, capital at the expense of labor, a political project that has dominated the policy agenda in most countries for the last two decades.

What are the implications of viewing globalization as neoliberal globalism for the debate over national currencies? The central point here is that there is no neoliberal position on national currencies and exchange-rate regimes. In many areas of public policy, a broad neoliberal position is easy to identify. A general belief in the efficacy of markets over state intervention leads to a wide range of policy prescriptions, such as deregulation, privatization, and liberalization of factor and product markets at all levels. However, there are some policy issues on which there is no neoliberal consensus. The governance of money and exchange-rate regimes provides an example where neoliberalism has no broad consensus position.[6]

Money has always been controversial. For some liberals, such as Hayek (1976), money should, like other goods, be left to the market to regulate. He therefore stressed the need for free banking—that is, to take the state out of controlling money issue (what he called the "denationalization" of money) and allow competing private banks to regulate the supply of money. Here money could flow freely within and between countries and private dollarization could occur. This view has its contemporary supporters (see Dowd, 1996) and is based on the view that market mechanisms should operate throughout the economy; the state monopoly of money resulted from the political temptations of seigniorage rather than sound economic welfare-enhancing reasoning.

For some, therefore, central banks at the national level should be abolished and the market left to regulate itself. This would not only deny national governments the means to exploit seigniorage, it would remove a moral-hazard problem resulting from the central bank's role as lender of last resort. This argument has also been extended to the international level where the activities of the IMF have been viewed as playing lender-of-last-resort roles and hence have been subject to moral hazard critiques (see Meltzer, 1998).

For other neoliberals, however, state-issued money is logical, and central banks are key economic institutions, but their governance is critical.[7] Recent neoliberal critiques have stressed the benefits of central bank independence (i.e., central banks removed from the threat of political manipulation or persuasion). Once independent, opinions have differed as to what central banks should actually do. Should they be subject to legislated monetary rules, as many Friedmanites have argued? Should they have some discretion but target monetary aggregates, as other monetarists argued in the 1980s?

Neither is there any agreement on the most appropriate exchange-rate regime. As we have seen, some contemporary neoliberals argue that fixed exchange rates, in conjunction with free capital mobility, provides for international stability by removing domestic policy autonomy and disciplining national governments to adopt global best practices. Some, notably Hanke through his writings in Forbes and the Cato Institute, have extended this to other 'harder' fixes such as currency boards and dollarization.

For others, flexible exchange rates are preferred. For example, Friedman (1953) advocates flexible rates on the grounds that the exchange rate is a price like any other and freely adjustable prices are a required feature for the efficient operation of capitalist economies. Mundell (1961), with equally impeccable neoliberal credentials, argues for the use of common currencies within optimal currency areas (which typically do not coincide with national borders) so that the microeconomic benefits of reduced transactions costs can be realized and economic efficiency thereby enhanced.[8]

Nor can a neoliberal position be defined in an oppositional way, that is, by establishing a clear non-neoliberal position that can then be used to define its counter. Thus, the Bretton Woods agreement, fashioned by Keynes and White, prescribed fixed exchange rates on the grounds that these, if operating in conjunction with capital controls, would provide for international stability and for domestic policy autonomy. Some Keynesians advocate a global money whereas others have strenuously opposed the euro project and the ECB; some, such as Arestis, do both.[9]

The reason that there is no consensus on a neoliberal or a non-neoliberal position on national currencies and exchange-rate regimes is because they constitute only one element in the policy mix; what works "best" (for both neoliberals and their opponents) depends critically on the wider policy and institutional environment. The context is crucial. The basic proposition of neoliberalism, that markets can and should be left to operate as freely as possible and that governments should be constrained, can be met by a variety of monetary institutions. The main argument is that governments should be disciplined by markets or constitutions (or both), but there are various institutional arrangements that might be compatible with this general aim when applied to the monetary sphere. Thus, neoliberals may disagree on which institutional arrangement is most appropriate theoretically or practically, but they do not disagree on the central problem that needs to be addressed.

For this reason, it is useful to view neoliberalism as applied to monetary institutions, not as having a well-defined policy position but as being "contingent." Contingent neoliberalism means that policies that are advocated by neoliberals may differ from country to country and from time period to time period, depending on the wider institutional setting. Some neoliberals, such as Friedman and Mundell, have been lifetime advocates of flexible and fixed exchange rates, respectively. However, neoliberalism also offers the possibility of advocating different policies in different times and places, depending on an assessment of how best to achieve neoliberal objectives in any particular case.

As a recent example of this contingency within neoliberalism's approach to money and monetary institutions, consider Helleiner's discussion (2005b) of "the strange story of Bush and the Argentine Debt Crisis." Helleiner builds a compelling case to show that when Argentina defaulted in 2001, it did so without opposition from the United States and, indeed, found the United States to be supportive of its default, including the write-down of foreign investors' financial assets by around 70 percent, one of the largest write-downs in history. One of the primary reasons for this position is, according to Helleiner, neoliberal ideology—a belief in letting markets work without government intervention so that if private investors make poor decisions, they should bear the responsibility for this rather than having a misallocation occur as a result of "moral hazard." All of this is persuasive.

What is more difficult to explain, however, is why the United States behaved so differently in the Asian crisis of 1997 and in previous crises when the necessity of the repayment of debts to foreign investors was enforced by the United States through the IMF much to the dismay of governments and IMF critics alike in Asia (Bowles, 2002). Helleiner provides an explanation for this, but what is important to draw out in the context of the argument being pursued here is that the response to the Asian crisis was also based on neoliberalism—on the belief in the sanctity of contracts and the need for their enforcement. However, for the contracts to be enforced, the borrowing countries needed to be bailed out by the IMF to enable them to make these payments. The difference between U.S. policy in 1997 and 2001 is not so much a difference between the Clinton and Bush Administrations, or of a transition from a non-neoliberal to a neoliberal ideology, but rather a transition between two versions of neoliberalism. In the Asian crisis. the version that dominated was that which had been in the ascendancy for the debt crises of the previous twenty years, namely, that debtor countries must be made to honor their debts no matter what hardships this might inflict on them. The upshot of this policy in the Asian crisis was that the IMF made its largest ever bailouts and emerged as a fledgling world central bank acting as a lender of last resort. This development, and the associated implications for the workings of the international financial system, alarmed many neoliberals in the United States, who became more concerned with the potential harm posed to the operations of the market by a more powerful IMF than by the violations of freely entered contracts by debtors. What worried neoliberals was that the disciplining role of markets was being lost by the size of IMF interventions. And, as Meltzer (1998) argued, "capitalism without failure is like religion without sin. It doesn't work." Policy changed, therefore, between the Asian and Argentine debt crisis because the main problem to be addressed had changed—enforcing contracts on debtors in the former and enforcing creditors to take responsibility for risk in the latter. Neoliberalism was dominant in both periods but contingent.

The implications of neoliberalism being contingent with respect to monetary institutions and exchange-rate regimes is that it must be analyzed on a case-by-case basis; the context matters, so whether neoliberals pressure for common currencies, for example, depends on their assessment of the particular conditions of a specific country. How "neoliberal globalism" expresses itself with respect to currency questions may differ from country to country.

Imperial monies and structures

> Contemporary warfare has traditionally involved underlying conflicts regarding economics and resources. Today these intertwined conflicts also involve international currencies, and thus increased complexity.
>
> (Clark, 2005)

The imperialism interpretation places primary focus on structures of power and on how institutional arrangements and policies are imposed by imperial powers for their own benefit. This extends to the monetary field. In the empires of the nineteenth century, the currencies used in the colonies were often direct descendants of the imperial power's currency. The monetary arrangements of the colonies were directly tied to those of the colonial powers. For example the sterling bloc and the franc zone were put in place by Britain and France with the dual purpose of bringing institutional stability and "good governance" to the colonies and facilitating trade and investment flows within the Empire. Of course, these two purposes were seen as linked. As Fieldhouse (1981: 311) explains, colonialism:

> attempts to describe what proved to be a brief period and transient condition that was experienced by most parts of Africa, and much of South-east Asia and the Pacific, during the period 1870–1945 ... Under colonialism a dependent society was totally controlled by the imperial power. Its government was in the hands of officials of the imperial state, its social, legal, educational, cultural and even religious life was moulded by alien hands and its economy was structured to meet the needs of European capitalism.

Monetary arrangements were typically a part of this structure.[10]

These power relationships may seem reasonably straightforward when imperialism was accompanied by colonial rule. Twentieth-century imperialism since 1945, and U.S. imperialism in particular, has, it is argued, followed a largely different path. It is, in Magdoff's words (2003), an "imperialism without colonies." It is no less imperialism, and monetary arrangements remain a critical component of imperial order. That is, international monetary arrangements and currency usage are part of imperial structures.

The view that the widespread international use of the U.S. dollar provides unique privileges to the United States is shared by many commentators. What differs, however, is their assessment of whether these privileges are (1) counterbalanced by significant costs, (2) are a by-product of providing an international public good, or (3) represent a "dollar empire."

Thus, with respect to propositions (1) and (2), some argue that being the issuer of an international currency has significant costs as well as benefits. As such, "hegemony" takes a benign form. In Kindleberger's analysis (1986), a hegemon is required to provide an international currency to facilitate global trade. An international currency, therefore, has the character of a public good, one that all can share and that imposes some costs on the provider, such as the need to provide the world with global liquidity when necessary by running trade deficits. Other costs include the dollar overhangs that arise when other countries amass large foreign currency reserves and that pose uncertainties and a loss of bargaining power for the hegemon. Thus, an international currency is not necessarily an imperial currency.

For others, however, the benefits to the United States of having its currency used widely throughout the world are large and constitute a part of an imperial structure; what is important is not the deterritorialization of money but the extension and reinforcement of the power of the U.S. imperial state that comes with greater "financialization" (Panitch and Gindin, 2005).

The interpretation of the global system as representing a "dollar empire" is advanced by Rowbotham (2000: 8). He argues that:

> the issue being discussed here is power. It is the power to control and direct economic activity, and thereby, ultimately, people. This is the power of money and of banking, the power of the Federal Reserve and especially the dollar, the power of the IMF and World Bank, the power of the World Trade Organization, the power of a few hundred Chief Executive Officers of the most powerful multinational corporations and the power of dominant governments. It is today's imperialism.

Thus, in the period of "imperialism without colonies," one of the central mechanisms for propagating empire is the international role of the dollar. This is seen as a part of a wider imperial structure geared to the maintenance of political and economic power in the hands of imperial states. There is no discussion of shared sovereignty here, just the imposition of undemocratic rule. As Rowbotham (2000: 9) argues, "with any degree of popular conviction and determination, and commitment by politicians to their own citizens, the Washington Consensus, the empire of the dollar and the power to dominate and draw an unjust profit from the world's economic activity will simply vanish."

For Rowbotham, the origins of this dollar empire go back to the Bretton Woods agreement where, according to his analysis, Keynes's proposals for a neutral international money—the "bancor"—and a framework for requiring equal adjustments by creditor and debtor countries were rejected by strong U.S. self-interest. The United States as the world's largest creditor country did not accept Keynes's proposal and put in its place a framework in which the dollar became the de facto international currency, a move strengthened by the closing of the gold window in 1973. It was thus U.S. self-interest that rejected a genuine internationalism but imposed a system designed to enhance U.S. global power.

From this position, Rowbotham argues that it was inevitable that debt would accumulate as creditor countries were under no pressure to reduce their surpluses. The result was Third World debt, and this was a major factor driving globalization. Third World countries borrowed in U.S. dollars and were forced to adopt export-oriented growth strategies to repay their debts. These debts are still on the books, despite the fact that there is no chance of their ever being fully repaid, and the Third World is still forced to generate hard currency funds by selling its commodities and its assets on world markets. The use of the dollar as an international currency has therefore enabled the United States, under the auspices of the IMF and the World Bank, to prise open developing-country markets, force trade and investment liberalization on them, and maintain this position by insisting on the sanctity of U.S. dollar-denominated debt.

The view that U.S. imperial power was advanced by the post-1945 international financial order put in place then is also advanced by Panitch and Gindin (2005), who further argue that the current phase of "financialization"—or what others might call the rise of global finance—contributes further to U.S. power. For Wade (2003), the international financial architecture represents the "invisible hand of the American empire." He argues (2003: 87) that "this is the paradox of economic globalization—it looks like 'powerless' expansion of markets but it works to enhance the ability of the United States to harness the rest of the world and fortify its empire-like power." Central to this "empire-like power" is the international role of the dollar. If a country wanted to create an empire, Wade argues (2003: 78), it would be beneficial to have

> no constraint, such as the gold standard, on [its] ability to create [its] currency at will, so that [it] can finance large current-account deficits with the rest of the world simply by selling [its] government's debt securities. Second, [its] currency must be the main international currency for foreign exchange reserves, international trade, and foreign exchange speculation. This ensures robust demand from the rest of the world to hold [its] assets ... This gives [it] more policy flexibility, especially freedom to run big deficits, than other debtors have.

Although a thought experiment, Wade regards these conditions as being present today.

Panitch and Gindin (2005) and Wade (2003) argue that the ability of the United States to finance its deficits by issuing its own currency provides the imperial center with a competitive advantage over other countries. Petras and Veltmeyer (2001) concur that the international role of the dollar provides direct benefits to U.S. firms. Among the advantages of U.S. MNCs, they include the fact that "the U.S. Treasury Department can finance the nation's huge current account deficit by issuing dollars—the major currency of exchange in world markets. No capitalist competitor has this privileged ability to finance its negative balances" (Petras and Veltmeyer, 2001: 64). As long as the U.S. dollar is the international reserve currency, the United States need never be concerned about IMF sanctions, as it alone borrows in the currency that it issues. And holders of the dollars abroad are exchanging their goods, to be consumed in the United States, for pieces of paper produced by the U.S. Treasury: an international seigniorage.

This line of reasoning suggests that U.S. imperial ambitions have been strengthened since the early 1970s when the Bretton Woods system collapsed (or, more accurately, was unilaterally ended by the U.S. decision to close the gold window) and at the same time as the United States made its transition from being a net creditor country to a net debtor country. The ability to finance trade deficits through seigniorage is regarded as strengthening the U.S. position in the world. This view is not only advocated by those of a left-Marxist persuasion but finds supporters on the right-mainstream. Just as there are those (such as Johnson, 2000) on the right who have argued that, in general, the United States has mismanaged its power to the detriment of the rest of the world, so this argument also has its supporters when applied to the case of international financial markets. This can be seen in the recent arguments of MacKinnon (2005), for example, which although never using the term—and for this reason included here with some misgivings—bear a striking resemblance to those analyses that explicitly examine imperialism.

He argues (2005: 3) that:

> in the 19th century, Britain was resented as the world's dominant creditor country that kept the rest of the world in thrall to the London capital market with the pound sterling being the key currency. But because Britain was then on the gold standard more or less on a par with other industrial countries, it had much less autonomy in monetary matters than does the U.S. in today's world of fiat national monies.

The problem for McKinnon is that the United States may use this autonomy, gained by "historical accident," to promote its own interests to the detriment of others. McKinnon argues (2005: 7–8) that "after World War II, the US had the world's only intact financial system ... because of the open U.S. foreign exchange and financial markets, the dollar naturally became the world's vehicle currency for (private) interbank transacting and the intervention currency that governments used for stabilizing their exchange rates ... This was quite natural given the history of the situation ... Because of this accident of history, the US dollar became the intermediary currency in international exchange between any pair of 'peripheral' monies."

No imperial design here, as argued by Rowbotham (2000) and Panitch and Gindin (2005): just nature and historical accidents. Nevertheless the outcome of this was (2005: 5; emphasis in original) that "the US *alone* can go deeply into debt to the rest of the world in its *own* currency" and therefore the United States alone is removed from the strictures of financial orthodoxy to which all other countries are subject. The result of this is that the rest of the world (with the exception of the eurozone) is exposed to financial fragility, with debtors facing crises if their currencies are attacked and creditors facing the risk of deflation with speculative capital inflows; there is thus both "fear of floating" and "conflicting virtue." These negative consequences are manageable, but "the unbalanced world monetary regime turns more malign when the centre country tends to act—either consciously or unconsciously—in an exploitative fashion" (2005: 32). The United States is able to do this because "the central position of the U.S. government gives it unusual leverage to influence policies in other countries" (2005: 33). That is, policies designed to liberalize capital markets prematurely and to "open their domestic financial markets in the interests of American banks, insurance companies, stock brokerages, and so on" (ibid.).

The United States has also, in McKinnon's opinion, exploited its position (again consciously or unconsciously) as the "international natural lender of last resort" (ibid) to borrow indefinitely for domestic purposes. As a result, the United States drains savings from poorer countries, places pressure on exchange rates, and uses its role as the supplier of the world's key currency to advance its own interests while exposing other countries to greater risks. In other words, the world financial system is organized to benefit U.S. capitalism—just as it supported European capitalism in the period of late-nineteenth-century European imperialism. Of course, while leftists-Marxists argue for anti-imperialist struggles, McKinnon calls for new rules to ensure that the United States acts more as a provider of an international public good than as—consciously or unconsciously—an exploiter. Despite the differences in terminology and responses, there is nevertheless a remarkable degree of agreement on the current role played by the U.S. dollar in the international financial system.

The characterization of the current phase of financial globalization as one that increases the power of the United States is, however, disputed by other analysts from both right and left. Here, the transition of the United States to a net debtor position is interpreted as significantly restricting its power. Arrighi (2005), for example, argues that the U.S. position as a debtor signals its decline. Ferguson (2001: 293; italics in original), in comparing the late-nineteenth-century imperialism with current U.S. dominance, argues that:

> perhaps the crucial difference between then and now ... is that Britain was a net exporter of capital while the United States today is the opposite. For the United States has used its dominance of the international bond market not to *export* capital—which in net terms it did until around 1972—but to import it. This greatly reduces the financial leverage of its foreign policy: for you cannot have "dollar diplomacy" without dollars. In short, the global hegemon of the present age of globalization has much less financial leverage than that of the first age. And this is one of the reasons why, although the United States has a few quasi-colonial dependencies, it cannot exercise the kind of formal and informal control over the world economy wielded by Britain in her imperial heyday.

Though there is broad agreement within this approach, therefore, that the international financial system with the central role in it of the dollar acts (by design or even unintentionally) to support the interests of the United States as the major imperial power, there are nevertheless differences in assessing how much power, in comparative historical terms, this provides the United States. For some, such as Wade and McKinnon, the absence of constraints such as the gold standard means that the United States is much more powerful than its British counterpart at the end of the nineteenth century; by focusing on the net debtor position of the United States since 1973, Arrighi and Ferguson reach the opposite conclusion.

These differences in comparative historical assessments aside, what are the implications of viewing the financial structure as a part of the structure of empire? The first and most obvious is that given that the role of the dollar as an international currency is a critical factor in the maintenance of U.S. economic dominance, it is one that the United States might be expected to defend. As an example of the pressures brought to bear to continue the role of the dollar as an international reserve currency and thereby maintain the privileges arising from it for the United States, consider the events surrounding the oil price shocks of the 1970s. In a fascinating piece of academic detective work, Spiro (1999: x) argues that "In 1974, [U.S. Treasury Secretary William] Simon negotiated a secret deal so the Saudi central bank could buy U.S. Treasury securities outside of the normal auction. A few years later, Treasury Secretary Michael Blumenthal cut a secret deal with the Saudis so that OPEC would continue to price oil in dollars. These deals were secret because the United States had promised other industrialized countries that it would not pursue such unilateral policies." That is, it was critical to the United States that the dollar remain an international currency and the United States broke its commitment to its allies not to use the dollar as a weapon in economic rivalry.

The importance of the international role of the dollar as a support for U.S. global interests has also led to analyses of current conflicts as being at least in part, if not mainly, driven by the United States's need to maintain this position. Thus, Saddam Hussein's decision in 2000 to price Iraqi oil in euros rather than in dollars was a move unquestionably designed to signal an act of defiance against the United States and, more questionably, has been interpreted as a major reason for the United States–led invasion (Clark, 2005). The decision of the Iranian government to accept euros in payment for its oil exports to Europe and Asia in 2003 and its subsequent 2004 decision to create an Iranian oil bourse denominated in euros (though its planned 2006 trading start date has been postponed) has similarly been seen as underlying the threat of United States–Iran confrontation (Clark, 2005).

Interimperialist rivalries have been interpreted as taking the form of rivalry between the euro and the dollar, a rivalry that peripheral countries, such as Iraq and Iran, have sought to exploit. Furthermore, members of the European Left have supported the euro precisely because they believe it will undermine the role of the dollar and hence U.S. power. For example, Monbiot (2003) argues that the international role of the dollar provides the United States with large benefits. As he states, "in order to earn dollars, other nations must provide goods and services to the United States. When commodities are valued in dollars, the United States needs do no more than print pieces of green paper to obtain them: it acquires them, in effect, for free. Once earned, other nations' dollar reserves must be invested back into the American economy. This inflow of money helps the United States to finance its massive deficit." If, however, a commodity such as oil was not priced in oil but in euros—a move that Monbiot considers might be feasible if Europe's two largest oil exporters, the United Kingdom and Norway, decided to switch to the euro—"oil importing nations will no longer need dollar reserves to buy oil. The demand for the dollar will fall, and its value is likely to decline. As the dollar slips, central banks will start to move their reserves into safer currencies such as the euro and possibly the yen and the yuan, precipitating further slippage. The US economy, followed rapidly by US power, could then be expected to falter or collapse." A seemingly technocratic discussion of international currencies therefore masks fundamental issues of power within the world (see also Hensmann and Correggia, 2005). The potential of the euro to rival the dollar, however, is dismissed as unrealistic within the foreseeable future by many (see, for example, Panitch and Gindin, 2005).

We would also expect that the power of imperial states would be seen in setting and controlling exchange rates with "market forces" less dominant than in other accounts. Thus, U.S. pressure led to the revaluationof the yen in 1985 and the South Korean won in 1989 and has recently been attempted with the Chinese renminbi (Bowles and Wang, 2006). It is not powerful international financial markets that are responsible for these realignments in exchange rates but the powerful U.S. government.

Those adopting an imperialist interpretation pay primary attention to the ways in which the dominant imperial power—first Britain and now the United States— uses the international monetary system to its advantage; the international monetary system reflects the power dynamics in the international—imperial—system itself. The focus is typically on the currency of the imperial power with the implications for non-imperial currencies less discussed. It is certainly the case that unofficial dollarization and the widespread use of the U.S. dollar is seen as conferring benefits to its issuing government. Carchedi (2001: 161) argues that official dollarization also provides considerable advantages to the United States, though "in spite of these advantages, up to now the United States has displayed a cautious attitude towards [this] development" because it also brings some costs. Nevertheless, he continues that official dollarization is likely to be important for the United States "as a strategy to hold back EU imperialism." Carchedi (2001: 165) is of the opinion that the EU is capable of challenging the United States on a number of fronts and that "the euro is one such challenge." We would expect to see, therefore, pressures for official dollarization as part of imperial structures even if it is more likely to be sold as "an aspect of a supposedly inevitable process—globalization" (Carchedi, 2001: 162). That is, discussions of the need for "good governance" in the form of dollarization in non-imperial countries need to be analyzed against the backdrop of an imperial international financial and monetary structure. Furthermore, this may be the site of inter-imperialist rivalries, particularly between the dollar and the euro.

Regional currencies

Regional currencies will form the bedrock of the next century's financial stability.

(Beddoes, 1999: 3)

The regional interpretation stresses the regionalized or triadic nature of production and trade. It highlights the differences between regions and analyzes the complex relationships between regionalism and globalization. Similar concerns are transferred to the discussion of monetary affairs.

The contemporary world can be read as a "tripartite world" (Bergsten, 2000) or a regional world rather than one of inter-imperialist rivalries. The decline of post-1945 U.S. dominance has led to a multipolar world order characterized by macro-regions centered on the major powers in each of these regions. This is based on a process of regionalization, the formation of regional divisions of labor based on technological and market-driven forces, and regionalism, a politically driven process of regional integration. This would be expected to result in the regional dominance of the leading currencies of each region. As an example of the type of evidence that might be used to support such a position, consider the shares of the U.S. dollar, the euro, and the yen in the invoicing of international trade in the United States and in selected European and Asian countries presented in Table 3.1.

Though this data, using an indicator commonly used to measure the importance of currencies as vehicles for trade, provides some evidence of regional currency blocs; it is clearly stronger in the case of the United States and members of the eurozone than it is in Asia. This points to the need to delve behind the numbers to examine the dynamics involved. Each of the three main regions (Europe, Asia, and the Americas) may follow different patterns of integration, with different histories and different outcomes. The differences may be especially clear in monetary affairs and in the implications for national currencies.[11]

Most obviously, in Europe—or, more precisely, in twelve of the fifteen countries forming the EU—a common currency, the euro, replaced national currencies on January 1, 2002. The process leading to the adoption of a common currency—and the abandonment of national currencies—was long and complex and has been the

Table 3.1 Shares of the U.S. dollar, the euro, and the yen in trade invoicing in selected countries

Country	Year	Currency share in export invoicing (%)			Currency share in import invoicing (%)		
		U.S. Dollar	*Euro*	*Yen*	*U.S. Dollar*	*Euro*	*Yen*
U.S.	2003	95	–	–	85	–	–
Japan	2001	52	–	36	70	–	24
Korea	2001	85	–	7	82	–	10
Malaysia	1996	66	–	7	66	–	7
France	2002	21	72	–	25	70	–
Germany	2002	18	71	0	21	73	0
UK	2001	29	15	–	38	10	–

Source: Goldberg and Tille (2005: 40)

subject of much academic analysis. A synthetic interpretation drawing on some of these sources is provided below.[12] Of course, it is not the only account possible but one that can be considered as representative of a significant part of the literature. The three most salient phases of the move to the euro, each characterized by a distinct objective, are briefly discussed, and the reasons and driving forces behind each of these objectives are analyzed.[13]

The EU (or European Community [EC] as it was then) did not devote much attention to monetary issues in its early years because the common market operated with practically fixed exchange rates by virtue of its member states belonging to the Bretton Woods exchange-rate system. When this system began to unravel in the late 1960s, it became evident that exchange-rate fluctuations could pose a problem for the proper functioning of the common market and would be particularly disruptive for the administration of the Common Agricultural Policy (McNamara, 1998: 98–104). To remedy the problem and to facilitate trade and promote further economic and political integration, in 1971 the EC adopted the Werner Report, an ambitious plan for economic and monetary union to be achieved in stages by 1980. The first stage, a modest scheme known as the "snake," which limited the range of exchange-rate fluctuations of the participating currencies, was launched in April 1972.

The objective of trying to establish a regional zone of stability in the midst of global monetary turbulence was not realized as member states pursued conflicting macroeconomic policy goals during an unprecedented period of stagflation. For example, while Germany pursued a restrictive monetary policy to control inflation, other member states implemented expansionary policies to try to stimulate growth and employment. The result was that the snake ran immediately into trouble. A wave of currency speculation pushed half of the participating currencies outside the established exchange-rate margins and, by 1974, the snake was reduced to a limited Deutschmark zone. Consequently, the goal of achieving monetary union was abandoned, though not for long.

In April 1978, German Social-Democratic Chancellor Helmut Schmidt and French President Valéry Giscard D'Estaing resurrected the idea because both thought that the adoption of a quasi-fixed European exchange-rate system would help them to reach preferred domestic economic policy objectives. Schmidt wished to adopt an expansionary policy with a view to the 1980 elections but had to overcome the doubts of some members of his coalition government and the Bundesbank's traditional commitment to price stability. As he saw it, German participation in a managed exchange-rate system would slow the appreciation of the mark (and thus help German industry retain competitiveness) and act as a constraint on the Bundesbank, pushing it toward the adoption of a less restrictive monetary policy. That is, movement to a pegged exchange rate would be an expansionary move.

According to Oatley (1997: 48–56), Giscard D'Estaing's committing the franc to a managed exchange-rate system was a way to enlist French industrialists in the struggle against inflation by convincing them that they could no longer hope to maintain international competitiveness by means of periodic devaluations and, hence, encourage them to resist any wage increases not reflecting improvements in productivity. That is, the movement to a pegged exchange rate would be a more deflationary, neoliberal move.

The outcome of this Franco-German initiative was the European Monetary System (EMS) that began to operate in March 1979. Its central component was the Exchange Rate Mechanism (ERM), limiting the exchange-rate fluctuations of most member currencies to plus or minus 2.25 percent of predetermined parities. The EMS proved more successful than the snake, although some currencies were repeatedly obliged to leave it and then devalue before rejoining (see Tsoukalis, 1977; Kruse, 1980; and Ludlow, 1982).

In 1987, EC member governments ratified the so-called Single European Act (SEA) that aimed at "completing" the common market by removing all remaining non-tariff barriers to the free movement of goods, people, services, and capital by the end of 1992. The success of this initiative gave new impetus to the integration process and enabled the European Commission to again put on the EC agenda the project of the economic and monetary union (EMU) to be achieved in three stages. The official justification for the project was that monetary union was a natural and logical complement of a single European market—a single market required a single currency.

After 1992, the EC became characterized by complete freedom of capital movements and a system of quasi-fixed exchange rates (the EMS), deemed necessary to facilitate intra-Community trade and thereby promote greater economic efficiency. As a result, member states relinquished their ability to conduct autonomous national monetary policies as required by the trilemma. The inconsistency of these three elements had already manifested itself during the 1980s, when some member states had either opted for flexible exchange rates and withdrawn from the EMS (e.g., the United Kingdom) or had been occasionally obliged to resort to capital controls (e.g., France and Italy). After 1992, however, the instrument of capital controls would no longer be available. Hence, if governments wished to retain their ability to make autonomous national monetary policy, they had to return to flexible exchange rates. If, on the other hand, they were willing to relinquish whatever national autonomy they retained in monetary policy, they might as well move from the EMS to full currency union.

Though a case could be made for returning to flexible exchange rates on the grounds that Europe did not appear to be an "optimum currency area" (Eichengreen, 1997), a number of factors combined to provide favorable conditions for the re-launch of the currency union project (see Dyson and Featherstone, 1999). First, and perhaps most important, currency union was the solution favored by EC officials, especially within the Commission (Verdun, 1999), and by those political leaders who perceived the *telos* of the process of European integration to be the formation of a European federation. Officially, the EMU was justified on the arguments that the single currency would lead to greater efficiency for the single market, eliminate transactions costs, and provide a stimulus to growth and employment (Cecchini, 1988; Commission of the European Communities, 1992; Emerson, 1992; Temperton, 1998). The contention was also advanced that monetary union would solve the trilemma by transforming an already weak national monetary sovereignty into "enhanced joint monetary sovereignty" (Commission of the European Communities, 1996: 12–15). There is no doubt, however, that the view that the adoption of a common currency would promote a European identity and thus contribute to the consolidation of the EC as a political union was paramount in the minds of the promoters of the project (Shore, 2000: 87–122). It was this realization, coupled with a divided public opinion, that led British and Danish politicians to opt out of EMU.

A second and important factor was that throughout the 1980s, European political elites, including social-democracies, had moved away from traditional Keynesian policies and converged toward neoliberal ones. Their penchant for "minimum government" made agreement on an SEA built around deregulation and liberalization easier, whereas their preference for low inflation facilitated agreement on the structure of EMU, particularly on the choice of the status (independence) and main objective (price stability) of the European Central Bank. Even trade unions supported currency union, limiting themselves to argue that as a counterweight to the perceived deflationary bias of EMU, the EC should make an explicit commitment to promote employment. A specific title to this effect was introduced in the 1997 Treaty of Amsterdam.

A number of more circumstantial variables also played a significant role in the choice of currency union.[14] For example, the fall of the Berlin wall and the consequent prospect of German reunification led some member states to regard reinforcement of EC institutions as the best way to avoid an institutionally weak EC being dominated by a larger Germany. The solution of a currency union was particularly appealing as Germany (or, more precisely, the Bundesbank) was already perceived as playing a leading role in the EMS (Giavazzi and Giovannini, 1989). Germany, for its part, traded its initial reluctance to adhere to EMU and thus relinquish the mark in exchange for unqualified support of reunification on the part of its EC partners. The adoption of a single currency was also regarded as necessary if the EC wished to be able to compete with the United States as an equal on the world stage. It was, after all, the perception that Europe was increasingly lagging behind the United States in economic growth that had led to the adoption of the SEA. Finally, and perhaps most important, domestic political and economic considerations also played a significant role. In Italy, for instance, the EMU—and particularly the need to meet the criteria for admission to its third stage—was regarded as an "external constraint" that would help Italy to bring its public finances under control by supplying clear objectives for fiscal policy and a supranational surveillance on progress to attain them (Croci and Picci, 2002).

To summarize, the EMU was officially justified as a logical next step after the completion of the common market, a step that would reduce transaction costs and thus increase trade and stimulate economic growth. These arguments, however, would not have been as successful—good economic counter-arguments also existed, most importantly that EMU would deprive national governments of their ability to use interest and exchange rates as instruments of economic policy—had it not been for the fact that the EMU was also, and primarily, a *politically* driven process. First, there was the desire on the part of EC officials to make another significant step forward in the process of integration, a step that arguably had the potential to increase Europe's role and visibility on the world stage and contribute to the formation of a European-wide "imagined community." Second, and most important, national leaders who could have blocked the project did not because they saw the EMU as an external factor that would help them attain domestic objectives (e.g., fiscal restraint in Italy, political reunification in Germany). The terrain of the euro will now be extended to include the ten accession countries of East-Central Europe as the result of another political decision by the EU.

According to this analysis, the primary driving force for the creation of the euro was regionalism, a state (or European elite) project designed to establish a new regional currency. As such, the specificities of the emergence of the euro mean that the dynamics of regional integration in Europe find no clear parallels in other regions. In Asia, for example, during much of the 1980s and 1990s, the process of regional integration was interpreted as being predominantly market-led, that is, a process of regionalization (Bowles, 2002). Embroiled in the military conflicts of the Cold War period, the countries of Asia did not participate in the wave of regionalism that proved popular with other developing countries in the 1950s and 1960s. When regionalism reemerged as a preferred economic policy in the 1980s and 1990s, Asia again lagged behind the rest of the world in terms of the formal political institutionalization of regionalism. Indeed, a distinguishing feature of Asian regionalism for many scholars was precisely the fact that the "region" itself was ill-defined (or capable of multiple definitions) and that the regionalism that was taking place was doing so through market-led, rather than government-led, integration processes. Stubbs (1995: 786), for example, argued that "although the state has been instrumental in nurturing business growth, regionalization in the Asia-Pacific region—unlike the other major regions of the world—has been driven by the private sector not by governments. Hence, the boundaries of the region do not coincide neatly with state boundaries. In many ways the region's governments are still trying to come to grips with the rapid economic changes that swirl around them."

The "regional economy" in Asia, and in a number of subregions, was therefore identified by economists and policy analysts as being based primarily on the activities of Japanese multinational corporations (MNCs) and of overseas Chinese businesses. These activities were highlighted as operating on the basis of a series of "networks" based on the production prerequisites of post-Fordism and the personal connections that facilitated and characterized much of the overseas Chinese diaspora. It was these business networks, rather than the existence of supranational political institutions, that led to the identification and integration of a "regional economy." This was also true at the subregional level. For example, "Greater China" was identified as one such subregion, comprising an international division of labor that integrated production in the southeastern coastal regions of China with companies in Taiwan and Hong Kong. Here, too, the impetus for economic integration was identified as largely business-driven rather than as state-driven. As Naughton (1997: v) writes, "firms, especially small and medium-size family firms, play central roles in the story, with government policies playing secondary, reactive roles."

Though the above analyses may underestimate the role of the state in promoting regional economic integration, they do make the valid point that Asian regionalism was based on a lower level of formal intergovernmental regional institutions and policies than were observed in other regions, most notably in Europe and North America. In this comparative sense, the above analyses are right to stress the relatively greater role of the "market" and relatively less importance of the "state" in regional integration in Asia than elsewhere, even if there has been a tendency to push the argument too far in that direction. Even so, there have been some state-led initiatives, such as the ASEAN Free Trade Area (AFTA) that came into effect in 1993 (Bowles, 1997). The ASEAN countries, under the "guidance" of the international financial institutions, had adopted trade and investment liberalization measures in the mid-1980s as a way to boost exports in the wake of the debt crisis of the early 1980s. At the same time, the appreciation of the yen had led to a rapid expansion of foreign direct investment (FDI) by Japanese companies. Japan's FDI grew at an annual average rate of 62 percent over the 1985–89 period. At the same time, the East Asian NICs were also investing heavily overseas with the ASEAN-4 (Indonesia, Thailand, the Philippines, and Malaysia) and China being favored destinations. As a result, FDI as a percentage of gross domestic product (GDP) quadrupled in the ASEAN-4 between 1985 and 1990. Having shifted to a strategy of FDI-sponsored export-led growth, ASEAN states were keenly aware of the need to ensure that the ASEAN as an investment site remained competitive. At the end of the 1980s, there appeared to be a significant threat to this in the form of competition from China; the former Soviet bloc following the dramatic events of 1989–91; the potential investment-diverting effects of greater European integration in 1992; and the NAFTA, particularly the threat of investment diversion to Mexico. The result was the ATFA.

Despite the increasing regional integration of Asian economies, there was little serious discussion at the time of the need for any form of common currency, along the lines of the euro, to further regional integration. The idea was raised but typically as a "long run" issue. The most important monetary innovation revolved around the possible development of a "yen bloc" (Frankel, 1991). This was partly a short-hand for a Japan-centered production network but also an expanded role for the yen in international transactions, an expansion encouraged by the Japanese government (through its aid policy, for example).

The idea of a yen bloc waned with the state of the Japanese economy but, in the aftermath of the Asian financial crisis of 1997, there have been further developments in regional monetary cooperation (Dieter, 2000). After the initial rejection of the idea of an Asian Monetary Fund, closer monetary and trade ties are now being actively fostered in the region; a new regionalism, geographically well-defined and located in East Asia and involving all of the major countries of this region, is now being forged. As Bergsten (2000) noted, the East Asian Economic Group has held summit meetings under the ASEAN+3 rubric (i.e., the ten ASEAN countries plus China, Japan, and South Korea), and a "Vision Group" was formed to advise on the future role and evolution of this group.

Regional monetary cooperation now includes bilateral swap arrangements between the region's central banks, the strengthening of financial surveillance, and a fledgling regional bond market (Nasution, 2005). These developments, arising from the post-financial crisis Chiang-Mai Initiative, has led to renewed speculation about a larger role for the yen and an eventual "Asian currency unit." For example, addressing the Asian Development Bank's (ADB) Board of Governors Meeting in 2004, ADB President Tadao Chino speculated on whether East Asia should "follow the global trend toward currency consolidation by moving to the adoption of a single currency over the long run" (ADB, 2004). President Chino continued by arguing that "in an increasingly globalized world, there is likely to be a greater synchronization of business cycles. Hence, the benefits of having fewer currencies to conduct cross-border business, especially at the regional level, are likely to increase" (ibid.). Thus, the increasing integration of regional trade and investment is seen as creating the conditions for East Asia to become a potential optimal currency area (though see Eichengreen, 2006 for a more skeptical view).

In the Americas, trade integration has taken place through the CUSFTA and NAFTA, with the more ambitious FTAA still at a stalled planning stage. Exchange-rate management, much less monetary union, has not been a part of the formal process of regionalism in the Americas. However, monetary issues, and dollarization in particular, have been prominent issues. Right-oriented governments in both Ecuador and El Salvador adopted the U.S. dollar, though their motivations differed. The dollar's adoption by Ecuador in 2000, following on its historic default on Brady bonds (restructured commercial bank debts) in 1999, was something of a desperate response to a country facing hyperinflation and a deteriorating external situation. In contrast, El Salvador's economy was suffering only a slowdown in growth but had sound "fundamentals," having had a fixed exchange rate with the dollar since 1994 and a highly open economy. The decision to officially dollarize came as an attempt to increase economic growth by eliminating the interest rate premium for domestic currency loans; by adopting the U.S. dollar, El Salvador hoped to reduce its borrowing costs and spur growth.

Though El Salvador and Ecuador provide examples of the adoption of other currencies by small countries, the idea has also been discussed in some larger countries, most notably Argentina, Mexico, and Canada. As previously outlined, Argentina adopted a currency board arrangement in 1991, with the U.S. dollar as the anchor currency in an attempt to stabilize its economy, but the option that caught most attention was its announcement in 1999 to consider the unilateral adoption of the dollar. In the wake of the contagion effects of the Asian financial crisis, and in particular the possibility that Argentina would have to match Brazil's devaluation, official dollarization offered the option of literally removing the possibility of a currency crisis by removing any exchange rate to defend. In Argentina, the choice of the dollar as the currency for potential unilateral official adoption is based as much on geography and the reality of U.S. power in the Americas as it is on economics. In fact, use of the euro as a common currency could be as justified as the dollar, given trade patterns and output co-movements (Alesina and Barro, 2001). The collapse of the currency board arrangement in 2001 ended this infatuation with dollarization.

Viewed comparatively, regional dynamics are quite distinct in each region. In Europe, the adoption of the euro can be seen as a primarily politically-driven process. In Asia, integration has been interpreted as a primarily market-driven process, though post-financial crisis regionalism may include closer monetary cooperation between the major states. The chances of this leading to a new regional currency are, however, remote at present. In the Americas, the dominance of the United States has made dollarization the main issue for other countries in the region. The implications for national currencies are, therefore, dependent on the region in which a country is located and on the regional dynamics in each case. Of course, monetary innovations in one region may lead to pressures for responses in other regions. The European example has influenced debate not only in the Americas but in other regions as well. Regional currencies are planned for West Africa and by the Gulf Cooperation Council.

Nevertheless, the regions and their dynamics remain distinct if interdependent. The relative insulation of these regions is reinforced by the fact that contagion effects are typically regional in character rather than global. Glick and Rose (1999), for example, argue that financial crises are contagious between countries that trade heavily with each other and these trade linkages are primarily regional in nature; there is much more evidence in favor of regional rather than global contagion. That is, financial markets, too, are regionally based rather than global. In similar vein, Larrain and Tavares (2003) find substantial regional differences in the determinants of real exchange-rate volatility.

Though comparativists are apt to stress how these regional tales differ, those coming from a traditional international economics background are more inclined to focus on the interdependencies and thus how these regional currencies can be effectively coordinated. For example, as Frankel and Roubini (2001: 6) have noted, "the short run volatility of G3 real exchange rates is one of the most robust—and to many observers disturbing—characteristics of the post Bretton Woods floating exchange rates experience." That is, how monetary relations can be structured in a "tripartite" world centered around three leading currencies is the main issue, with lesser regional players being influenced by this. Thus, for some, the appreciation of the U.S. dollar against the yen in the mid-1990s was a major contributing cause to the Asian financial crisis (Bergsten, 2000). In this reading, exchange-rate crises are at least as much due to the results of misalignments between the major regional currencies as they are due to new powerful global financial markets. The task becomes better coordination but one that offers the prospect of worldwide financial stability, with coordination between the major regional currencies allowing other countries in those regions to also obtain stability by linking with, or adopting, those currencies (Beddoes, 1999).

Thus, the economic arguments for the emergence of regional currencies rest on the regionalized nature of trade, production, and even finance. To this are added the political dynamics of regionalism, though here the emphasis is often of the differences between the regions in this respect. The triadic nature of the world political economy was perhaps more strongly asserted in the 1990s than it has been since as a result of Japan's economic stagnation and the apparent rise of Brazil, Russia, India, and China (the BRICs). In currency terms, this shift has meant either greater emphasis on the possible emergence of an Asian currency unit rather than a focus on the yen or an emphasis on the regional role of the euro but a more extended role for the U.S. dollar. Much of the regional currency literature is also premised on the proposition that the emergence of regional currencies is not a step on the route to a global currency but a permanent feature reflecting the current regionalized economic and political structures. In this respect, the debate over regional currencies differs from that over regionalism in general as surveyed in Chapter 2 in that, in the latter, the links between regionalism and globalization were much more contentious.

Conclusion

The four interpretations of globalization surveyed in Chapter 2 have been shown in this chapter to have distinct implications for analyzing national currencies. These implications have been both for how the past, especially the period since 1945, should be interpreted and for what the future might hold.

As in Chapter 2, within each category a variety of arguments can be found. In some cases, this is a matter of strong and weak versions. For example, in the *globalization* interpretation, some authors hold a strong position that globalization will lead to distinct pressures for the disappearance of national currencies for efficiency or credibility reasons, for example. However, other subscribers to the view that globalization has weakened nation-states are much less inclined to conclude that this means that national currencies will disappear. This weaker version argues that nation-states have lost some important control over the value and uses of their currencies but not enough to lead them to forsake them altogether. This best describes one end of the bipolar view wherein national currencies are preserved with flexible exchange rates, but the issuing state has little control of the currency's value in the face of powerful international markets. For others, such as Cohen (2004), states' power has been reduced to the extent that they are now oligopolists rather than monopolists, but this is unlikely to lead states to abandon their currencies completely.

In the *globalism* interpretation, the strong and weak versions are couched in terms of the extent to which international financial markets have affected states' abilities to manage their national currencies. In the strong version, supported by authors such as Fligstein (2001), international financial markets have had little or no effect; in the weak version, these markets have limited state action but, crucially, these limitations have been the result of states ceding this power to markets, with reversals entirely possible technologically if the political will exists.

In the *imperialism* interpretation, the main difference between authors is in their assessment of whether U.S. power has increased as a result of the collapse of the Bretton Woods system and the abandonment of gold as a peg, as McKinnon

(2005) and Wade (2003) argue, or whether the emergence of the United States as the largest net debtor constrains their power, as Ferguson (2001) and Arrighi (2005) contend.

These arguments are summarized below in Table 3.2, together with their implications for national currencies.

To analyze which of these four interpretations best identifies the particular "forces of globalization" acting on national currencies requires analysis of specific cases; appeal to data alone will not guide us here. That is, it is the interpretation of trends and data that is critical. If, for example, a country in South America dollarized, what would this indicate about the relationship between globalization and national currencies? Would it show that international financial markets are now so powerful that countries have limited choices and had best delegate their monetary sovereignty to more credible central banks? Would it indicate that policy makers had choices but chose this option to lock in neoliberal reforms? Would it indicate that the country had become inserted more fully into the U.S. empire? Would a process of regional integration provide the best explanation? The fact of dollarization alone would not illuminate the relationship between globalization and the national currency unless we were also able to explain the dynamics of this fact and thereby throw light on the meaning of globalization. That is, we need to analyze case studies in more detail to enable us to tease out which of the forces of globalization are most evident and therefore which implications for national currencies are most persuasive.

In the second part of this book, we analyze four case studies. The case-studies approach will enable us to see which of the forces of globalization and which of the four interpretations best explains the debate in each of the case studies. To accomplish this, we can draw out from the discussion in this chapter eighteen key questions for analysis that can be asked in each of the case studies. Of course, some questions will be more relevant for some cases than others but, taken together, they can be used as an entry point into the country-specific debates.

Arising from the *globalization* with weakened nation-states interpretation, we can ask in any case study:

1   What is the extent of "unofficial dollarization?"
2   Have there been pressures by global or exporting firms (or both) for currency unions or dollarization (or both)?
3   What have been the responses to currency volatility or currency crises (i.e., is there a credibility issue)?
4   How have levels of trade integration changed?
5   Have business cycles become more synchronized with major trading partners?
6   Have there been discussions of shared or delegated monetary sovereignty?
7   Have alleged technologically or efficiency-driven "historical trends" been a part of the discussion?
8   Have subnational political entities been part of the debate?

Table 3.2 The implications of interpretations of globalization for national currencies: summary

Globalization	Globalism	Imperialism	Regionalism
Supraterritorial currency or currencies (common currencies or official dollarization) suggested by: • efficiency (transaction cost) arguments (Mundell) • trade integration and OCA theory (Frankel) • endogenous OCAs (Rose) • credibility and institutional endowments (Hanke) • fear of floating (Calvo) • new global governance and a world currency needed to overcome international financial market volatility (some neo-Keynesians) Idea of inevitability of move towards fewer currencies Bipolar view—exchange-rate regime choices limited to two (hard fixes such as dollarization OR completely flexible exchange rate with no control by states of a currency's value) De-territorialized currencies with significant unofficial dollarization in some cases. End of state monopoly power in many cases (Cohen)	Viability of national currencies Monetary disunification (Pomfret) International financial markets have not weakened nation-states (Fligstein) Nation-states have ceded, not lost, power (Helleiner, Bienefeld) Same old trilemma; new policy environment Trend is reversible (with capital controls, for example) (Blecker) "Contingent neoliberalism"—no single neoliberal position (e.g., Mundell vs. Friedman) Neoliberal policy prescriptions vary by context; domestic conditions are critical. In some cases giving up national currencies may be advocated, in other cases not	Dollar as an international currency provides U.S. state with power over others (by design—Rowbotham; by accident—Wade and McKinnon) Dollar as an international currency provides benefits to U.S. firms (Petras and Veltmeyer) U.S. power increased in post-1973 era (Wade and McKinnon) U.S. power reduced in post-1970s period when US became a large net debtor country (Ferguson and Arrighi) Possible inter-imperial rivalries expressed in fight for market share between the U.S. dollar and the euro and in pricing of key international currencies Imperial powers seek to extend use of their own currencies through both unofficial dollarization and, possibly, official dollarization	Regional currencies emerging reflecting triadic nature of production and trade Financial crises and contagion are regional in nature (Gillick and Frankel) The euro as an exceptional event driven primarily by political factors Asian monetary regionalism post-1997 Asian financial crisis and possibility of Asian single currency (ADB) Possibility of dollarization in the Americas Main issue is coordination between the three main regional currencies (Bergsten) With successful coordination of three main regional currencies, other countries' currencies can lock onto their regional currency

Arising from the *globalism* with contingent neoliberalism interpretation, we can ask:

9   How much do national borders matter economically?
10 To what extent has policy autonomy been given away rather than taken away?
11 Has "inevitability" been invoked primarily to limit alternatives (as opposed to being a technologically determined outcome)?
12 How has "contingent neoliberalism" been applied in this case?

Arising from the *imperialism* interpretation, we can ask:

13 Have states been subject to imperial pressures?
14 What has been the policy on the pricing of key commodities?
15 What have been the responses to currency debates by the imperial powers?

Last, arising from the *regionalism*-is-more-important interpretation, we can ask:

16 Are there specific regional dynamics in evidence with respect to currency debates?
17 What role is played by supranational political bodies?
18 Is market-driven regionalization a significant force?

Part II

Case studies of four systemically significant currencies

In this part of the book, I analyze trends and currency debates in four countries. The countries chosen—Australia, Canada, Mexico, and Norway—have been chosen as illustrative of countries with systemically significant currencies. Globalization has the potential to affect national currencies in terms of both scope and intensity. That is, globalization may have impacts on the number of national currencies (i.e., the scope), but the significance of many or all of the currencies affected may be strictly limited for the operations of the overall currency system in its present form (i.e., the intensity). In the case studies analyzed here, in contrast, the currencies can be thought of as systemically significant. As noted in Chapter 1, the four currencies are the sixth, seventh, tenth, and twelfth most traded currencies in the world. That is, these countries are important for both the scope and the intensity of globalization's impacts. The creation of the euro has already resulted in a major change in the way in which the world's currency system operates. If we want to examine whether further changes are likely in the wake of this, as a result of the forces of globalization, we must analyze the future of national currencies of a similar standing in the currency system. The prospects for the Australian and Canadian dollars, the Mexican peso, and the Norwegian krone will tell us a good deal about the future of the present currency system. Specifically, the case studies will enable us to analyze which particular forces of globalization are present in each case, how strong they are, and what their implications might be.

As also discussed in Chapter 1, each of the four countries are political economies that have always been integrated into the wider world economy while, at the same time, striving to foster national development. As such, they are countries wherein the dual forces of globalization and national development might be thought to be most keenly found and, therefore, to offer rich analytical terrain for our question.

The four chapters that follow are each organized as follows. An introductory section provides a brief history of the country under consideration, stressing the linkages with the international economy and the phases of national development. The next section focuses on the exchange-rate regimes and monetary institutions used during this history, and the third section highlights the major trends and policy debates of the last twenty years. These sections therefore provide the background within which currency debates and trends can be analyzed. The debates over the future of the national currency are then discussed in detail. In the concluding section of each chapter, these debates are then analyzed in terms of their correspondence with each of the four interpretations of globalization set out in Part One of the book. Guided by the eighteen questions given at the end of Chapter 3, I analyze which of the forces of globalization are evident in the main contours of the debate in each country and provide an assessment of their importance and plausibility.

In the concluding chapter, comparative conclusions based on the case studies are drawn.

4   Australia

The decision to float the dollar, 20 years ago today, did not send Australians dancing into the streets, but it should have.

(Editorial, *The Australian*, December 9, 2003)

Overview of Australian development

When Britain declared sovereignty over Australia at Sydney Cove in 1788, the invaders viewed the land as *terra nullius*, an empty space (Dyster and Meredith, 1997: 17). Australia was brought into the orbit of the British Empire, its extensive land was used to supply British industry, and its economic structure and development were framed by the needs of the imperial center. Capitalism took root, land was appropriated, and a laboring class was formed within this wider structure of imperial dependency. Australia, like other colonies, became a staple economy, that is, one based on the export of raw materials. In the 1820s, it became profitable to ship wool to Britain (Maddock and McLean, 1987: 6), and wool became the first staple and the largest export earner for most of the nineteenth century (ibid.: 26). Other staples, such as wheat, were soon to follow, as were minerals. The repeal of the Corn Laws was instrumental in forging "economic complementarity" between Britain and Australia (Leaver, 2001: 4). Coal, "the fundamental source of energy for the industrial revolution" (Dyster and Meredith, 1997: 18), was discovered at the end of the eighteenth century. Copper and gold were also discovered, the latter leading to the gold rush of the 1850s, which tripled the non-aboriginal population in a decade (ibid.: 27) By the 1870s, Broomhill (2007: 4) argues, the Australian colonies "had achieved a higher level of capitalist development and political independence than many other colonial societies." Production and export of gold peaked in 1903 (Dyster and Meredith, 1997: 19). By then, Australia had also entered the silver, lead, and zinc markets.

Following British "discovery," the course of the nineteenth century saw the exchange of resources for people; as staples left Australia, labor flowed in. Between 1788 and 1914, around 1.3 million people had emigrated from Britain to Australia. More than one-half of them did so with fares paid by the British or colonial governments (ibid.: 20). British immigrants still accounted for around three-fourths of all new immigrants in the early twentieth century (Pope, 1987: 42).

The gold rush had also attracted Chinese migrants, but this migration was barred following an agreement in 1888 by all of the governments in Australia. This was followed in 1896 by a further agreement that excluded all immigrants who were not "white" (Dyster and Meredith, 1997: 23).

This resulted in a high wage policy as it reduced the flow of migrants from lower wage economies. The high demand for labor drove up wages in Australia, providing a home market for manufactured goods; export of these goods was not competitive, and tariffs were introduced to protect producers for the domestic market (ibid.: 26). The expansion of the domestic market was financed to a significant extent by capital inflows from Britain, used to fund industry and infrastructure (such as railways). In the 1870s, Australia accounted for one-eighth of British overseas investment; in the 1880s, this rose to one-fourth and, for much of the latter half of the nineteenth century, foreign capital accounted for one-half of Australia's gross domestic capital formation (ibid.: 34).

Being tied into the international economy meant that Australia experienced the typical volatility that characterized staple economies, namely, the booms and busts of the international cycle. The wool slump of the 1840s (as a result of the textile crisis in Britain) was replicated in the 1890s depression as commodity prices fell, with Australia adversely affected again (Broomhill, 2007: 5). However, this time it was compounded by its "debt crisis" with "a severe balance of payments deficit, declining terms of trade, soaring foreign debt burden and virtually static economic growth" (Dyster and Meredith, 1997: 41). It was against this backdrop that the six colonies voted for federation and formed an Australian political union and economic common market on January 1, 1901. New Zealand abstained, but the door was left open for New Zealand to join later should it wish (ibid.: 60).

The new confederation was already well integrated into international goods and capital markets. However, it was deliberately selective in its integration into international labor flows, and "when Australia became a single and independent country in 1901 [the White Australia] policy was one of its explicit foundations" (ibid.: 25).

Labor markets were affected not only through the "White Australia" immigration policy. The 1890s had seen a spate of strikes and industrial conflicts. Labor had been weakened during the decade and, in 1901, only 5 percent of wage earners were union members (ibid.: 61). Furthermore, manufacturing was in its infancy and not significant at all on the world scene.

However, as Pusey (1991: 215) notes:

> in Australia, the Labor Party had emerged from a strong trade union movement as a powerful force well before Federation in 1901 and, more importantly, before the process of industrialization had really got under way. Labor emerged as a political force in conditions where capital was sharply divided between the "Free Traders" (representing large overseas-owned and controlled mining, shipping, and agricultural commodity exporting enterprises that cared only about reducing wages) and, on the other hand, the "Protectionists" (local small industrial and service industries that were

willing to work with the trade unions). The bitter outrage over the maritime, coalminers', and shearers' strikes of 1890 seems, together with ensuing industrial upheavals of the 1890s and the continuing disunity of capital, to have "allowed the state sufficient elbow room to establish its authority in the field of industrial relations" in a way that provides a "striking example of the relative autonomy of the state." No one doubts that the enormous authority of the state in this area of industrial relations was anything less a keystone of Australia's national development in the twentieth century and the principal means of resisting pressure, changing private behaviour, and of quite decisively forming the social structure.

This is an assessment shared by historians of all political hues.[1]

The system of centralized industrial relations and wage determination, accompanied by industrial protection and selective immigration, formed the basis of the so-called "Australian settlement."[2] It amounted to the construction of a political economy which sought to constrain capital-labour conflict and to define the terms of, and distribute the benefits from, Australia's integration into the international economy.

The contours of this development strategy were clear, but the balance between reliance on commodity exports and the encouragement of manufacturing for the domestic market continually shifted. The first half of the twentieth century, punctuated by two world wars, the Great Depression, and a change in the international balance of power as Britain declined and the United States became the leading Western power, all had ramifications for the newly formed country of Australia.

Australia responded in a variety of ways. First, trade diversification away from complete reliance on Britain was sought as trade with the United States, Germany, and Japan all increased (Dyster and Meredith, 1997: 68). Protectionism continued into the 1920s as tariffs encouraged import, substituting industrialization. The Brigden Report of 1929 argued that tariffs had been beneficial for Australia's development and standard of living (ibid.: 99).

However, domestic protectionism was not much of an insulation against the depression of the 1930s. As international commodity prices fell, Australia was faced (again) with high external debt, a reduction in foreign trade, and reduced capital inflows. Britain took measures to ensure that Australia did not default on any of its debts, including removing the NSW government (Broomhill, 2007: 6–7). Unemployment rose to perhaps as high as 30 percent of trade union members in the early 1930s (Maddock and McLean, 1987: 16), and real gross domestic product (GDP) fell by more than 11 percent (Dyster and Meredith, 1997: 127).

Australia joined with other colonies in resurrecting the Imperial Preference scheme at the Ottawa agreement of 1932, which sought to insulate the British empire from the international chaos surrounding it. By 1935, Britain still accounted for more than one-half of Australia's exports (Leaver, 2001: 5); wool, gold, butter, and wheat still made up the bulk of these exports (Dyster and Meredith, 1997: 148–9).

In the 1950s, Australia remained firmly in the Anglo-Saxon world, with Britain dominant in terms of trade volumes. However, relations with Asia were more contradictory. Australia supported the United States in Korea and was later to do so in Vietnam as well. Australia followed the U.S. lead (not that of Britain) in denying diplomatic recognition to the People's Republic of China, though it nevertheless did seek to sell its wheat there. When Australia joined the GATT, it specifically excluded Japan from consideration, and when it announced universal import restrictions in March 1952, it stated that they applied equally to all countries except Japan, against which even stricter controls operated than had been the case in the later 1930s. Imports from Japan fell below 1 percent in the early 1950s. However, exports to Japan continued to be important and constituted the second largest market by the mid-1950s. In 1963, Australia agreed to refrain from discriminating unilaterally against Japan (ibid.: 207).

Australia experienced high growth for most of the postwar period up until the world crisis in the early to mid-1970s. During this "golden age," the Treasury worried about the "problem of continuous growth" (ibid.: 234), and Australia became known as the "lucky country" (Broomhill, 2007: 1). Growth was accompanied by a shift in the relative importance of Australia's trading partners. Britain's preeminent position was lost and, by 1966, Japan had replaced Britain as the largest market for Australian exports, and the United States had replaced Britain as the largest source of imports (Dyster and Meredith, 1997: 249). A similar pattern was evident in the sources of foreign direct investment (FDI), with Britain's dominant position in the 1950s being replaced in the two subsequent decades by the United States and Japan, respectively (Bryan, 2004: 116).

During the "golden age" period, Australia did not follow the trade-liberalizing policies adopted by other OECD countries. Between 1950 and 1976, Australia's share of world trade fell by half from 2.8 percent to 1.4 percent (Dyster and Meredith, 1997: 254). The protectionist ingredient of the "Australian settlement" remained central and was supplemented by the new mechanisms of Keynesian macroeconomic control (see Bell, 1997: 63–4). Protectionism also encouraged continued large inflows of FDI, and the fear over a loss of economic sovereignty was raised (Broomhill, 2007: 9).

The end of the golden age and the onset of the crisis of the 1970s and 1980s opened the door for a rethinking of the Australian development path to that point. Persistent current account deficits had resulted in high levels of foreign debt by the end of the 1980s (Dyster and Meredith, 1997: 277). In 1988, the Department of Trade estimated that to stabilize foreign debt, the current account deficit needed to fall to 2.5 percent of GDP, requiring Australia's exports to grow at double their historic rate. As primary products could not be expected to grow this fast, this meant that manufactured exports would need to grow by 15 percent per year (ibid.: 278). The declining terms of trade meant that "by 1985 Australia had to export 75 per cent more by volume than it did in 1955 just to fund a given level of imports" (Bell, 1997: 84).

The 1970s and 1980s, therefore, saw a major crisis, with stagflation and continued current account deficits. This experience was by no means unique to

Australia among OECD countries, and the policy response was also similar to that adopted in many countries. As Bell (ibid.: 80–99) argues, the level of the welfare state, the power of unions, and the protection of industry were argued to be policy and institutional choices that needed to be changed to put Australia on the path to international competitiveness. Just as in the earlier periods of restructuring in Australian history, namely the 1890s depression and the 1930s depression, the post-1970s period again relied on the state to play "a major transformative role in the process of change and restructuring" (ibid.: 63).

Brief history of exchange-rate regimes and monetary institutions

The new country of Australia adopted a new currency but with an imperial reference, the Australian pound. It was initially fixed at par against its imperial counterpart, the British pound, and was subsequently faced with some of the same crises. Dyster and Meredith (1997: 101) argue that when Britain returned to the Gold Standard in 1925, with the British pound overvalued by approximately 10 percent, Australia was forced to make its first conscious decision about its exchange rate. The two currencies had always been officially interchangeable, though the smaller economy's pound often exchanged in practice at a slight discount. If Australia devalued against the British pound in 1925, it was felt that this would weaken confidence in Australia. Given Australia's foreign debt at the time, it would also lead to an increase in the debt burden. Devaluation was therefore an unattractive option for reasons that bear some similarity to the "fear-of-floating" hypothesis advanced many decades later. In the end, Dyster and Meredith (1997: 101) argue that "for a reason similar to Britain's—reputation—Australia overvalued its pound in 1925."

This situation was not, however, sustainable. Foreign creditors did lose confidence in the Australian pound, the official parity notwithstanding. In the 1930s, foreign creditors insisted in being paid in sterling or in gold (ibid.: 134). The banks, therefore, had to discount the Australian pound if it was used for payment. As Dyster and Meredith (1997: 134) report, in January 1931, the Australian private banks forced the federal government to concede that the discounted market rate was also the official rate. This was the first currency devaluation in Australian history. The Australian pound moved upward in December 1931 to a ratio of 125:100, where it stayed until the international realignments caused by the U.S. decision to suspend convertibility in 1971. Australia's exchange-rate regimes since 1931 are shown in Table 4.1.

The new exchange rate for the Australian and British pounds was maintained for nearly four decades. Thus, when Britain again abandoned gold in September 1931 and the pound sterling devalued, the Australian pound followed suit. Similarly, when the pound sterling was devalued again in 1949, the Australian pound followed again (ibid.: 189). This pattern was broken, however, in the British devaluation of 1967. This time, the Australian dollar, as it had now become, did not follow but remained fixed against the U.S. dollar even though the sterling link

Table 4.1 Exchange-rate regimes in Australia, 1931–2007

12. 1931–12. 1971	Fixed (against sterling)
12. 1971–9. 1974	Fixed (against U.S. dollar) with changes
9. 1974–11. 1976	Fixed (against trade weighted basket)
11. 1976–12. 1983	Variable (set daily against trade weighted basket)
12. 1983–6. 1986	Clean float
6. 1986–2007	Managed float (occasional interventions by RBA)

Source: Schedvin (1992: 550–2) and Kearney (1997: 88)

continued but at the new rate[3] (Schedvin, 1992: 550). By this time, the importance of Britain as a trading partner had fallen and been eclipsed by the rise of the United States.

The decision to fix against the U.S. dollar did not relieve policy makers of choices to make, however, as the 1970s brought an end to the postwar exchange-rate order. The first decision was how to respond to the devaluation of the U.S. dollar in 1971. When the U.S. dollar was devalued by 7.89 percent in 1971 against gold, the Australian dollar did not follow and became fixed against the U.S. dollar at the new rate (a scenario repeated when the U.S. dollar was devalued again against gold in 1973) (Schedvin, 1992: 551).

The oil-price shocks of the 1970s led to severe balance of payments problems for Australia. In 1974, Australia responded by devaluing the dollar by 12 percent, raising tariff rates (Dyster and Meredith, 1997: 271) and now fixing against a trade-weighted index. There was a further 17.5 percent devaluation in 1976 (ibid.: 272), with the exchange rate now set on a daily basis by the triumvirate of the Minister of Finance, the central bank governor, and the Treasury Secretary.

This system continued until 1983, when the Australian dollar was floated. At first this was a clean float, though since 1986 there has been some intervention by the Reserve Bank of Australia. Nevertheless, this intervention is minimal, and Kearney (1997: 89) argues that the current exchange-rate regime represents "a relatively clean float by international standards."

The Reserve Bank of Australia, as an institution, dates only from 1960 (Linklater, 1992: 26). The Commonwealth Bank was established in 1912 under the ownership of the federal government (ibid.: 5). Though it was responsible for note issue, it had few of the other functions of a central bank. Indeed, the prevalent view among the (non-Labor) political elites was that "the bank should not compete unfairly with the privately owned banks in Australia, let alone dominate them" (Dyster and Meredith, 1997: 134).

The post-1945 period, with the associated Keynesian ideas for economic policy management, saw an expansion in the power of the Commonwealth Bank; and macroeconomic objectives, including currency stability, were now part of its mandate (Schedvin, 1992: 63). The bank was brought fully under government direction, and the government's view was to prevail in the event of any differences with the board. Over the next decade and a half, the functions of central banking were gradually separated from those of the commercial activities, culminating in the Reserve Bank Act of 1959 and the formal commencement of the Reserve Bank of Australia a year later. In line with global trends, the Bank shifted to targeting monetary aggregates in the mid-1970s. These were abandoned in the mid-1980s, and inflation targeting was introduced in 1993 (MacFarlane, 1999; Bell, 2004).

Summary of recent trends and policies

In line with other OECD countries, inflation that had been one of the central policy concerns of the 1970s had been substantially reduced by the 1990s. Unemployment remained a central concern during the 1980s and reached more than 10 percent in the latter part of that decade and the early 1990s (see Le and Miller, 2000). This was a consequence of a recession that then-Prime Minister Keating argued that "Australia had to have" (Bell, 1997: 157). Since the mid-1990s, however, economic growth rate averaging more than 3 percent per annum and sixteen consecutive years of growth have significantly reduced unemployment to a 30-year low of approximately 5 percent, though the extent to which official figures underestimate the true level of unemployment is a point of contention (see Mitchell and Carlson, 2001). Debate has subsequently focused more on the quality of the jobs that have been produced as Australia has experienced a large increase in the number of casual jobs, jobs that signal a change in the stability of the employment relationship that characterized the "Australian settlement" (see Burgess et al., 2006). Australia's growth rates are shown below in Figure 4.1.

The dominant policy issue of the 1980s, however, was the current account deficit and the drive for international competitiveness. It was this underlying problem that led then-Finance Minister Keating to issue his famous warning in 1986 that Australia was in danger of becoming a "banana republic." In the run-up

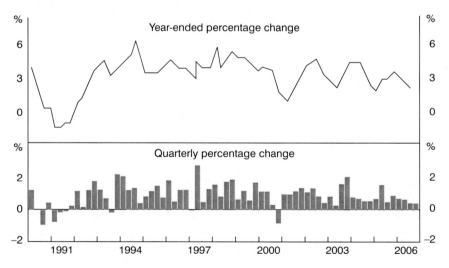

Figure 4.1 Australia: real GDP growth 1990–2006 (Source: Edey, 2007)

Figure 4.2 U.S. dollar/Australian dollar exchange rate, January 1971–April 2007 (monthly data) (Source: Federal Reserve Bank of St. Louis, 2007; research.stlouisfed. org)

to this remark, the Australian dollar, now floating freely, had in fact been sinking freely as indicated above in Figure 4.2.

The need to reduce the current account deficit through a competitive manufacturing sector (for both export and import replacement) was the central policy question that dominated the 1980s. The international competitiveness agenda and the associated neoliberal policy reforms intended to contribute to it have continued to be central policy issues though the 1990s and into the 2000s. Perhaps strangely, however, concern over the current account deficit has largely evaporated. This "problem" has not been "solved" but has rather been downgraded from the status of a major problem by policy makers and academics alike. Australia's current account deficits remain relatively large and have been consistently around 5 percent of GDP for the last decade, but the ability to finance them has not raised the level of concern that it did in the 1980s. When Paul Keating made his famous banana republic speech, Australia's net external debt to GDP ratio was around 33 percent; by the end of the 1990s, it was beyond 40 percent (Gruen and Stevens, 2000: 56). The current account deficit became viewed, as Gruen and Stevens (2000: 58) write, as "the dog that didn't bite" (see also Belkar et al., 2007 for review).

Indeed, policy discussions even shifted from "problems to be solved" to "miracles to be explained" (see Parham, 2002). In particular, Australia's rate of productivity growth has been relatively high and has been attributed to microeconomic reform and changes in the regulatory environment to a more liberal regime.

One policy issue in the 2000s has been that of asset inflation, in some ways reminiscent of the asset boom of the mid-1980s, which accompanied financial deregulation (see Bell, 1997: 172–7; 2004). The property market boom in particular has raised questions about the Reserve Bank's handling of the economy and its interest rate policies in particular. One area where the Reserve Bank's policies have received very little criticism, however, is in the area of exchange-rate policy, to which I now turn.

The contemporary currency debate

During the 1990s and 2000s, the Australian dollar went on a roller-coaster ride. As Figure 4.3 shows, the Australian dollar depreciated sharply against the U.S. dollar in the wake of the 1997 Asian crisis and reached historic lows in 2001, at one point crossing through the psychological barrier of A$1 = U.S.$ 0.5. Since 2002, the Australian dollar has appreciated rapidly against the U.S. dollar, regaining by 2007 the value that it had reached a decade earlier. There have, therefore, been sharp falls and a rapid rise in the relative value of the Australian dollar, both adding up to considerable volatility. The period of the sharp fall also coincided with the birth of the euro.

What is remarkable is that, despite this recent history, the flexible exchange-rate regime still enjoys overwhelming support in Australia. Indeed, Melinda Cilento, Chief Economist at the Business Council of Australia, rightly commented that "in terms of the floating exchange rate regime, I suspect that you would struggle to find someone that doesn't support it."[4]

That is, despite the fact that the rapid changes in the exchange rate has entailed gains for some sectors and losses for others and a volatility that might inhibit corporate planning, this has not led to any discernible pressures among the business community for greater currency stability; the flexible exchange rate has more or

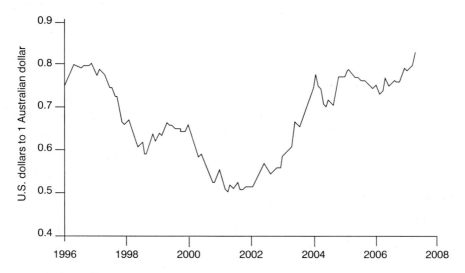

Figure 4.3 U.S. dollar/Australian dollar exchange rate, January 1996–April 2007 (monthly data) (Source: Federal Reserve Bank of St. Louis, 2007; research.stlouisfed. org)

less universal approval among them. The media may have reported the decline in the Australian dollar in headline-grabbing ways, but this did not seem to have translated into any desire to change the exchange-rate regime among business (or, indeed, the public).[5] Similarly, the rapid rise in the value of the dollar against the U.S. dollar since early 2003 has not led to any business backlash despite the fact that some sectors, such as manufacturing exporters and, especially, Australian farmers whose commodities are priced in U.S. dollars on international markets, were adversely affected by this.[6]

One reason for this may be that in an economy with high foreign ownership, manufacturing firms have been able to offset currency volatility through intra-firm trading practices. Examining manufacturer's export price behavior in the 1980s, Menon (1994: 51) concludes that:

> the large and non-transitory changes that commonly occur with floating exchange rates could create price differentials in the prices measured in the home and host country currencies that would easily outweigh the differentials in tax rates that would normally exist between countries—a factor that has been traditionally regarded as the major motivation to engage in transfer pricing. Our pass-through estimate of close to one for the [chemical, petroleum and coal products] and [transport equipment] industries suggests that during the period of prolonged depreciation of the AUD, the objectives of shifting excess profits and providing parent companies with cheap purchases in their home currency, by keeping AUD prices relatively unchanged in the face of currency movements, could have been achieved simultaneously. An important conclusion ... is the need to give due recognition to the dominant role played by multinational corporations in the international trade of certain industries, and in particular their ability to respond to volatile floating exchange rates through the machinery of intra-firm trade.

Among academics and policy makers, there has been widespread agreement that the flexible exchange rate did what it was supposed to do—depreciate so that Australia could weather the turmoil around it and avoid a recession. The fact that export growth continued and buffered the economy from negative demand shocks was taken as evidence of the wisdom of having a flexible exchange-rate regime. A volatile exchange rate might be an inconvenience, but it was one that was worth having. Ross Garnaut (2003), economic advisor to Prime Minister Bob Hawke at the time of the decision to move to a flexible exchange rate, has subsequently summed up the general opinion neatly:

> The powerful tendency for the floating dollar to depreciate in adverse times and to appreciate in times of buoyant external conditions contributed to the exceptional stability of Australian economic growth during the subsequent two decades. It is hard to imagine the sharp decline in terms of trade in 1985–86, the Asian financial crisis of 1997–98 or the U.S. 'tech wreck' and recession of 2000–01 being negotiated without recession, as they were, without the large

dollar depreciations and lifts in net exports that were experienced in these times. Even in the recession of 1990–91, the effects of the largest decline in domestic demand since the Great Depression on output and employment were moderated to some extent by exchange rate depreciation and an exceptional lift in net exports.

However, this general appeal to external conditions notwithstanding, understanding the movements of the Australian dollar has proved elusive to both academics and to the Reserve Bank. Indeed, there is general acceptance that there is no model of the exchange rate that can plausibly explain the recent path of the Australian dollar.[7] In light of this, some politicians wondered whether international speculators were adversely affecting the Australian economy through excessive exchange-rate volatility. This provided one context within which issues concerning exchange-rate regimes and monetary unions were raised.

The forum for this was the inquiry by the House of Representatives Standing Committee on the Economy, Finance, and Public Administration into "International Financial Markets: Friends or Foes?" that was set up in March 1999 in the wake of the Asian crisis and that reported two years later. The Committee (2001: 31) noted that there was concern over the "unexpected weakness of the $A. With the economy still growing quite rapidly and the economic fundaments still very sound, the Committee said there was no apparent reason for the dollar's dramatic slide to record lows in international exchanges."

The question was whether this "unexpected weakness" might be overcome by the use of a shared currency that provided insulation against any currency contagion. Possible currency arrangements were adoption of the U.S. dollar, joining a new Asian currency, or the creation of an ANZAC dollar with New Zealand. The first of these options was raised by the Australian Stock Exchange (ASX), which "tentatively canvassed the idea that Australia might study the advantages of 'dollarization'" (ibid.: 33). The committee was right to use the adjective "tentative." The ASX was also responsible for suggesting that the progress of an Asian currency be monitored with a view to possible Australian participation. However, the ASX agreed that the emergence of such a currency was unlikely.

The ASX, though raising these shared-currency alternatives as possible areas for study, was much less tentative—indeed, was positively firm—in viewing the flexible exchange rate as of considerable benefit to Australia. Here it argued that "the Australian government has important economic policy instruments at its disposal. The use of these tools is at world-class standards, as reflected in our economic performance during the Asian financial crisis in the past two years ... Given the importance of these policy tools, *ASX suggests that it is vital that we maintain the Australian dollar rather than become part of a monetary union with one or more other nations*" (ASX, 1999: 2, emphasis in original). This accords with the view of the Reserve Bank that "unequivocally indicated the flexible exchange rate as the main reason for the Australian economy's resilience in the crisis" (2001: 14). Others added the strength of the Australian banking system and prudential regulation as explanatory variables, but the flexible exchange rate was seen by all as a critical policy choice that allowed the Australian economy to insulate itself from the economic malaise that surrounded it and to avoid an exchange-rate crisis.

Furthermore, the argument has been made that "the international financial markets appeared to make a clear distinction between the Asian currencies that were tumbling in value and the Australian dollar so that 'contagion' was largely avoided" (Meredith and Dyster, 1999: 320). The Australian dollar did continue to fall against the U.S. dollar as indicated in Figure 4.2, though its decline on a trade-weighted measure was far less dramatic. Though the Australian dollar was certainly not unaffected by the Asian crises, it did avoid some of the worst problems. There would be little point in inviting contagion through some form of currency arrangement with Asia.

The third possibility raised in the Committee's Report was that of an ANZAC dollar. This possibility was driven not so much as a response to contagion from Asia but as a response to a debate initiated by New Zealand. The issue of currency union had been considered briefly in New Zealand in the early 1990s as a result of the signing of the Maastricht Treaty. In 1999, the New Zealand Treasury published a paper on currency union, taking as its starting point the European debate (Coleman, 1999).[8] However, the New Zealand debate was sparked into life primarily by the New Zealand Chamber of Commerce, which commissioned a study by the Institute of Policy Studies (IPS) in Wellington on the merits of New Zealand's joining a currency union with Australia or of adopting the U.S. dollar

The authors of the IPS study, Grimes, Holmes, and Bowden (2000: ix) asked whether New Zealand should "remain the smallest industrialised country to run an independent monetary policy." They argued that it should not and considered both an ANZAC dollar and adoption of the U.S. dollar. The former garnered the greatest public attention and was the primary focus of the study.[9] New Zealand has a monetary history very similar to that of Australia—a member of the sterling bloc at the end of the nineteenth century, fixed exchange rates for much of the rest of the century, and a move to floating exchange rates in 1985. However, the authors argued that it was time for New Zealand to consider monetary union. They advanced many arguments in support of this, but the three main reasons were as follows.

The first was that the volatility in the value of the New Zealand dollar that resulted from the greatly increased size of international capital flows led to misalignment and reduced the ability of the Reserve Bank to manage the economy. The second was that the world was moving in the direction of regional currency blocs (as a response to currency volatility) and that Australasia should not be left out of this global trend. The third was that New Zealand businesses were in favor of it, as it would increase their competitiveness in the Australian market. Grimes et al. (2000: 104) summarize their findings from their survey of 400 firms as follows: "Business respondents are strongly positive towards an ANZAC currency union. A total 58% of respondents were Positive or Very Positive towards union (almost a half of these being in the latter category. Only 14% indicated that they were Negative or Very Negative (half being in the latter category); the rest were Neutral. Thus, of the 298 firms that were non-neutral regarding the issue, 80% were in favour of currency union." These figures were taken to indicate high levels of interest in currency union by the business community, which served to raise the profile of the issue even if the presentation of the results provides an interesting example of how to turn 58 percent support into 80 percent support by a judicious manipulation of the data.

The issue gathered further momentum during 2000 as the New Zealand dollar, following the same trend as the Australian dollar, reached record lows against the U.S. dollar as shown in Figure 4.4.

As the New Zealand dollar fell to another all-time low against the U.S. dollar of 41.3 cents in September 2001, Prime Minister Helen Clark raised the topic of monetary union in a speech to U.S. investors in New York. She noted that monetary union might attract more investment into New Zealand and end the decline of the New Zealand dollar (Brockett, 2000). Drawing on the European experience, she further argued that "if the largest countries in Europe see benefit in a currency merger, what is so sacrosanct about the currency of a country with 3.8 million people. It might be one of those things that becomes inevitable as we have closer economic integration with Australia" (quoted in Dore, 2000).

However, while Prime Minister Clark (who had previously been skeptical of a joint currency) now invoked historical inevitability as an argument for a currency union on one side of the Tasman Sea, on the other side no such inevitability was perceived. Within a week of Clark's suggestion, the reply from Peter Costello, the Australian Treasurer, was that "the Australian government is not proposing any

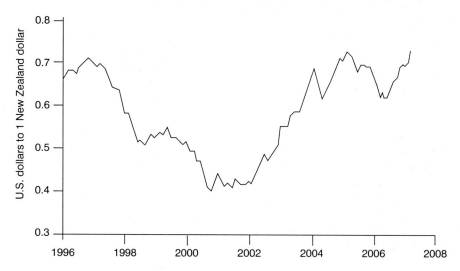

Figure 4.4 U.S. dollar/New Zealand dollar exchange rate, January 1996–April 2007 (monthly data) (Source: Federal Reserve Bank of St. Louis, 2007; research. stlouisfed.org)

change to the Australian currency or to our monetary arrangements. We're not interested in any new currency, any third currency. Now if someone came along and said we would like to adopt your currency and your monetary arrangements we would look at them. But no such request has been made" (quoted in van Beynen, 2000). Neither was it likely to be made. Political considerations made a currency union with Australia the only viable option for New Zealand; asking for permission to adopt the Australian dollar was not.

The Asian crisis spurred research into the problems and pitfalls of fixed exchange-rate regimes and possible solutions to exchange-rate crises. In 2001, the Reserve Bank of Australia held its annual conference on *Future Directions for Monetary Policies in East Asia*. The focus was on fixed versus flexible regimes for East Asia, with only one paper on Australia. This looked at the case for a monetary union between Australia and New Zealand but was written by a former employee of the Reserve Bank of New Zealand working in the United States.[10]

The Argentine currency board crisis in 2001 further undermined support for joint currency arrangements in New Zealand (Neill, 2001), whereas the idea of an ANZAC dollar was officially pronounced dead in November 2002 by New Zealand's Ministry of Foreign Affairs and Trade (see Hosking, 2002). New life was breathed into the idea, however, in 2003, the year of the twentieth anniversary of the Closer Economic Relations (CER) agreement between the two countries. New Zealand business interests continued to push the idea with Canterbury Manufacturers' Association chief executive John Walley, for example, arguing that a currency union could reduce the volatility in the value of the New Zealand dollar (then rising rapidly). Furthermore, former Reserve Bank governor and at the time National Party finance critic Don Brash also supported a joint currency (King, 2003).

The Australian response this time was not so dismissive. Indeed, Peter Costello himself used the European experience to speculate on the possibility of a joint currency. Speaking to the Auckland Chamber of Commerce, he said that he was often asked about the prospects of a single currency. He responded that "if the 12 countries of Europe … have a single currency, is it so hard to imagine a single currency across the Tasman? The answer is no" (quoted in Fabro, 2003: 12). Costello went on to immediately add that neither country was actively working on a single currency proposal.

The debate over an ANZAC dollar, or of adoption of the Australian dollar, was an issue with some profile in New Zealand. And the issue still has some momentum, with proponents of some form of currency union still raising the flag. It was raised, for example, at the Australia–New Zealand Leadership Forum in May 2004. The conference cochairs, Margaret Jackson, Chair of Qantas, and Kerry McDonald, Chair of the Bank of New Zealand, both advocated a single currency (see Taylor, 2004). It resurfaced again in April 2007 when New Zealand's National Party leader, John Key, backed a single currency. By this time, however, Prime Minister Clark had returned to a more skeptical position and rejected the suggestion (see O'Sullivan, 2007).

However, in Australia, the issue was very much one of musing at the margins even during the most active stage of public discussion in 1999–2001. The consensus in both the academic and policy-making worlds was firmly in favor of maintaining the Australian dollar and the flexible exchange rate. In general, neither the European example nor the decline in the value of the Australian dollar to its historic low in 2001 did anything to dent this position.

Indeed, the advent of the euro was seen as boosting the profile of the Australian dollar rather than heralding its demise. Private-sector bank economist, John Edwards, chief economist at the HSBC in Sydney, proclaimed the rise in the importance of the Australian dollar as the result of the abolition of European competitor currencies. In a Report entitled "The Fifth Global Currency," Edwards (1998: 2) argued that "the increasing integration of Europe and the coming recovery in Asia ... is about to catapult the Australian dollar to a new status as the fifth global currency" from its then-eighth-placed position. Furthermore, he added, "over the next four or five years, the world's most frequently traded currencies will be reduced to the U.S. dollar, the euro and yen—with the Australian dollar, Swiss franc and the Canadian dollar vying for fourth place."[11]

Furthermore, some Australian academics were still advocating that it extend its role as a regional currency by being adopted by small Pacific Islands. Thus, de Brouwer (2000: 167) advocated that other countries in the Pacific follow the example of Naura, Kitibati, and Tuvalu in adopting the Australian dollar. Such a move was justified by the "stabilizing properties of the Australian dollar and the solid performance of Australian monetary policy over the past decade." And this despite the 25 percent depreciation against the U.S. dollar in 1999.

The future of the Australian dollar was therefore bright, monetary policy sound, and the flexible exchange rate working, the euro and the pressures on the "Aussie battler," as commentators affectionately termed the Australian dollar, notwithstanding.

Though the IPS study in New Zealand argued that international capital mobility made currency union with Australia (or dollarization with the United States) desirable to offset currency volatility, in Australia many academics argued that, given this capital mobility, it was impossible to have a fixed exchange rate anyway and that a flexible rate was necessary. Though this assessment is common among mainstream economists (see Garnaut, 2003, for example), it is also shared by more radical political economists. Bryan and Rafferty (1999), for example, argue that a flexible exchange rate is inevitable in the era of globalization. For them, the international trading of the Australian dollar has indeed made it, as Edwards argued, a global currency. This results in a "diminishing association between the Australian dollar and the territory of Australia. The dollar is used, for example, in derivatives contracts that have no association with either Australia or companies of Australian origin. The clear implication is that the value of the dollar has but a partial connection to Australia (and to the balance of payments current account)" (1999: xxvi). The fact that international investors determine the value of the Australian dollar puts it well beyond the control of the national government; the extent of international capital markets makes a flexible exchange-rate regime inevitable. An agreement on the flexible exchange-rate regime therefore exists across the political spectrum.

Analyzing the debate

In terms of the "forces of globalization" invoked during the debate in Australia, very little reference was made to the "inevitability" of a global trend toward fewer currencies as a result of globalization or following the example of the euro (or both). These reasons were invoked in the New Zealand debate but played little role in Australia. Indeed, to the extent that "inevitability" played a role, it took the form of arguing that a flexible exchange rate was inevitable, given the expansion of international financial markets. This argument is made by Bryan and Rafferty, who argue that "more critical than any ideological shift was the recognition that the old order of fixed exchange rates was unsustainable and that the international market for Australian dollars was overwhelming the domestic regulatory practices of the RBA" (1999: 127). As they state, "there was no real choice but to float the dollar" (1999: 128). Subsequently, trading in the Australian dollar had become so large (with 60 percent of trade in the Australian dollar taking place outside Australia by 1995) that it no longer is determined by the performance of the Australian economy but has become determined more by international investors' preference (Bryan and Rafferty, 2000: 51). This view also found support from mainstream private sector economists, such as Edwards. The implication of this for Bryan and Rafferty is that the value of the currency lies beyond the control of the nation-state and, in this sense, "the Australian dollar has been 'denationalized' in a territorial sense" (2000: 46), with government policy ineffective in exchange-rate management; a change of exchange-rate regime (other than perhaps outright dollarization?) would not be possible even if it were desirable. On this reading, the bipolar view has apparently held sway in Australia since 1983.

However, whether the flexible exchange-rate regime has been so widely supported because it is seen as being inevitable is open to question. What is surprising about the Australian debate is how little attention has been paid to the possibility of currency union and how little criticism there has been of the exchange-rate regime despite a period around the turn of the millennium when the Australian dollar was falling to new lows. The consensus view in favor of the retention of the Australian dollar and the continuation of the flexible exchange-rate regime is better explained by the concept of "contingent neoliberalism." That is, the flexible exchange rate has enjoyed such widespread support because it is seen as an integral part of a neoliberal paradigm shift that began in the early- to mid-1980s.[12]

To understand why a flexible exchange rate has become an icon of neoliberal orthodoxy in Australia, it is necessary to go back to the decision to float the dollar in 1983. This decision was, in essence, the first step in dismantling the so-called "Australian settlement," the social compromise between capital and labor that saw rising living standards based on natural resource exports and a protected domestic sector with centralized wage bargaining. This "settlement" had used a fixed exchange-rate regime, as indicated in Table 4.1.

The policy of a fixed exchange rate and tariffs meant that, according to Anderson (1987: 165), "for the last fifty years Australia has been more protectionist towards its manufacturing sector than perhaps any other high-income country except New Zealand. This difference between Australia and other industrial countries became especially marked following the substantial post-World War II reductions in tariffs on manufactured goods imported by Western Europe, the United States and Japan."

This view is also supported by Emy (1993: 12), who argues that "for 40 years after 1945, Australia was protected by high tariff walls from the impact of dynamic changes in the world economy. Other countries industrialised, and adapted successfully to the accelerating pace of change in the global economy, while Australia stood still." As a result, "in 1983, Australia (along with New Zealand) was the most highly protected economy in the world" (ibid.: 18).

In 1983, however, the newly elected Labor party under Bob Hawke changed the pattern of Australian economic development. Neoliberalism, often known as "economic rationalism" in Australian parlance (see Pusey, 1991), was introduced in Australia. The subtitle of Pusey's book, *A nation-building state changes its mind*, highlights the change from state-sponsored development to market-led restructuring, a change in paradigm that Pusey (1991) shows was thoroughly inculcated in the upper echelons of the Canberra federal bureaucracy.

The move from fixed to flexible exchange rates was an absolutely central part of this change in paradigm. First, the facts. During 1983, the Australian monetary authorities found it increasingly difficult to maintain the exchange rate in the face of high capital inflows. The newly elected Labor Party had devalued the A$ by approximately 10 percent on coming to office in March. However, speculative capital inflows led to this being almost entirely reversed over the course of the summer. There followed intense debate about how best to respond. Treasury secretary John Stone was the most notable among those who opposed any movement away from a fixed rate regime. According to Kelly (1992: 84), Stone's argument was that "the dollar would become a speculators' toy; it was inappropriate for a nation of Australia's size to float its currency; the exchange rate was a weapon of policy and should never be surrendered to the markets."

Reserve Bank officials, and some of Stone's own staff, however, felt otherwise. The forward exchange rate was floated in October 1983. Then, on December 9, "it was decided to float the dollar and abolish exchange controls in the face of a massive wave of speculative capital inflow that was wrecking attempts to manage the exchange rate and money supply. In a radical stroke, the Australian financial system was thrown open to world market forces as part of the seemingly inexorable process of global financial liberalization" (Bell, 1997: 143).

The decision to float the dollar was not simply a technical economic decision. It was much more than a short-term technical fix to be used in "crisis management" but signaled a dramatic change in Australian economic policy, as the basis of the "Australian settlement" was now directly challenged and a new neoliberal economic agenda gradually emerged as dominant. A central part of this agenda was that Australia would need to integrate into the world economy and be subject to its disciplines; the float was a key component of this.

This much is clear from the words of Labor Party Finance Minister Paul Keating (quoted in Kelly, 1992: 86–7) at the time: "One of the things is that … the coalition [the opposition party] … have never lived with the discipline of a floating exchange rate. … The float is the decision where Australia truly made its debut into the world and said, 'O.K., we're now an international citizen.'"

The shift to "the discipline of a floating exchange rate" meant that, in Bell's words (1997: 144), "the ALP, a party with a long tradition of antipathy to 'money capital' had accepted the 'banker's agenda' … The markets were delighted. In 1984 Keating was even awarded a special prize from Euromoney magazine – Finance Minister of the Year."

This assessment of the shift in political dynamics is widespread. Gratton (1994: 41), for example, argues that "the decision [to float] was extremely bold, not just in economic terms, but in political ones as well. … The float set the Labor Party bravely on the course of economic rationalism." For Meredith and Dyster (1999: 323), "the decision to float the Australian dollar in December was the shot from the starting gun in Australia's move to 'globalization.'" Thus, the float is seen as marking a shift in policy toward globalizing the Australian economy, with globalization seen as a domestic policy choice rather than an externally imposed constraint. According to Kelly (1992: 76), "the float transformed the economics and politics of Australia. It harnessed the Australian economy to the international marketplace—its rigours, excesses and ruthlessness. It signaled the demise of the old Australia—regulated, protected, introspective." And, in Kelly's words once more (1992; 77), "the float had a psychological significance almost greater than its monetary effects. It sealed the de facto alliance between the government and the financial markets."

The decision to move to a floating exchange rate was therefore regarded as a major—*the* major, according to Treasury secretary at the time, John Stone— economic decision of the postwar period.[13] It signaled an abrupt change in economic policy and a new shift in Australian politics. The "discipline" imposed by the foreign exchange markets would lead to measures to introduce discipline into many other areas of economic policy in the quest for a neoliberal restructuring of the economy in order to more fully integrate into global markets. According to Gratton (1994: 42–3):

> the medium- and longer-term consequences of the float have affected every area of economic policy. It put a discipline economically on the Government, which could also be turned into a political discipline. The fact that the local and international markets delivered their view on economic policy meant that the Government was forced to be responsible. To be otherwise would invite damaging consequences. This argument could be used to some effect against ministers wanting to spend, and with backbenchers who were exerting pressure for this or that policy.

The disciplines imposed by the float were argued to be strong and binding. In Kelly's opinion (1992: 94), "the floating rate and exchange control abolition meant that currency and capital markets would test every major economic policy decision made by Australia. The nation would be under permanent examination with savage consequences for failure. ... During the 1980s the discipline imposed by the markets through the float and capital movements imposed severe policy changes on Australia. It forced Labor towards small government, real wage cuts, lower taxation and industry deregulation."

In the period after 1983, the discipline imposed by the float and the change in political direction chosen by the Hawke and then Keating governments led to a wave of neoliberal economic reform. After 1983, "many of the regulations that governed the behaviour of the Australian economy were questioned and a great number were swept away or radically altered. Economic policy shifted towards a greater role for market forces and a disengagement from the economy by the State" (Meredith and Dyster, 1999: 268). This trend was accelerated by the conservative coalition governments under John Howard after 1996. A neoliberal revolution had been born, and its birth was marked by the change in exchange-rate regime.

It is the reductions in tariffs, the move toward enterprise wage bargaining and away from centralized wage bargaining, and the deregulation of industry, which followed on from the float, that have been commonly identified as the reasons behind the Australian "productivity miracle" (see Productivity Commission, 1999, and Parham, 2003).

A floating exchange rate has become entrenched as an icon of neoliberal orthodoxy. Twenty years after the decision was taken, the lead editorial in *The Australian*, under the heading of "Celebrating two decades of reforming government," could look back on the Hawke and then Keating years and state that "by floating the dollar and lowering tariffs, they opened up the economy, forcing both management and workers to compete internationally."[14] This was why Australians should have been dancing in the street.

The disciplining role of international financial markets with a flexible exchange-rate regime remains an article of faith within Australian policy-making circles. For example, the Treasury explained to the House of Representatives Standing Committee on Economics, Finance, and Public Administration that "governments have to pay attention to the views of international financial markets. That is certainly true and there is, therefore, a discipline that is placed on governments through the operation of international financial markets. It is difficult to run an argument that there is something wrong with that discipline" (2001: 28–9).

One of the main reasons, therefore, that there has been so little debate in Australia about monetary union is because a floating exchange-rate regime has been a central part of the neoliberal agenda for the last twenty years, a regime that is argued to have brought the discipline of markets to all areas of the Australian economy. It was the decision to float the dollar and have its value determined by market forces, rather than by government decree, that started the neoliberal revolution. To renege on that policy now is barely imaginable for policy elites and business leaders.

From its beginnings, Australia had attracted attention as a social experiment led by a reformist government (Maddock and McLean, 1987: 21). The model of national development that had been adopted was one based on high levels of government involvement in the economy through industrial policy, labor market regulation, protectionism, and exchange-rate determination. However, Australia's relative standing in the international per capita GNP league tables fell from being one of the richest countries—if not *the* richest—in 1900 to within the top twenty by the end of the 1970s.[15] With an international recession and the evident catching-up of countries in Southeast and East Asia, Australian policy makers were faced with choices to make. They choose neoliberalism, and the floating of the exchange rate marked this choice. As one of the chief architects of the float, Ross Garnaut, has argued, "the floating of the dollar and the abolition of exchange controls on December 9, 1983, told Australians that Bob Hawke's Labor government was serious about economic reform. It was neither the most difficult nor the most important of the many Hawke reforms. But it was necessary and dramatic" (Garnaut, 2003). Others view the float less modestly and regard it as the "most crucial decision of all" (Pierson, 2002: 183).

The absence of a significant debate over the exchange-rate regime, therefore, has much to do with the domestic consensus among policy elites that neoliberalism was best served by the "discipline" of a flexible exchange rate. "Contingent neoliberalism," therefore, has considerable explanatory power in this case. The other *ism*, imperialism, has much less so. Australia's history indicates how it has been tied into the sterling bloc and how its economic structure was framed to meet the needs of the British Empire. The shifting international power structure in the postwar period led Australia to replace the link with sterling to one against the U.S. dollar, even changing the name of its own currency from the pound to the dollar. Australia has, therefore, clearly tied itself in monetary terms to historic superpowers. However, though it fell within their orbit it has not, in the contemporary debate, played a significant role in determining its exchange-rate policies. Certainly there has been no pressure placed on Australia to dollarize or even to link more closely to the U.S. dollar. In the post-September 11 period, the Howard government has moved Australia decisively toward closer political and economic ties with the United States. One outcome of this has been establishment of the Australia–United States Free Trade Agreement that came into effect in January 2004. As Ranald (2007) explains, this Agreement came about in an effort to put Australia's economic relationship with the United States on the same close footing as its political relationship as the Howard government became a staunch supporter of the "War on Terror." Australia can be regarded, therefore, as becoming more closely integrated with and dependent on U.S. power. However, this integration and dependence has not had any implications for monetary affairs and, in the extensive policy and public debates over the content and desirability of the Free Trade Agreement with the United States, Australia's monetary sovereignty has not been an issue. Closer monetary integration with the United States through dollarization, for example, was simply never a point for discussion or ever a U.S. demand. The post-September 11 reconfiguration of Australia–United States relations has not included a monetary dimension.

In the larger picture, Australia can be seen as being integrated into the imperial structures of first Britain and then the United States. However, Australia can also be seen as a subimperial power itself. Thus, as Broomhill (2007: 15) argues, "Australia's emergence as a developed capitalist economy under the hegemonic umbrella of the British imperial empire had resulted in the adoption in the late [nineteenth and early twentieth centuries] of a racist and colonialist role itself within its own sphere of influence in the South Pacific region." One result is that the Australian dollar is used by a number of small Pacific Island countries, a region in which Australia has played a historic role. However, there has been no big push to extend the role of the Australian dollar in the contemporary period. Garnaut (2000: 21) suggested that an ANZAC dollar, rather than the Australian dollar, might be attractive to small countries in the region and, if adopted, might provide some monetary stability in what Australian foreign policy saw as an increasingly worrisome "arc of instability" to its north. However, nothing has come of this; Australian interests in the region have been served through more traditional mechanisms, such as the deployment of peace keepers and advisors (in East Timor and the Solomon Islands). The "re-emergence of Australian neo-colonialism and militarism" in both Southeast Asia and in the South Pacific" (which Broomhill, 2007: 15, observes) has not been matched by Australian "dollar imperialism."

The one case where the use of the Australian dollar could perhaps have been extended was New Zealand. Even here, though, as discussed above, Australia has been a reluctant participant in the currency union debate with New Zealand. Perhaps this is deliberate. Bob McMullen, the ALP shadow Treasurer in 2003, was reported to be in favor of such a union but argued that Australia should not be seen as pushing this too hard for fear of raising concerns over "Australian imperialism" in New Zealand.[16] The alternative explanation for Australia's reluctance to enter the debate is that it simply does not regard this as an important issue or the gains from extending the use of the Australian dollar to be that great. This seems more plausible.[17]

The regional context of the debate does seem to be important, however. That is, a further reason for the relatively low level of debate in Australia is that, New Zealand aside, there are no obvious regional neighbors with whom Australia could join in a monetary union. That is to say, the absence of regionalism as a strong force can be seen as limiting Australia's monetary options.

Geography has long been recognized as an important influence on the country's political economy. Indeed, Australia's distinctive economic history was attributed in Geoffrey Blainey's influential 1967 book to the "tyranny of distance." Though in a globalized world distance has shrunk, it is still commonplace for Australians to regard their country as being "eight hours from anywhere" and surrounded by a "moat." Australia remains isolated geographically from its historic imperial allies, first the United Kingdom and, since 1945, the United States, and remains culturally isolated from its geographically closer (but still non-contiguous) Asian neighbors.

Australia has a long history of ambiguity in terms of its relations with its Asian neighboring countries (see Leaver, 2001). As Beeson (2001: 45) has written:

Australia has always been a long way from "home" and often painfully conscious of its isolation and potential vulnerability. The sense of being strangers in a strange land, surrounded by peoples of whom they knew little other than that they were different, alien, and possibly hostile, shaped much of Australia's early international relations. Indeed, it is still possible to trace the continuing influence of such insecurities and uncertainties in contemporary politics.

Of course, Australia did embark in the 1990s under Prime Minister Paul Keating to seek an "engagement" with Asia and to more closely integrate itself with the rest of the "region," a policy that is reflected in the country's changing composition of exports. Nevertheless, this integration was problematic even before the current Howard government's tempering of the explicit "engagement" policy. For example, as APEC withered as a regional force, Australia's attempts at greater integration with Southeast Asia through a linking of the CER and AFTA were initially rebuffed by the ASEAN.[18] Australia is not included in the ASEM meetings and suggestions to expand the current ASEAN+3 to include Australia and New Zealand in an ASEAN+5 formula came to naught. Australia has, however, been included as one of the sixteen countries in the recently initiated East Asian Summits, the first two of which were held in 2005 and 2007. Australia has also signed bilateral free-trade agreements with Singapore (2003) and Thailand (2005). However, political tensions in the relationship between Australia and her Asian neighbors have been evident, especially over East Timor and following John Howard's threat in 2002 to undertake "pre-emptive" action in the region if this was felt necessary for security reasons. An AFTA-CER Closer Economic Partnership agreement was signed in 2002, and a free trade agreement is planned for 2007. However, in general, Australia's post-2002 stance has been to pursue closer political and economic relations with the United States rather than with Asia, consideration of free-trade agreements with China and Japan notwithstanding.

Though this points to the problematic path of economic integration in the region in general, and Australia's place within it, more telling from the point of view of the topic of this chapter is the fact that there is no obvious currency in Asia with which Australia might wish to join. An "Asian Currency Unit," though talked about as discussed in Chapter 3, is not a near-term possibility. For New Zealand, it does have an obvious larger currency neighbor with which it might join—Australia—and this has undoubtedly played a role in stimulating the New Zealand debate. In Australia, however, this condition is missing. Approximately 57 percent of Australia's exports in 2006 were destined for East and Southeast Asian countries, but there is no obvious regional currency with which Australia could join.[19]

The regional context, therefore, provides some explanatory power in analyzing the nature of the Australian debate. Even here, though, in terms of the "forces of globalization" identified in Chapter 2, it is the *absence* of regionalism, not its presence, that gives it importance.

5   Canada

I predict a North American currency bloc within five years; it is inevitable.
(Sherry Cooper, Chief Economist, Nesbitt Burns,
January 30, 1999, *The National Post*)

If you look at the way currencies are consolidating around the world, I don't think the Canadian dollar can exist in 10 years.
(Thomas Courchene, Queen's University, January 13, 2003, *The Buffalo News*)

Of all the billions of people on this planet, only a handful of separatists and Canadian economists believes that the world's only superpower, the United States, is about to give up its dollar and band together with Mexico and Canada to create a new euro-style currency.
(John McCallum, Liberal M.P. and former Royal Bank of Canada Chief
Economist, June 2, 2001, *The National Post*)

Overview of Canadian development

European "discovery" of what is now Canada probably began in 1497 with Cabot and in 1540 with the arrival of Jacques Cartier in what was later to become Quebec (Pomfret, 1993: 11–13). Settlement did not occur for another century and was centered on the East Coast. Hoping to find a new sea route to Asia, the British and French instead found a land with rich fish stocks. This provided the initial motive for settlement, though this was soon supplemented with, and then surpassed by, the fur trade. This trade, financed and organized by Europeans but undertaken in conjunction with the native population, provided the economic basis of the area over at least two centuries (see Trigger, 1985). Supported by colonial monopolies, the fur trade led to the expansion to the interior of the country and was the focus for commercial and political rivalry between the British and French.

The "new lands" were firmly tied into the European imperial trading patterns with cod, fur, and then timber being the staples that supplied the European markets. However, though European empires profoundly influenced the path of economic development, so did the geographical proximity to the newly independent United States. Goods, labor and capital all flowed across the border. From the mid-nineteenth century onward, trade and economic policies can be seen as being influenced by the contradictory pressures exerted by imperial linkages, continental integration, and nation building.

Britain's conversion to free trade in 1846 led to a reassessment of trading relationships in the Canadian provinces as preferential access to the British market was phased out. The response was the 1854 Reciprocity Treaty with the United States that resulted in free trade in many goods across the border, though not in manufactured goods, which were excluded; their protection was subsequently raised under the Cayley–Galt tariff (Pomfret, 1993: 94). The Treaty lasted for twelve years until it was cancelled, by the United Staters, in 1866. By this point, Canada was on the eve of being constituted as a federation under the British North America Act of 1867. The initial thrust of the new government of the new country was "nation building." To this end, a package of policies collectively known as National Policies was designed to provide an economic basis for the east–west political union. These policies were, therefore, intended to offset the pull of north–south economic integration. The policy package consisted of tariffs to protect domestic industry, immigration policies to encourage immigration (from European countries),[1] land policies to facilitate the settlement of the Prairies, the building of the transcontinental railway system, and fiscal policies (which have subsequently become enshrined as "equalization payments" intended to limit interprovincial disparities).

By 1900, Canada was attracting thousands of new immigrants, the prairies had been settled, the agricultural economy was flourishing as a result of the post-1896 "wheat boom"—Canada's new staple—and three transcontinental railway routes had been completed. How much of this can be attributed to national policies remains doubtful. Net migration was negative in the three decades after 1870 and became positive only after the wheat boom. The settlement of the prairies occurred only after this time as well and was owed at least as much to the expansion of continental agriculture following changes in low-rainfall farming techniques as it was to government policies (see Norrie and Owram, 2002: 206). The succession of staples did, however, provide "leading sectors" around which the rest of the economy developed providing a distinctive quality to the path of economic development (Watkins, 1967).

By the end of the nineteenth century, Canada's per capita gross domestic product (GDP) was significantly below that of Australia and the United States but it would rapidly rise from 60 percent of the U.S. level in 1895 to 80 percent by 1913 (Norrie and Owram, 2002: 190). An integrating national economy, based on natural resources and industrial capacity, was being formed, and the liberal Laurier government felt confident enough in 1910 to propose a new free trade deal with the United States This was defeated in the 1911 election as the protectionist Conservative Party was brought to power. Canada's role as a supplier of agricultural products meant that it prospered economically during the First World War, with the substantial munitions production contributing to manufacturing exports. The Great Depression took a heavy toll, with trade falling, real output decreasing by 30 percent, and unemployment rising to more than 25 percent of the workforce (ibid.: 317). The continental depression saw Canada revert to the British Empire as a source of economic security, and it was the host nation of the Ottawa conference in 1932 that negotiated the reintroduction of imperial preferences; Canada's exports to Britain briefly surpassed those to the United States (ibid.: 333).

Though protectionism characterized much of Canada's pre-1945 trade policy, capital flows were relatively free. As a result, Canada was tied into London as a financial center and attracted large inflows of foreign direct investment from the United States, especially into the mineral and mining industries and in manufacturing.[2] In 1913, Britain accounted for 75 percent of foreign capital (direct and portfolio) in Canada; by 1960, the United States accounted for 75 percent (Pomfret, 1993: 82). The pattern of reliance on high capital inflows and foreign direct investment into industry continued in the post-1945 period, though it was now accompanied by a commitment to the multilateral trade liberalization process that gradually brought tariffs down.

Canada, like other OECD countries, experienced the "golden age" of postwar growth with historically low levels of unemployment. The composition of trade evolved from a heavy reliance on natural resource and agriculture commodities to a mix that included manufactured goods, automobiles being the most important among them. This mix continued to be marked by sharp, historically rooted, regional variations with Ontario, and to a lesser extent Quebec, remaining as the centers of industrial activity, agriculture dominant on the prairies, and (after 1945) oil and gas and timber being based in the West.

The postwar period also saw the development of a welfare state that, though less extensive than those found in Europe, nevertheless served to distinguish Canada from its southern neighbor. In important respects, the passing of the 1948 Canada Health Act served as a post-1945 nation-building equivalent of the post-confederation National Policies. However, the high levels of foreign ownership led to increasing questions in the 1960s and 1970s about the economic basis of the "nation," whereas the election of the Parti Quebecois in 1976 and the repatriation of the Constitution in 1982, without the consent of the Quebec provincial government, has led to continual strains in the political union.

The economic strains were evident in the 1970s as Canada was faced with stagflation and unemployment rose, and continued to do so, through the 1980s and early 1990s. With both oil-producing and oil-importing provinces, the country struggled to contain the frictions that inevitably arose with rising oil prices. Like other countries, in the 1980s Canada responded to the challenges posed by the economic problems by shifting to neoliberalism (see McBride, 2005).

Brief history of exchange-rate regimes and monetary institutions

Under the Currency Act of 1854, the Province of Canada was permitted to keep accounts in either the decimal system of dollars and cents or the British system of pounds, shillings, and pence. The Province had proposed the former, but Britain was willing only to confirm the Act if the provision was included for the British system to be used as well (Powell, 1999: 7). The exchange rates between the

Province's coins and the pound and the U.S. dollar were also set. These rates prevailed through Confederation (when government Dominion notes convertible into gold were first issued), and Canada operated on the Gold Standard from 1854 until 1914 (Bordo, 2000: 5; Powell, 1999: 14). Convertibility was suspended on the outbreak of war, and Canada did not return to the Gold Standard until 1926, following Britain's lead both in this and in maintaining pre-war parities. This proved just as difficult to sustain as it did in Britain with the onset of the Great Depression, and Canada suspended gold exports in 1931 (ibid.: 24).

The dollar was subject to a managed float for the rest of the 1930s until war broke out again. Then exchange controls were introduced to essentially fix the value of the dollar. In the aftermath of the war, fears of importing inflation from the United States led the Canadian government to revalue the dollar and fix its value in 1946. However, this was followed by a devaluation in 1949 but, in the next year, capital inflows and rising exports fueled further inflationary concerns. This led to the decision to float the dollar again in 1950 (Powell, 1999: 37). Over the next two years, exchange controls were repealed as well.

The abolition of exchange controls notwithstanding, the float was not a pure one, with occasional interventions by the Bank of Canada.[3] As it was, Canada, as an International Monetary Fund (IMF) member, was departing from the fixed exchange system that the Fund put in place as part of the Bretton Woods agreement and that led to Canada being regarded as "something of a maverick" (Powell, 1999: 42) and being subject to "repeated criticism by the IMF and other authorities" (Bordo, 2000: 7).

In 1961, the Government wished to lower the value of the dollar and tried unsuccessfully to fire the Bank governor, James Coyne; he resigned later anyway, and the government then found that the dollar was being pressured to lower levels than it wanted. In May 1962, the government, therefore, came back into the fixed exchange-rate fold (Powell, 1999: 45). The return to a fixed exchange rate did not last long when, under further inflationary pressures, the government reluctantly decided to float the dollar in 1970. Though this was intended as a temporary measure, within three years the Bretton Woods system had broken down, and Canada became part of the fold again—because other countries moved to flexible exchange rates themselves. The history since 1931 is summarized in Table 5.1 below, and confirms what Helleiner (2005a) has termed Canadian policy makers' "fixation with floating" and their "unusually strong commitment to a floating

Table 5.1 Exchange-rate regimes in Canada, 1931–2007

October 1931–September 1939	Managed float
September 1939–September 1950	Fixed (against U.S. dollar and the pound) with changes
October 1950–May 1962	Managed float
May 1962–May 1970	Fixed (against U.S. dollar)
May 1970–2007	Managed float (occasional interventions by the Bank of Canada)

Source: Derived from Powell (1999), Bordo (2000)

exchange rate regime" (ibid.). With the Canadian dollar being fixed for only nineteen years since 1931, this assessment is an accurate one.[4]

In the midst of the Depression, the Bank of Canada was established as Canada's central bank on the advice of a government-appointed independent commission. The establishment of the bank, in 1935, is attributed by Bordo and Redish (1987) to have resulted from the political pressure to combat deflation, from the need to have an institution capable of engaging in international monetary coordination, and as a part of a nationalist agenda. Bank of Canada notes were issued in this year, and private bank notes were phased out (Powell, 1999). Consistent with international trends, the Bank's post-1945 mandate was based on Keynesian demand-management objectives. These were replaced by inflation objectives in the 1970s as the Bank flirted with monetary targets and, later, by inflation targeting.[5] In 1988, Governor Crow announced that the target inflation would be zero. Subsequently, this has been revised to 1–3 percent per annum range.

Summary of recent trends and policies

The economic history of the last two decades has been dominated by two issues: free trade with the United States and debt and deficit reduction. The renewed interest in free trade with the United States was initiated by Canada in 1985 and led to the signing of the Free Trade Agreement in 1989. The arguments made in favor of this agreement were that it would secure access to the U.S. market and provide the necessary competition for Canadian manufacturers. One overriding concern within Canadian policy-making circles has been Canada's allegedly poor productivity performance *vis-à-vis* the United States.[6] The Free Trade Agreement and, later, the NAFTA in 1994 were intended to provide a part of the competitive and deregulated framework within which this poor performance would be addressed by firms. A consequence of the trade agreements has been a rapid increase in the value of trade between Canada and the United States, as indicated in Table 5.2. Also indicated in Table 5.2 is that the proportion of Canada's exports destined for the United States increased rapidly from 1989, when the CUSTFA was signed, to a peak of more than 85 percent in 2000. Since then, however, the higher value of exports notwithstanding, the share accounted by the United States has fallen back to the levels of two decades earlier.

Table 5.2 indicates the growing dependence of Canada on the U.S. market throughout the 1990s, a dependence further emphasized by the fact that the export sector was Canada's main growth driver during much of the 1990s when domestic demand was relatively restrained and when, as a result, Canada's export:GDP ratio rose dramatically from 25.7 percent in 1989 to 45.6 percent in 2000.[7]

The reason that domestic demand was restrained during this period was that governments targeted the budget deficit and the national debt as the most important economic issues of the day to address; in short, the macroeconomic framework was changed. Though debt reduction was a goal of the Conservative governments in the early 1990s, it was only with the election of the Liberal Party in 1995, and under the direction of then-Finance Minister Paul Martin, that any success was

Table 5.2 Canadian exports 1985–2006: total (US$ millions) and U.S. share

Year	Total exports	Exports to U.S.	U.S. share of exports (%)
1985	119,061	93,793	78.78
1986	125,172	97,647	78.01
1987	131,484	99,764	75.88
1988	143,534	105,292	73.36
1989	146,963	108,024	73.50
1990	152,056	111,565	73.37
1991	147,669	108,616	73.55
1992	163,464	123,377	75.48
1993	190,213	149,100	78.39
1994	228,167	181,049	79.35
1995	265,334	205,691	77.52
1996	280,079	222,461	79.43
1997	303,378	242,542	79.95
1998	326,181	269,336	82.57
1999	365,233	309,194	84.66
2000	422,559	359,551	85.09
2001	420,730	352,165	83.70
2002	414,056	347,072	83.82
2003	400,175	330,468	82.61
2004	429,134	350,769	81.74
2005	453,060	368,577	81.35
2006	458,167	361,309	78.86

Source: Statistics Canada (various)

achieved in this respect. The national debt, which was approaching 70 percent of GDP, was reduced, and budget surpluses have been recorded. In fact, prior to 1997, the federal government had run a budget surplus in only two of the previous thirty-six years, whereas a surplus has been recorded every year since (including some relatively large ones), and the debt has fallen to around 40 percent of GDP. Since moving back into black ink territory, the government has become more concerned with preserving public health-care.

As shown in Table 5.1, Canada has had a floating exchange-rate regime since 1970. After a few years of relative stability, the trend of the Canadian dollar against the U.S. dollar has been generally downward. This downward trend is illustrated in Figure 5.1, though there have been some periods of reversal in this trend, particularly in the late 1980s–early 1990s and since early 2003.

Figure 5.1 U.S. Dollar/Canadian dollar exchange rate January 1971–March 2007 (Source: Pacific Exchange Rate Service: fx.sauder.ubc.ca)

The rise in the value of the dollar during the late 1980s and early 1990s coincided with the high interest rate policy followed by Bank of Canada Governor John Crow in his pursuit of a zero inflation target, a policy that caused high unemployment and attracted widespread criticism from the center-Left (see, for example, MacLean and Osberg, 1996). The continuing decline of the dollar after 1995, even though neoliberal policies had been implemented to change the macroeconomic and competitive frameworks through deficit reduction and free trade, also brought criticism on the Bank and calls for a change in the exchange-rate regime, this time predominantly from the Right. The rise in the value of the Canadian dollar since the beginning of 2003 has been accompanied by the exchange-rate regime debate largely disappearing.

The contemporary currency debate

The most recent debate over the Canadian dollar sprang to life in 1999.[8] It was initiated by a number of academic studies and by the Quebec sovereignist parties.[9] The debate was soon to be joined by a range of others, including government leaders and the Bank of Canada, and was kept alive by a whole series of interviews, opinion pieces, and editorials in the press (especially *The National Post*) for the following four years.

The initial academic studies were those produced by Thomas Courchene and Richard Harris (1999) for the conservative think tank, the C.D. Howe Institute, and by Herb Grubel (1999), a Reform Party M.P. and academic economist, in a publication by the right-wing Fraser Institute. Both publications argued for the creation of a common currency in North America, termed the NAMU (North American Monetary Unit) by Courchene and Harris, and the Amero by Grubel.

Both analyses took as their starting point the emergence of the euro, the discussions of dollarization taking place elsewhere in the Americas, and the fall in the value of the Canadian dollar. Courchene and Harris (1999: 3) argued that "the introduction of the euro in January 1999 represents a watershed in the annals of economic and monetary history. At one level, the advent of the euro signals the denationalization of national monetary regimes; at another, it signals that, in a progressively integrated global economy, currency arrangements are a supranational public good, one that is arguably consistent with a twenty-first-century vision of what constitutes national sovereignty."

This argument, that the euro had fundamentally changed the way in which monetary arrangements were being reconstituted in an integrating global economy, was one that surfaced again and again in the Canadian debate. The birth of the euro was seen as heralding a trend, or more strongly, as signaling a destiny.

Furthermore, Courchene and Harris argued that this vision of "twenty-first-century national sovereignty" was being pursued in the Americas and that dollarization was a trend for much of Latin America. Canada should join this trend quickly to avoid being excluded from the wave of the future. The twist added to this argument was that though, on the one hand, the trend toward dollarization elsewhere in the Americas (in Argentina and Mexico in particular) was marginalizing Canada and would likely lead to the demise of the Canadian dollar, on the other hand, this same trend offered an opportunity to Canada to exercise leadership and to protect its national interests. For though the rest of the Americas would likely go along with dollarization, Canada would favor a monetary union in which it would continue to have some say in monetary governance. Hence, if Canada joined in the debate, there would be more chance of persuading the United States to follow a more cooperative approach to monetary governance along European lines. In short, Canada's influence could be used to design a common currency rather than an acceptance of dollarization.

Both Courchene and Harris (1999) and Grubel (1999), therefore, took seriously the task of developing new proposals for common currencies and used the European experience as their comparative case. Courchene and Harris (1999: 22) drew explicit parallels with the European model and argued that "the easiest way to broach the notion of a NAMU is to view it as the North American equivalent of the European Monetary Union and, by extension, the euro. This would mean a supranational central bank with a board of directors drawn in part from the central banks of the participating nations." Grubel (1999: 5), in discussing the governance structure for the Amero, proposed that the three NAFTA signatories adopt a common currency, with each member country appointing members to a North American central bank "governed by a constitution like that of the European Central Bank." Such an arrangement would be in the interests of the United States, according to Grubel, as it would enable the new north American currency to compete with the euro. And, he argued, the United States joined the WTO, the IMF, the World Bank, and the NAFTA, all of which required the United States to "surrender a significant degree of national sovereignty" (1999: 21).

Though proponents argued that this change of exchange-rate regime might be the trend of the future, they clearly also saw it as a highly desirable one: desirable because the flexible exchange-rate regime had, in their eyes, served Canada poorly. These arguments, however, had little to do with international developments and paid virtually no attention to the European debates and experiences. The focus here was firmly on perceived failures in Canada and the poor performance of the economy relative to the United States. A number of arguments were advanced why the flexible exchange-rate system had served Canada badly: it increased business costs, reduced investment, and lowered productivity growth.

Courchene and Harris argued that the case for a flexible exchange rate—that it provides a shock absorber for the Canadian economy—was overrated. First, they argued that though in 1998 "the Bank [of Canada] ... put a positive spin on the dollar's fall, arguing that it is serving as a buffer to offset falling commodity prices and ensuring that Canada's level of economic activity is likewise buffered. But the buffering argument can account for only a small part of the exchange rate movements of the past decade or so" (1999: 7). Second, the shock-absorber argument relied on Canada's being an optimum currency area. They argued that, in fact, there were a number of regional economies constituted on north–south lines that cross the Canada–United States border. An exchange-rate movement that benefited manufacturing-oriented Ontario in response to an external shock did not necessarily benefit natural-resource-exporting Alberta, for example. Both effects mean that "the presumed buffering qualities of flexible exchange rates are overestimated" (1999: 14).[10] Grubel also made the argument that a flexible exchange rate did not really give Canada much monetary independence anyway, as the Bank of Canada was forced to follow the interest rates set by the Federal Reserve.[11]

Further, the buffering effects were likely to be of less importance in the future as the Canadian and U.S. economies became more integrated. Courchene and Harris argue that "at the aggregate level, Canada is integrated with the United States to a greater degree with respect to trade than the average EU member is to the EU. Hence, on economic integration grounds, the argument for a common currency is at least as compelling from Canada's vantage point as that for the average EU member" (1999: 11).

In an appeal to the "efficiency arguments," it was also argued that a fixed exchange rate would reduce transactions for businesses and lead to greater investment in Canada. This latter outcome would occur if both the depreciation of the Canadian dollar and its volatility could be ended. The depreciation of the dollar could reduce investment in Canada by discouraging firms from making the capital-intensive investments necessary for productivity growth. Though introduced only as "a hypothesis meriting further research than a conclusion" (1999: 9), the argument that currency depreciation causes low productivity growth soon became a central part of the debate over the appropriate exchange-rate regime for Canada. It became known as the "lazy manufacturers" hypothesis—the idea that the manufacturing sector had a lower productivity growth rate than that of the United States because it sought to compete on the basis of a depreciating dollar rather than by innovation. Grubel (1999: 14) was more forthright in making the same point, arguing that the depreciating dollar provided "temporary protection" to industries and thereby led them to "postpone the required downsizing and investments to raise productivity" and had slowed the rate of structural change in the economy. By linking the exchange rate with the ongoing productivity debate, the proponents of a change in exchange-rate regime hit a raw nerve in the policy community and garnered much attention for their cause.

The depreciating dollar also hit a raw nerve with the public as each new low invited unflattering comparisons between the Canadian and U.S. dollars. This led, according to Courchene and Harris, to a process of "market dollarization" as firms and individuals sought to "flee the uncertainty and volatility of the Canadian dollar" (1999: 15). Grubel, too, argued that "the private sector in Canada is moving rapidly in [the] direction ... [of the] private dollarization of commerce" (1999: 37).

The link between exchange-rate volatility and misalignment and low productivity growth relied on an asymmetry. When the exchange rate was overvalued for a significant period, Canadian firms, as a result of the free trade agreement with the United States and later the NAFTA, would shift production southward. However, when the exchange rate was undervalued, they would find it more difficult to keep their best employees and would suffer a "brain drain." The result according to Courchene and Harris was that "firms may exit in the periods of overvaluation, and workers may exit in periods of undervaluation" (1999: 10). In the former periods, Canada tended to lose manufacturing jobs; in the second, it lost the most skilled human capital. The outcome of this process over time was that Canada became more and more reliant on its natural resource industries. To have flexible exchange rates and free trade, therefore, are "inherently inconsistent" (1999: 11) and prevented Canada from taking full advantage of the free trade agreement with the United States.[12] To these arguments, Grubel also added that the elimination of exchange-rate risk would reduce Canadian interest rates by 1 percent (1999: 10).

These arguments spurred academic debate, were widely aired in the media, and dove-tailed with debates taking place in the parliamentary arena where it was not just the most conservative political party at the time (the Reform Party, for whom Grubel was an M.P.) but also the sovereignist Bloc Québécois that pushed the issue. Indeed, the sovereignty movement in Quebec came to see greater Canadian economic integration with the United States as a means of easing the transition costs of a move to a separate (or at least decidedly more sovereign) Quebec (Parizeau, 1999: 8). Proposals for Quebec sovereignty had always raised difficult issues of what currency would be used after independence and how continued use of the Canadian dollar could be negotiated with the rest of Canada (see Helleiner, 2004b).[13] With the adoption of a common North American currency, the proponents of sovereignty believed that this source of uncertainty would be removed, facilitating the redrawing of political boundaries within a larger economic unit. The Bloc Québécois introduced a motion in the House of Commons to study a common currency for the Americas in March 1999, a motion that was defeated by 175 votes to 67 but, much to the chagrin of the Liberal government, the Banking Committee of the Senate did discuss the issue one week later (see Bellavance, 1999; Aubry, 1999). The sovereignist leadership continued to argue that a common currency or dollarization was a sensible option for North America and used the European experience for comparison. The Parti Quebecois's Bernard Landry supported it, and Bloc Québécois leader Gilles Duceppe was also an advocate, arguing that "I think within 20 to 25 years, we'll have a common currency for the three Americas, that we'll have a free trade zone for the three Americas as it is in Europe, … that's where Quebec sovereignty will be located" (quoted in Ditchburn, 1998).

These political dynamics added a new dimension to the debate so that government members and policy makers had to consider not simply economic theory but political calculations in their pronouncements. The debate between economists, however, largely ignored this particular political dimension. Instead, opponents of monetary union focused on the economic benefits of a flexible exchange rate and on the political prospects for shared monetary governance in North America.

The leading opponents of a common currency have been economists with Canada's banks, most notably John McCallum when he was chief economist with the Royal Bank, and economists with the Bank of Canada, such as John Murray, James Powell, and Lawrence Schembri. Successive Governors at the Bank of Canada, Gordon Theissen and David Dodge, also periodically entered the debate by affirming their belief that Canada's flexible exchange-rate system had served the country well. Other opponents can be found on different ends of the policy spectrum. Among them are Mario Seccareccia, an economist at the University of Ottawa, whose work was published by the Left-leaning think tank, the Canadian Centre for Policy Alternatives, and David Laidler, an internationally known monetary economist with the University of Western Ontario and a Canadian Bankers Association Scholar and Fellow-in-Residence with the conservative C.D. Howe Institute.

Each of the points advanced by the proponents was countered by their opponents. To refute the claim that a flexible exchange rate had inhibited Canada–United States trade, opponents of a common currency-dollarization pointed out that the rapid increase in trade between Canada and the United States during the 1990s had occurred under a flexible exchange-rate regime. Common currencies were *not*, therefore, required to spur trade integration. As Seccareccia (2002: 9) argued, "already more integrated than most of the countries of the EMU, with almost 90 per cent of our trade being with the United States, it would be difficult to envisage still further growth in what is a share that has practically reached its upper limit!"

The view that Canada was already unofficially dollarizing was also examined. This view, expressed by Courchene, Harris, and Grubel, was also circulated in the media with *The Globe and Mail* proclaiming that "Canada, by osmosis, has already adopted the US dollar."[14] Certainly, in the business sector, exporters to U.S. markets are typically paid in U.S. dollars, and imports are also typically invoiced in U.S. dollars. However, beyond this, the evidence for unofficial dollarization is weak. Seccareccia (2002: 5), for example, found that there had not been "any dramatic shift in the holding of foreign currency-denominated deposits by Canadians over and above what one would normally expect from the growing share of foreign trade out of GDP." Similarly, Murray and Powell (2002: 1) argue that "existing data suggest that informal dollarization is proceeding at a very slow (to non-existent) pace. Indeed, by many measures, Canada is less dollarized now than it was twenty years ago, and bears little resemblance to those economies that are typically regarded as truly dollarized."

For the multinationals, or "global firms," as some would prefer to call them, it is certainly the case that many larger corporations have adopted a dual accounting system in which they report their activities in both Canadian and U.S. dollars.[15] A major reason for this is that Canadian equity markets are argued to be too limited to support the financing needs of large corporations. Thus, corporations turn to U.S. markets to raise funds, a move that requires meeting U.S. accounting practices and financial reporting standards. This provoked debate about the extent to which corporate Canada was "hollowing out" and heading south of the border. The implications of this, for the currency debate, are that Canadian firms are argued to be increasingly operating in U.S. dollars and therefore that a dollarized economy might "naturally" evolve as a result of corporate activities. The head of the Toronto Stock Exchange (TSX), Barbara Stymiest (2002: 15), refuted the hollowing-out hypothesis and argued that "in 1997, for example, 49 Canadian companies were listed solely on a U.S. exchange—the NYSE, Nasdaq or Amex—and the number went up to 53 in the following year. Now, only 35 Canadian companies are solely listed in the United States—down better than a third from the peak. The number of Canadian interlisted companies—that is, companies listed on both the TSX and a U.S. exchange—is down, too, from 213 to 184. There are 11 fewer on the NYSE, 30 fewer on the Nasdaq."

Though these data cast further doubt about alleged trends in Canadian companies listing abroad, it should also be noted that, not surprisingly, it is the largest companies that are listing (solely or cross-listing) on U.S. exchanges. Furthermore, the TSX has sought to move beyond the borders of Canada for its clients, is open to U.S. investors, and lists some forty foreign companies, including Sony, British Airways, and General Motors (see Macklem 2002: 45). Thus, even if there were no trend toward Canadian companies' listing in the United States, it is also the case that the TSX is pursuing a continentalist and global strategy itself.

One of the most common arguments used by opponents of monetary union was that a flexible exchange rate was best suited to Canada because it continued to be an economically distinct national economy and, as such, secured macroeconomic benefits from a flexible exchange-rate regime. It was argued that because Canada relied relatively more heavily on commodity exports than did most other industrialized countries, its currency depreciated in times of global economic slowdowns, as commodity prices weakened. The Bank of Canada, in its analysis, pointed out that it is this feature of the Canadian economy that distinguishes it from the U.S. economy and why a flexible exchange rate serves as a useful adjustment mechanism in the face of external shocks (see Murray et al., 2002).

The Bank of Canada's exchange-rate equation modeled the relative value of the Canadian dollar (against the U.S. dollar) as a function of the commodity terms of trade, the energy terms of trade, and the Canada–U.S. short-term, interest-rate differential. In the words of Murray (2000: 53), "not only does the equation fit the data with surprising accuracy, it is also remarkably robust" (see also Antweiler, 2002; Bailliu and King, 2005). Thus, movements in the exchange rate could be explained by economic fundamentals and were not signals of "policy errors" or the result of "speculators."

Furthermore, adopting a common currency would not remove the need for adjustments to be made; it would merely move them to areas other than the exchange rate, such as nominal wage flexibility or labor mobility, wherein there were likely to be, at least in the short run until labor is sufficiently weakened, more protracted struggles and higher output costs. The flexible exchange rate, therefore, speeded adjustment (Murray, 2000: 54). The fact that the United States and Canada did not meet some of the central criteria for an optimal currency area added weight to the argument that independent national currencies and a flexible exchange rate were more appropriate (Dean, 2001).[16] These arguments concerning the asymmetries of external shocks, the asynchronicity of business cycles, and the degree to which labor markets adjusted to shocks were all used to support the economic case for an independent currency and a flexible exchange rate.

The flexible exchange rate–low productivity link was also refuted. According to Murray (2000: 56–7), "the biggest flaw in the productivity debate ... is the presumption that productivity growth in Canada has fallen behind that of the United States. Although earlier data painted a rather grim picture, more recent evidence suggests that Canadian performance has been roughly equal to that of the U.S, and perhaps superior. This is especially true of one focuses on multifactor productivity, as opposed to labour productivity, and includes the entire business sector in the sample, as opposed to just the manufacturing sector." Even using the older numbers, some were not convinced. McCallum (2000: 17) argued that Canada's inferior productivity performance was due to performance in just two sectors of the economy and could not, therefore, be generalized to an argument about Canadian industry as a whole.[17] Furthermore, opponents argued that the "lazy manufacturers" hypothesis should be rejected at both the theoretical and empirical levels. At the theoretical level, the hypothesis implied that Canadian firms were not profit maximizers and, therefore, the hypothesis was inconsistent with one of the basic tenets of neoclassical economics.

To these economic arguments, the political dynamics of currency union suggested by the proponents' analysis were also subject to scrutiny. In making their proposals, proponents attempted to sell North America as if it was comparable to Europe and to suggest that joint sovereignty over monetary policy was possible in the same way in which it was exercised through the European Central Bank. To suggest that the regional political superstructures for European monetary governance were capable of being applied to the North American case was, however, an inappropriate usage of the euro example opponents argued. For example, McCallum (2000: 2) argued that "the European Union model, in which independent states share decision-making and sovereignty, is alien to American thinking and American history," and he described the United States as being "light years" away from allowing any other country a formal role in formulating U.S. monetary policy.[18] Helleiner (2004a) questioned whether it would be easy to have influence over monetary policy even if Canada did become, as proponents suggested, the thirteenth District of the Federal Reserve system.

However, while the academics and policy institutions debated, the issue became more widely discussed in public and business circles. Two factors led to this wider debate. The first was the continuing depreciation of the Canadian dollar, which kept the issue in the news.[19] The second was the decision by parts of the media, especially *The National Post*, to make the issue newsworthy. Concern over the level of the dollar intensified as the currency fell. As Harris (2001b: 36) noted, "most Canadians see a large depreciation of their currency as a policy 'mistake' even if, while the currency has been depreciating, the Bank has hit its inflation targets." Indeed, CIBC World Markets chief economist Jeff Rubin argued that the 60-cent Canadian dollar was an important psychological threshold and that if this threshold is broken, in his view, "the days of the Canadian dollar are going to be limited" (quoted in Rubin, 2001: C1). Canadians would simply no longer be willing to live with an increasingly noncredible currency. The Canadian dollar hit an all-time low of 61.79 cents U.S. in January 2002.

Certainly concern over the level of the dollar was evident in the business community though, importantly, there was no consensus that Canada should have a fixed exchange rate let alone use a common currency or adopt the U.S. dollar. There are clear divisions within the business sector in terms of their responses to exchange-rate movements. For example, many resource-based industries benefited from a declining dollar, and this boosted their competitiveness in the U.S. market; Canada's $10 billion exports of softwood lumber to the U.S., for instance, were aided by the depreciating dollar in the face of other trade restraints imposed by the United States. Thus, though these firms might be willing to support a stabilization of the exchange rate, the rate at which any monetary union came about would be of critical concern. Conversely, many high-tech firms, faced with importing information technology (IT) equipment from the United States priced in U.S. dollars and competing for labor in a continental market, were hurt by the depreciating dollar as it has pushed up their costs and made it difficult to recruit and retain highly skilled, mobile workers. The impacts on the two sectors have been reversed since 2003 with the rapid appreciation of the dollar since then.

Divisions between business interests are also evident from surveys conducted by the Canadian Federation of Independent Business. Given concern over the value of the dollar and the prominence of dollarization debates, it asked its members (made up of small and medium-sized firms) for the first time in its 2002 Business Outlook whether the low value of the dollar benefited their firm. Some 23 percent responded that the lower dollar helped them, whereas 31 percent saw a higher dollar as being of more benefit (38 percent reported no effect one way or the other). Similar divisions are also present in larger firms, which were described as being "all over the place" in terms of their response to the depreciating dollar.[20]

Furthermore, while meetings held by Chambers of Commerce across the country were very keen to hear about why the dollar was depreciating, this was much more of an interest in the level of the Canadian dollar than about the exchange-rate regime per se. As Helleiner (2004a) points out, business organizations came out generally in favor of the flexible exchange rate.

The media coverage of the debate was considerable, largely spearheaded by *The National Post*, a newspaper started by Conrad Black in 1998 and which on the front page of its first edition declared that it was time to "Unite the Right" in Canadian politics to defeat the Liberals (see Cobb, 2004). The *Post* came into being very much with the aim of setting the agenda, and the future of the dollar was one issue that it chose to profile through editorials and opinion pieces. Remarkably, even studies by academic economists Frankel and Rose (2000) became headline news—because they had predicted that Canada's economy could grow by 37 percent if it adopted a currency common with that of the United States (see Hunter, 2001). The award of the Nobel Prize in Economics in 2000 to Canadian Robert Mundell, known as the "father of the euro," was given wide coverage, interviews were given, and a debate with Milton Friedman on exchange-rate regimes was reported.[21]

However, in 2003, the top news story of the year was the remarkable (and unexpected) 20 percent-plus appreciation in the value of the Canadian dollar.[22] The proponents of currency union sought to keep the debate alive, with Sherry Cooper, for example, penning a piece in *The National Post* under the title "Dollarization not dead yet." Here she repeated the argument that the historical trend toward currency blocs was still relevant and added that Canada should lock into a relatively low value of the U.S. dollar before the appreciating Canadian dollar adversely affected Canadian exports (Cooper, 2003). Terence Corcoran, an editorial writer with the *Post* who had done much to promote the debate, argued that other currencies had also appreciated so that "the Canadian dollar's rise ... is far from a ringing endorsement of Canada's economy" (Corcoran, 2003: FP11); in any case, he continued, the case for dollarization rested on the volatility of the dollar, not its level.

However, the rising dollar had pulled the rug from under the debate. In March 2003, the *Post* reported that in its poll of business leaders, "respondents were ... asked about whether Canada should seriously consider adopting the U.S. dollar and 41% agreed. That was down from 49% almost two months earlier. In November, 2001, 54% of respondents favoured dumping the loonie for the U.S. dollar" (Marr, 2003). In October 2003, a poll conducted by the Centre for Research and Information on Canada reported decreasing support among the public for a common currency (down from 53 percent to 45 percent between 2002 and 2003) and for dollarization (down from 35 percent to 23 percent over the year).[23]

Within academic and government circles and among the wider public, the debate effectively died when the dollar started its rapid appreciation shown in Figure 5.1. The fact that the rising dollar cost an estimated 52,000 jobs in the manufacturing sector in 2004 (and an estimated further 100,000 manufacturing jobs in 2005) did not revive interest in the topic from business or labor leaders.[24] Certainly there is concern in some business circles about the effects of the appreciation of the Canadian dollar, an appreciation that continued through 2007 when it reached its highest level against the U.S. dollar for thirty years. However, these are the concerns of manufacturers and exporters about the level of the exchange rate, not a reconsideration of the exchange-rate regime.

The post-September 11 security concerns have changed the way that the North American "region" is seen, with a common security perimeter and border issues receiving considerable attention. There has been an increasing interest among policy elites on both sides of the Canada–U.S. border to push a "deep integration" agenda with harmonized security a part of this. Among proposals floated in this regard is a call for "building a North American community." This call, made by the Independent Task Force on the Future of North America,[25] covers both security and economic dimensions. With respect to the latter, a customs union, greater regulatory harmonization, and increased labor-market mobility are proposed to create a "North American economic space" and a "seamless" continental economy (see Independent Task Force, 2005), both of which are viewed as not needing any form of currency union; this remains conspicuous by its absence.

Analyzing the debate

The argument that the "forces of globalization" produced an "inevitable" trend to fewer currencies both within the Americas and the world was one that was advanced regularly in the Canadian debate. Proponents of monetary union cited the euro as representing a "watershed" in monetary history and ushering in new conceptions of economic sovereignty. The view that the Canadian dollar would inevitably disappear was frequently voiced in the media. Even opponents of monetary union conceded that a trend toward fewer currencies might be underway and that this was problematic for the continued existence of the Canadian dollar. John McCallum (2000: 7), then chief economist at the Royal Bank, and prominent advocate of a flexible exchange rate, conceded "that in a world that would otherwise have only three currencies, it is unlikely that the Canadian dollar would constitute the fourth. However, to the extent that the reader agrees that the benefits of the status quo exceed the costs, the implication is that Canada should not seek to speed up this grand historical process that is allegedly leading to only one, two, or three currencies."[26]

As well as the example of the euro, the interest in dollarization in other countries in the Americas, with Ecuador and El Salvador unilaterally dollarizing and Argentina and Mexico openly debating it, added further weight to the idea that there was a "trend" toward fewer currencies. The interest in Latin America in dollarization quickly evaporated with the Argentine crisis of 2001, and the supposed trend disappeared with it. There have been sporadic attempts to revive the issue, though with the inevitability of the trend no longer asserted. For example, Terence Corcoran (2005) argued in the *Post* that rising oil prices were leading to potential "Dutch disease" problems in Canada and that a common currency could help prevent this. Gilles Duceppe (2006), the Bloc Québécois leader, also raised the issue again in 2006. However, as Benjamin Tal (quoted in Perkens, 2007), an economist at CIBC World Markets, remarked with respect the Canadian dollar's future as an independent currency, "when the dollar is low, everybody's talking about it. Now, nobody is talking about it."

There is also little evidence that unofficial dollarization in Canada has been occurring, which might support the "globalization" view that there was an "inevitability" about the end of the Canadian dollar as a result of private sector activities. The data suggest that unofficial dollarization in Canada has been limited and that there has been no clear trend over time. Certainly, the business sector, though keenly interested in the level of the Canadian dollar, has had no unified position on whether the exchange-rate regime should be changed. There has been no concerted effort on behalf of the business sector to support a change to a fixed exchange-rate regime or for a common currency. It is more accurate to say that the business community has been divided on the issue and has thus been unable to reach a consensus position, rather than that the business community has been opposed to a change in regime, even if the balance has fluctuated with the variations in the value of the dollar as the polls of CEOs show.

The argument that trade integration requires a common currency is also problematic. For one thing, the data presented above demonstrate that trade has increased substantially under a flexible exchange-rate regime. Second, around 60 percent of Canada–U.S. cross-border trade is intrafirm trade and, for these firms who are both major exporters and importers, exchange-rate changes lead only to internal transfers for some of these firms.[27] Third, the levels of trade integration with the United States have been overestimated. Work by Weir (2007) examines the extent to which cross-border trade between Canada and the United States consists of the same goods moving across the border at various stages of their production process. The implication of this is that if this trade is high, trade figures are inflated as they record the value of the good in each cross-border movement. That is, each good is counted the number of times it crosses the border, whereas only the value-added is included in the calculation of GDP figures. Thus, to the extent that cross-border trade is in goods that are subsequently re-exported, the export:GDP ratio will be overestimated, and the degree of integration of the Canadian economy into the continental economy will be exaggerated. Weir (2007) argues, on the basis of his examination of the data, that the reliance of the Canadian economy on the U.S. market is approximately one-fifth rather than the oft-quoted one-third.[28]

The argument that globalization will inevitably lead to the demise of the Canadian dollar cannot, therefore, be sustained by appeal to historical trends, rates of unofficial dollarization and business interests, or the prerequisites of trade integration.[29] It might be argued that though globalization does make some form of monetary union inevitable, it makes it more likely. This, in my opinion, would occur only if there was a decisive shift in favor by the business community, a shift that is certainly possible (and which was the basis for the free trade agreement in 1989) but not at this point evident even though business interests have shown much interest in "deep integration."[30]

The credibility argument, one of the forces of globalization identified by the globalization view, posits that dollarization offers a solution to the fear of floating felt by issuers of noncredible currencies and the nonsustainability of conventional fixed exchange-rate regimes in the face of powerful international financial markets. Though typically applied to developing countries, echoes of this debate can be found in the Canadian debate. For proponents, the decline in the value of the Canadian dollar was taken as evidence of long-standing government mismanagement of the economy. This was reinforced by media coverage that fed into public anxiety during the period when the currency depreciated.[31] Grubel (1999) suggested that the performance of the Federal Reserve was better than that of the Bank of Canada and that monetary policy set by the Fed would be more credible. However, though the noncredibility argument was implicitly invoked in this way, it was not linked to the bipolar view of exchange-rate regimes associated with globalization.

In fact, the advocates of a monetary union did not rule out the possibility of a fixed exchange rate. A monetary union may be preferred but it was not the only option. And the reason it was preferred was not because of international capital markets. For Grubel, the main problem with fixed exchange rates was that "the government's commitment to fixed rates is too easily reversed as different parties form government or a new economic ideology takes hold" (1999: 25). A monetary union, just like the free-trade deal, imposes constraints on domestic governments. This is the reason why a monetary union is preferred, not because international capital markets make them impossible to implement even though they punish "domestic mismanagement" (ibid.).

Courchene and Harris are even more robust in their defense of a fixed exchange rate. They argued that there were contemporary examples of fixed exchange rates that worked well; they cite pre-euro Austria–Germany and Netherlands–Germany (1999: 18) and continue by arguing that appropriate complementary policies "could make a fixed Canada–US rate one of the most stable and viable such regimes anywhere" and therefore represents a "feasible option for Canada" (1999: 19).

The critique of government policy can best be seen as constituting a part of the contingent neoliberalism, or globalism, argument. That is, much of the debate in Canada can best be understood as arguments between neoliberals as to the best way to impose the discipline of markets on governments and economic agents and which exchange-rate regime was most likely to do this. Proponents argued that monetary union would not only change the investment behavior of Canadian industry but would have wider impacts on Canada's institutional structure, making it more "flexible" and "efficient." A common conservative critique of the Canadian institutional framework has been that, in comparison to the United States, Canada is less flexible and less dynamic and relies more on a welfare state (in the form of both "corporate" and individual welfare). Implicitly, the argument is that Canadian economic institutions and policy had "failed" with the result that Canada had a persistently higher level of unemployment, and a lower productivity growth rate than in the United States. It is this more generalized sense of policy failure that the proponents of a common currency sought to address. If adjustments to differential economic performance by the United States and Canada could no longer be channeled through the exchange rate, they would have to be addressed by greater flexibility in other markets, such as the labor market. Tying in with the U.S. monetary order would, therefore, force Canadian institutions to adapt and to become more like those in the United States: labor markets would need to become more flexible (implying a reduction in trade union power), firms would need to be more innovative, structural change would have to occur more quickly, and governments would be generally less interventionist.

Courchene and Harris (1999: 6), for example, argue that "under a fixed exchange rate regime, it might have been possible to isolate the sources of the relative decline of Canadian living standards and so to identify the more likely policy repairs." These policy repairs would include measures to make labor and product markets more flexible, as "a fixed rate regime ... implies a wholesale transformation in the way an economy responds to various shocks, whether external or policy induced" (ibid.: 4). The aim of moving to a fixed exchange-rate regime is, therefore, to encourage, or more strongly to force, the "wholesale" institutional changes necessary to make price- and wage-setting mechanisms more flexible. In short, for markets to impose more discipline.

This point was also made by Grubel. He argued that the adoption of a common currency would lead to greater labor market discipline in Canada "where unionization is about 35 percent of the labour force, much higher than that in the United States" (1999: 12). The flexible exchange rate had

> contributed to a lack of labour-market discipline and interfered with the rational adjustment to a more appropriate mix of industries. Excessively generous unemployment insurance benefits, high rates of taxation, inflation, permanent subsidies to ailing industries and regions, misplaced agricultural policies, and other government measures are also to blame for the poor performance of the Canadian economy. The main point is that flexible exchange rates and national monetary sovereignty have not been able to compensate for the problems caused by these policies. In fact, because they masked the effects of some problems, they contributed to their strength and persistence.
>
> (1999: 17–18)

The proposition that agents in the Canadian economy needed to be exposed to greater market discipline and that a flexible exchange rate was not helpful to this, found support in the business community. A member of the Business Council on National Issues argued that "we need a Schumpeterian process of creative destruction to increase income so an exchange rate which acts as a shock absorber may be inappropriate."[32] In less academic terms, business economist Sherry Cooper (2002: D5) made essentially the same point when she argued that "the reality of dollarization is difficult. It is a tough-love reality in that it will force us to truly compete through innovation and productivity-enhancing investments."

The advocacy of a change in exchange-rate regime in Canada was made possible because though Canada's current flexible exchange-rate regime has long historic roots, it is one that has no association with neoliberalism. Thus, the decision to float the Canadian dollar again in 1970 came about as the dollar was coming under pressure from large capital inflows, and the pressures for appreciation, it was argued, could no longer be resisted. However, there was no association of this return to floating rates with exposing Canada to the discipline of the international market, no association with the launch of a neoliberal project.

When the decision was taken to float the dollar, concern was expressed at the time that, despite the government's argument that returning to a floating rate would help to fight inflation, the float would "encourage, as it had in the late 1950s, an unsatisfactory mix of financial policies" (Lawson as quoted in Powell, 1999: 49). These concerns were evidently borne out. As Norrie and Owram (1996: 420–1) argue, "unfortunately, Canadian authorities did not avail themselves of this opportunity to reduce inflationary pressures. Inflation did come down in 1970, a direct result of the appreciation. But the money supply grew very rapidly, from the float through to 1975, in the range of 10–15 percent."

Laidler (1999: 14) writes in similar terms that:

> Canadian monetary and fiscal policy were totally incoherent in the early 1970s. The dollar was initially floated to relieve inflationary pressures emanating from the balance of payments, but within a year or two, expansionary fiscal and monetary policy were more than compensating for this. A monetary order based on money growth targeting was instituted in 1975, but it broke down in the early 1980s. Thereafter, monetary policy moved in fits and starts toward the pursuit of price stability as an ultimate goal, while fiscal policy delivered a constant stream of budget deficits until the early 1990s.

The float did not bring discipline; neither was it associated with a neoliberal revolution. In fact, quite the opposite, as Canadian government policy reached new interventionist heights. For example, The Canada Development Corporation was set up in 1971 to promote investment by Canadians in Canadian companies whereas the Foreign Investment Review Agency was set up two years later to screen FDI for its benefits to Canada (see Norrie and Owram, 1996: 424). Furthermore, the year after the float saw a substantial expansion of unemployment insurance. The neoliberal "paradigm shift," to use McBride's description (2005), in Canada did not occur until the early 1980s, and the basis for the debate in Canada in the late 1990s and early 2000s was whether a change in the exchange-rate regime would add to the neoliberal market disciplines being brought to bear on economic agents.

For some neoliberals, macroeconomic self-discipline had already been realized. This is the position of Laidler, writing for the same conservative C.D. Howe Institute as Courchene and Harris. He argued (1999: 15) that

Canadian macroeconomic policy changed in the 1990s. Inflation targets were instituted, were adhered to, and became credible; fiscal policy turned to deficit and debt reduction, and now poses no threat to the future stability of monetary policy. In macroeconomic policy, it seems, cause and effect do not run from a fixed exchange rate to disciplined monetary and fiscal policy but from a domestic political decision in favour of fiscal and monetary discipline to a coherent policy mix that need not include a fixed exchange rate. In Canada, the fundamental domestic political decision in favour of macroeconomic policy discipline has already been taken, and we could gain nothing further on this front by now adopting a fixed exchange rate.

McCallum (2000: 8) shared this opinion. In his rhetorical question to the pro-monetary unionists, he asked, "If you think that a flexible exchange rate results in fiscal and/or monetary indiscipline, how do you explain the fact that, over the past decade, Canada has taken giant strides to greater policy discipline under a flexible exchange rate regime?" McCallum clearly believed that policy discipline had been achieved under flexible exchange rates. As he put it, "Flexibility is a good thing—providing one has the discipline" (2000: 4). It is not, therefore, an argument about whether "discipline" is a good thing but simply whether it is present. With discipline present, the flexible exchange rate made economic sense because Canada's structural economic differences from the United States allowed the exchange rate to act as an important shock absorber.

For others, such as Grubel and Courchene and Harris, however, more discipline was needed and could be exacted by a fixed exchange-rate regime. They do not believe that the government's policy switch in the mid-1990s to impose monetary and fiscal responsibility is irreversible or represents a strong enough commitment to small government, especially as it was performed by a federal Liberal government. Thus, the currency debate in Canada has been dominated by arguments between neoliberals about what role the exchange rate might play in promoting policy discipline. For some, monetary and macroeconomic discipline has already been achieved, and a change of exchange-rate regime is not needed. As Laidler (1999) put it, Canada has a stable "monetary order" and had lower inflation rates than the United States for much of the last decade. The monetary regime should, therefore, be left well alone. For Courchene and Harris, however, a common currency is needed to foster a "wholesale" change in Canadian institutions; for them, a common currency can act as a neoliberal Trojan Horse.

Others joined in the debate, with those of a more left orientation opposing monetary union and, perhaps ironically in view of their critique of the Bank of Canada's policies, particularly under John Crow, defending the flexible exchange-rate regime and the Bank of Canada. Currency union was supported, however, by the Quebec sovereignty movement, which has typically been seen as having a social democratic orientation. The argument that common currencies as part of macro-level economic globalization foster political fragmentation would seem to be supported by the Quebec sovereignist position. However, even here, some caution is required. As Helleiner (2006) has documented, the modern Quebec independence movement started in the 1960s, and it has never advocated a separate currency for Quebec. During the 1960s through to the early 1990s, the official position was that an independent Quebec would use the Canadian dollar. In the mid-1990s, dollarization or a North American currency were supported. Helleiner attributes much of the motive for these positions to the desire to avoid monetary instability in a post-independence Quebec. However, this fear was evidently as real in the 1960s as it was in the 2000s. The rise of a post-1980s "globalization" has not dictated any change in policy here, comments about the "new" power of international financial markets notwithstanding. The changes have been in the extra-Quebec currency of choice and the mechanism of adopting it rather than a response to globalization. The choice of currency has more to do with what was happening elsewhere (in the Americas and in Europe) than with any change in the operation of international capital markets, even though sovereignists appealed to this to justify their arguments in the most recent debates.

The left analysis has also been concerned that monetary integration would result in a loss of national autonomy and be one more step in the process of Americanization. The concerns over "national identity" were also important for opponents of monetary union and resonated with the wider public. In an important sense, the 1990s concerns over identity and autonomy over economic policies as represented in the monetary union debate were counterparts of the 1970s debate over identity and autonomy over economic policies that were evident in the debate over the foreign ownership of productive assets in Canada[33] and in the free trade debate of the 1980s. However, there was little in the way of analysis of how monetary union or dollarization might feature as part of U.S. imperialism per se. In fact, it was the political Right who came closest to this as a way to demonstrate that it might be in the United States's interests to pursue such a project! It was Grubel (1999) who argued that a North American currency might appeal to the United States so that it could take on the euro. Sultan (1999: C5) argued that "Americans will greet these ideas [for currency union] with a yawn, but we can point to continental economic integration, and possibly appeal to their sense of empire."

This assessment of U.S. disinterest was real. Though the United States may have been wary of dollarization in some Latin American countries for fear of becoming embroiled in currency crises and having to bail out insolvent financial institutions, no such concerns could have been relevant in the Canadian case. And yet, still there was disinterest. Given the politically sensitive nature of the debate in Canada, perhaps this is understandable at the highest policy-making levels, particularly as members of the Canadian political Right were willingly doing their running for them. However, the issue of dollarization was of no interest in the United States. It seems that though the role of the dollar in the global economy plays an important part in supporting U.S. power, countries such as Canada still have considerable autonomy in their choice of exchange-rate regime and currency. There is no "imperial pressure" constraining their choices within fairly wide limits.

Nevertheless, the regional context was clearly important in the Canadian debate. Sharing a border with the world's largest economy, the issuer of the world's most widely used currency, and the only superpower, made discussions of a new currency arrangement naturally focus on the United States The debate was on the adoption of a regional currency. The debate was over what forms of regional monetary governance were possible. This compared forms of monetary governance in Europe and North America and concerned the extent to which the institutions of the former could be replicated in the latter. The proponents of monetary union couched their arguments in these terms (as opposed to dollarization) to present a possible regional model that provided more appeal to Canadians than subjugation to the U.S. monetary authorities, even though the realism of such proposals is open to considerable doubt. The nature of the regional dynamics was important, though even here domestic factors shaped the way in which regionalism entered the debate.

6 Mexico

with Juan Carlos Moreno-Brid

The unexpectedly wide debate provoked by the proposals in favour of a North American monetary union or the adoption of a currency board reflects, more than the actual soundness of their arguments, ideological dogma or the simple desperation of businessmen, bankers and even workers to find rapid remedies to cure the instability of the financial system and prices in the Mexican economy.

(Ibarra and Moreno-Brid, 2001: 16–17)

Overview of Mexican development

The attraction of silver meant that Mexico was incorporated into European imperial orbits during the sixteenth century. The brutality that accompanied Spanish colonialism also brought with it economic transformation. Moreno-Brid and Ros (2004: 1) write that "by the end of the 18th century Mexico was probably one of the most prosperous regions [areas] in the world. It was surely one of the wealthiest Spanish colonies in America, with an economy whose productivity was possibly higher that that of Spain herself. Output per capita (in 1800) was around half that of the US, and Mexico's economy was less agricultural, with an advanced mining industry and a significant manufacturing sector."

From Mexican Independence in 1810, when Spanish rule was overthrown, to the Mexican Revolution in 1911, however, Mexico's relative position declined significantly. During this century, Mexico was frequently buffeted by internal and external political pressures and by numerous changes in economic policy and orientation.

Independence was accompanied by an economic slump as silver production fell. There were attempts to stimulate other parts of industry with, for example, a government-run bank financing the development of cotton-spinning industries in the early 1830s (Bazant, 1991: 13). The bank's funding came from protectionist tariffs (ibid.). These efforts at industrialization were, however, insufficient to stimulate an economy ravaged by continued internal and external instability. Texas declared independence in 1836 and joined the United States in 1845. Further treaties after wars with the United States meant that by 1867, Mexico's northern border was moved southward to the extent that Mexico had lost half of its territory (though less than 2 percent of its population) (Bazant, 1991: 22).

Civil war, continued interventions by European imperial powers, periodic capital flight, and ambiguous relations with the United States continued to plague nineteenth-century Mexico. Among the causes of conflict with the United States was the Mexican government's decision in the 1870s to establish a ten-mile duty-free zone along the border with the United States to encourage settlement (Katz, 1991: 68). However, relations were ambiguous. In the 1870s, highly favorable concessions were also given to U.S. (and European) companies to provide incentives for foreign direct investment (FDI) into the oil and railway sectors (Katz, 1991: 69–70). This included subsidies to railway construction that amounted to one-half of their total costs (Moreno-Brid and Ros, 2004: 9). This contributed to producing an economic boom in the last decade-and-a-half of the century as annual gross national product (GNP) growth rates averaged 8 percent and exports as a percentage of GDP tripled (Katz, 1991: 74; Moreno-Brid and Ros, 2004: 9).

The inequalities—regional and class—that the economic boom generated, together with the end of that boom in the early 1900s, provided the economic backdrop to the Mexican Revolution of 1910–11. The Revolution sought to establish a more egalitarian development path though the extent to which it was successful in this has been questioned by economic historians. Womack (1991: 200) argues that the struggles of the Revolution led to the consolidation in power of a regional faction (from the northwest) of the bourgeoisie. What followed, he concludes, was "a long series of reforms from above, to evade, divide, diminish and restrain threats to Mexican sovereignty and capitalism from abroad and from below."

Post-revolution Mexico, therefore, can be seen as a state long penetrated by international capital, attempting to construct a nationalist, soft authoritarian form of capitalism. It was inevitably a path full of contradictions, not the least of which were in the economic relations with foreign capital and with the powerful neighbor to the North. Mexico continued to be a producer of raw materials, primarily for the U.S. market. Mexico became the world's second largest oil producer in the early 1920s, though by the end of the decade, oil production had fallen, and Mexico had been overtaken as a producer by Venezuela (Meyer, 1991: 226). In 1930, as in 1900, the trade:GDP ratio was 20 percent, though the United States accounted for an increasing share of this trade over the period; by 1930, the United States accounted for 70 percent of Mexico's imports and 80 percent of its exports (Meyer, 1991: 221). The Revolution had not immediately changed the pattern of export-led development (Knight, 1991: 241).

Mexico did, however, change track in the late 1930s and in the post-1945 years. Underpinning this change was the formation of the Partido Nacional Revolucionario (PNR) in 1929, eventually renamed the Partido Revoluncionario Institucional (PRI) in 1946, a party that brought political stability to Mexico through its hegemonic control (see Moreno-Brid and Ros, 2004: 12). The state began to play a larger role, signaled by the nationalization of the oil companies in 1938. Compensation was eventually agreed with the United States for the expropriation of U.S. oil companies' assets in 1941, an agreement that included the provision of credit by the United States for support of the peso (Knight, 1991: 286). Agrarian reform and import substitution policies supported by protectionism became other central parts of government policy.

Knight (1991: 324–5) argues that "by some standards Mexico's import substitution policies met with resounding success. Between 1940 and 1960 the GDP grew ... [at] an average annual [rate] of 6.4 per cent. ... By the late 1970s manufacturing represented nearly one-quarter of the GDP and ... the industrial sector as a whole accounted for 38.5 per cent of national output. It was this performance that came to be known as the 'Mexican miracle,' an exemplary combination of economic progress and political stability in an area of the developing world." According to Moreno-Brid and Ros (2004: 14) nothing less than "a complete overhaul of the economy and society took place from 1940 to 1980."

The "miracle" was, however, soon to end. The import-substitution strategy had been expensive to foster and overseas borrowing had risen substantially as a result. In 1976, capital flight and balance of payments pressures led to a massive depreciation of the peso (Moreno-Brid and Ros, 2004: 17). This appeared as but a temporary setback when Mexico's own oil reserves were announced. Thus, the higher oil prices caused by OPEC action in 1979 encouraged further borrowing but, when the world economy went into recession in the early 1980s, Mexico's crash came. In 1982, Mexico found itself with an inflation rate of 100 percent, a huge government deficit (equal to 18 percent of GDP), a plummeting currency, and an inability to pay its international debts (see Smith, 1991: 380–3). This was met with a "very orthodox, stabilization-first strategy" (Moreno-Brid and Ros, 2004: 19) but, within four years, Mexico was hit by the oil price shock of 1986 that "dramatically cut off a major part of the country's main source of foreign exchange and fiscal revenues" (ibid.: 19).

The response adopted to the instability and crises of the 1980s involved another policy shift, this time to a more radical neoliberalism and a return to an export-led strategy, culminating in Mexico's entry into NAFTA in 1994. The effects of this are briefly reviewed in Summary of Recent Trends and Policies.

Brief history of exchange-rate regimes and monetary institutions

During the 1870s, which many regard as a previous wave of globalization, Mexico did not adopt a currency board as some colonies did or follow the move to join the Gold Standard as many of the core imperial states did. Instead, Mexico remained on the silver standard, a decision that resulted in a 26 percent real depreciation of the peso during the 1890s and contributed to the export boom of the period (Moreno-Brid and Ros, 2004: 9).

With the Mexican Revolution came a new period of state building that included the creation of the central bank in 1935. The Bank operated as a part of the hegemonic state apparatus put in place by the PRI during the import-substituting strategy of economic development that lasted until the debt crisis of the early 1980s. The Bank was granted formal independence in 1994.

During the first four decades of its existence, the Bank of Mexico was charged with maintaining a fixed exchange rate, a role that it played with a large measure of success. However, this was first challenged in 1967 and, for the last three decades, Mexico has switched exchange-rate regimes several times. The exchange-rate crisis in 1976 resulted in the devaluation of the peso; from its fixed level of 0.0125 pesos to the U.S. dollar, the peso fell to 0.0226 to the U.S. dollar between August 1976 and April 1977. The devaluation of the peso, dramatic though it was at the time, merely marked the beginning of a continuous decline in the nominal exchange rate punctuated with a series of dramatic collapses.

The next dramatic collapse came in 1982 when, as discussed above, Mexico was forced to renege on its international debt repayments. The currency crisis saw the nominal exchange rate collapse from 0.0264 pesos to the U.S. dollar in January 1982 to 0.1181 pesos to the U.S. dollar in July 1983. Exchange controls were briefly reintroduced, and a fixed rate was restored. However, in 1986, the exchange rate was under attack again, and the peso fell from 0.5989 to 1.017 to the U.S. dollar.[1]

In response to these currency collapses, Mexico adopted a number of different regimes in an effort to provide an anchor for the control of inflation. Edwards (1997: 8) describes the next period as follows: "[B]etween 1988 and 1994 Mexico modified its exchange rate system several times, moving first from a completely fixed rate to a system based on a preannounced rate of devaluation – with the actual devaluation set below the ongoing rate of inflation – and then to an exchange rate band with a sliding ceiling. … Until October 1993 … the actual peso/dollar rate was extremely stable, remaining in the lower half of the band."

In 1990, Mexico signed on to the Brady debt reduction plan, and entry into NAFTA was being negotiated. There appeared to be the prospect of some stability,

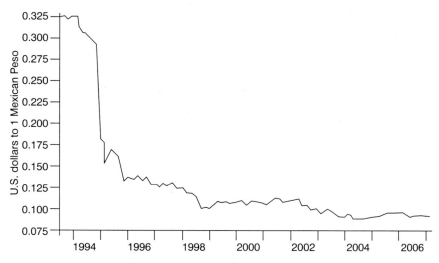

Figure 6.1 U.S. dollar/peso exchange rate July 1993–March 2007 (Source: Pacific Exchange Rate Service: fx.sauder.ubc.ca)

but this proved to be elusive as again the currency crashed. Mexico found itself embroiled in yet another currency crisis, the so-called Tequila crisis in 1994, in which the crawling band had ultimately to be abandoned, the peso devalued by 50 percent as shown in Figure 6.1.

The real costs to the economy were also high, as GDP fell by 6 percent and the financial system was left in ruins.

Since this crisis, Mexico has not attempted to go back to a fixed exchange regime but has moved to an increasingly free float. With inflation falling to single digits, the nominal exchange rate entered a period of stability from 1999 onward, as shown in Figure 6.1. The financial system has been repaired (and privatized) while the reputation of the Bank of Mexico as an overseer of the monetary affairs of the country has been to a significant degree reclaimed. As an indicator of this, Mexico issued twenty-year bonds in 2003; in 1995, the maximum maturity was one-year dollar-denominated *Tesobonos*. In 1995, two-thirds of Mexican debt was held by foreigners; by 2006, this had fallen to 40 percent, with Mexican nationals holding 60 percent of net public-sector debt (see Fisher, 2006).

The major periods in Mexico's exchange-rate regimes are summarized in Table 6.1.

Summary of recent trends and policies[2]

The policy shift to neoliberalism in the 1980s, following the debt crisis of 1982, drew on structures put in place decades earlier. Maquiladoras, for example, owed their origin to policies developed in the 1960s (Harris, 1993: 162). Their growth was inversely related to the level of the peso but, by the late 1980s, this sector

Table 6.1 Exchange rate regimes in Mexico, 1931–2007

1931–1934	Fixed versus the U.S. dollar, periodically adjusted.
1935 –March 30, 1938	Fixed.
March 31, 1938 –February 2, 1939	Free floating as the Bank of Mexico announced (March 31, 1938) the suspension of the free convertibility of the peso with gold or foreign exchange.
February 3, 1939–1976	Fixed versus U.S. dollar, adjusted periodically.
1976–1982	Floating versus U.S. dollar.
September 1982–1983	Full exchange-rate controls. Two rates: i) a so-called, controlled one for selected banking/debt operations, ii) a free one for the rest of the transactions.
1983–1987	Fixed with devaluations.
1987–1994	Pre-announced crawling peg, aimed at controlling inflation.
1995–2007	Managed float.

Source: A. Guillén (2004) and Villareal (1981)

accounted for 25 percent of Mexico's manufactured exports (Harris, 1993: 162). Most of this came from U.S. companies attracted to Mexico by the duty-free incentives and the low labor costs. There were, therefore, some strong roots on which to base the new strategy. Even so, as Harris (1993: 158) has written, most of the maquiladora growth prior to the mid-1980s "took place almost by default and without substantial government stimulation. Successive administrations emphasized issues of economic independence, rather than interdependence, and industrialization to supply the domestic market rather than external demand." Nevertheless, Moreno-Brid and Ros (2004: 23, emphasis in original), argue that "current trends in the trade *pattern* and industrial *structure* are largely an extrapolation of the past."

In terms of trade volumes and the policy environment, however, there have been large changes. From the mid-1980s onward, the PRI government abandoned its protectionist policies and turned to neoliberalism as the solution to Mexico's economic ills. Mexico joined GATT in 1986 and, adopting the array of policies recommended by the Washington Consensus, introduced a program of rapid trade liberalization, privatization, and deregulation. By 1990, Mexico had become one the world's most open developing countries. Entry into NAFTA on January 1, 1994 cemented the neoliberal policy reforms, an explicit objective followed by the Salinas government (1988–94) that argued that NAFTA would impose international legal and extra-legal constraints that would deter any attempt by subsequent governments in Mexico to return to trade protectionism.

The main economic debates in Mexico over the last decade have centered around whether the experience of NAFTA has been positive or negative for Mexico. The positive argument rests on Mexico's performance since NAFTA, having been marked by small budget deficits, low inflation, and a surge in non-oil exports and FDI. Mexico's exports and the volumes going to the United States have surged, as indicated in Table 6.2.

Though oil revenues have decreased from around one-fourth of total exports in the early 1990s to one-half of that level, manufactured exports have taken an increasing share of exports. Manufactured exports now account for 85 percent of total exports, with more than one-half of these coming from the maquiladora sector. The bulk of Mexico's non-oil exports originates in no more than 300 businesses, most of them linked to multinational corporations (MNCs). This has facilitated a rapid increase in intra-industry trade as firms have specialized production across the United States–Mexico border. Fiess (2004: 16) reports that "according to Bruehlhart and Thorpe (2001), between 1980 and 1998, the unadjusted Grubel–Lloyd index (3-digit SITC level) for manufacturing products between the US and Mexico grew from 0.36 to 0.61. Mexico's dramatic shift in intra-industry trade with the US is predominantly explained by increased vertical intra-industry trade in textiles and apparel, and auto industries."

This export growth has resulted in Mexico being among the top ten countries in terms of increasing its share in the world (non-oil) market. Indeed, in the period 1994–2001 (the most recent year for which comparative data is available), Mexico was second only to China in increasing its share of world manufactured exports.

Table 6.2 Mexico's exports 1985–2006: total (US$ millions) and U.S. share

Year	Total exports	Exports to U.S.	U.S. share of exports (%)
1985	22,105	8,954	40.5
1986	16,120	7,574	47.0
1987	20,526	8,252	40.2
1988	20,765	12,102	58.3
1989	22,975	15,553	67.7
1990	26,838	18,418	68.6
1991	42,688	33,912	79.4
1992	46,196	37,420	81.0
1993	51,886	43,068	83.0
1994	60,882	51,855	85.2
1995	79542	66,336	83.4
1996	96,000	80,541	83.9
1997	110,431	94,379	85.5
1998	117,539	103,002	87.6
1999	136,362	120,262	88.2
2000	166,121	147,400	88.7
2001	158,780	140,564	88.5
2002	161,046	141,898	88.1
2003	164,766	144,293	87.6
2004	187,999	164,522	87.5
2005	213,711	183,052	85.7
2006	231,997	212,313	91.5

Source: 1985–89: The Mexican Handbook: Economic and Demographic Maps and Statistics, 1994; 1990–2006: INEGI. http://dgcnesyp.inegi.gob.mx/cgi-win/bdieintsi.exe/NIVJ10#ARBOL

With respect to FDI, the neoliberal policy shift saw performance requirements for foreign investors progressively removed and, by 1993, 91 percent of branches of economic activity had been opened to majority participation by foreign investors. The result was a doubling of the FDI:GDP ratio from 2 to 4 percent over the decade of the 1990s.

Though these trends are used by supporters of Mexico's recent policy, as encapsulated by NAFTA, other trends are highlighted by those who view Mexico's path as having a negative effect on Mexican development. Thus, economic growth has been disappointing, with GDP growing at a rate significantly below its historical average and insufficient to generate the number of jobs required by the country's expanding labor force. Investment rates have been below the level required to produce the 5 percent annual level of growth needed to provide full employment.

Though manufacturing sector jobs have increased, there has been a net job loss in the economy as the agricultural sector has shed more than 1 million jobs. The result has been the increase in the informal economy and in emigration to the United States that has reached record levels. Indeed, Cypher and Delgado Wise (2007) describe Mexico's economy as one now best described as a "labour export-led" model. They argue that to emigration must be added the export of labor through the macquidora sector and through the "disguised macquidora sector" where the latter refers to domestic firms that use macquidora-produced inputs in their exports. As a result, they argue (2007: 28), "Mexico, in effect, exports cheap labour in several guises – a 'primarization' process even more backward than the export of basic agricultural commodities or raw materials."

The net result has been that instead of closing the real per capita GDP gap with the United States, it has widened. In the late 1980s, Mexico managed to begin to reduce this gap, but this improvement was short-lived as the economic crisis of 1995 widened it once more. Since then, there has been little change, and the current GDP per capita difference between the United States and Mexico is comparable to its level in the 1950s.

The contemporary currency debate

Though Mexican policies have, as illustrated, undergone considerable change over the last sixty years, traditionally, the topic of formal dollarization was never included as part of the discussions of Mexican economic policies. However, this dramatically changed in the late 1990s when dollarization became the subject of an intense debate. Local and foreign academics, policy advisers, editorialists, highly placed government officers, and prominent CEOs of Mexican industrial and financial firms intervened in heated discussions on this matter. Indeed, in 1998–99, the speculation on dollarization acquired such intensity that the President—Ernesto Zedillo—formally stated that Mexico would continue then and in the future with its traditional exchange-rate policy based on a managed float of the peso against the U.S. dollar.

Why was dollarization begun to be seen as a practical and perhaps commendable option for Mexico? A key element behind the sudden interest in it was the by-then rather successful price stabilization performance of the Argentinean economy under its currency board. Moreover, the adoption of the euro as a common currency for various countries in Europe on January 1, 1999 was another factor that helped to fuel the debate. And finally, as various analysts and businessmen argued, after more than ten years of drastic macroeconomic reforms to size down the state, Mexico should proceed toward a monetary integration with the United States. Such monetary integration would limit even more the degree of intervention of the state in the Mexican economy by eliminating its capacity to alter the foreign exchange rate. It was also an opportune moment as Mexico was coming to an end, in 2000, of a Presidential term and electoral cycles had led to previous currency crises; dollarization might offer the opportunity to prevent another episode.

In any case, in 1998–2000, the Mexican press was swamped with articles examining the pros and cons of dollarization. On the one hand, and in brief, its advocates argued that the adoption of the U.S. dollar as the local currency was a necessary and logical step for Mexico after NAFTA. They saw dollarization as a way to strengthen Mexico's preferential position in trade and investment with the United States. They argued that, given the vast proportion of domestic financial assets and liabilities already denominated in dollars, formal dollarization would merely give legal recognition to the *de facto* highly dollarized status of the Mexican economy. Finally, they saw in it a guarantee for long-run price stability given that it would ensure prudent monetary and fiscal policies. Though they admitted that in principle a floating exchange-rate regime may be useful for developing countries, they pointed out that in practice it was inadequate for Mexico, given the traditional lack of a credible commitment from its monetary authorities to maintain price stability. Supporters of this measure did differ on their considerations of the time horizon to move forward with dollarization. The more radical ones believed the sooner the better. More moderate supporters considered that Mexico needed to carry out a number of economic reforms for implementing dollarization. They estimated that, in practice, dollarization in Mexico would not be a reality for at least a decade.

On the other hand, its critics argued that dollarization would hinder Mexico's economic development. Its actual costs in terms of bringing about an increased vulnerability to external shocks would far outweigh its potential benefits in reducing the rate of inflation. The main costs that they identified included the elimination of the possibility of implementing an independent monetary and exchange-rate policy and the loss of fiscal revenues associated with seignorage. In addition, they said that given that the Bank of Mexico would not be able to act as a lender of last resort, under dollarization Mexico would be prone to more frequent and deeper banking and financial crises. And, owing to country risk factors, real interest rates would fail to come down to the United States levels (see Moreno-Brid and Rozo, 2000).

One of the first indications that dollarization was becoming a relevant topic for debate in Mexico occurred in September 1998, when the Centro de Estudios Económicos del Sector Privado (CEESP)—a major private sector think-tank—published a report with a formal proposal to adopt the U.S. dollar as Mexico's currency (see CEESP, 1998). However, in fact, the Mexican government had already started to examine the merits and drawbacks of dollarization (see Chapa and Angel, 1999). As Friedland (1998) reported in September 1998:

> During the past few weeks, Finance Minister José Angel Gurría and Central Bank Governor Guillermo Ortiz have instructed their technical teams to study how the dollar-linked currencies of Argentina and Hong Kong are faring amid the global economic turmoil. Finance-ministry and central-bank officials have held meetings with private economists and columnists here to discuss

the pros and cons of tying the peso to the dollar as a first step to monetary integration with the United States.

In October of that same year, Alfonso Romo, CEO of PULSAR, a major holding group, gave a public lecture in Monterrey stressing Mexico's need to join a monetary union with the United States. Perhaps the moment when pressure for dollarization reached its peak was in March 1999, when the Mexican Council of Businessmen (CMHN) in their annual meeting with the President explicitly made the central point of its presentation the argument that dollarization should be implemented soon in Mexico. The CMHN is the voice of the Mexican entrepreneurial elite, its membership limited to the fifty most powerful business leaders and a membership joined only by invitation of the existing members.[3] Carlos Peralta, CEO of IUSA telecommunications holding group, was among the various businessmen who backed CMHN President Clariond's plea for a fully dollarized system. Clariond argued that "sustaining a currency like Mexico's has an enormous cost. Living with its fluctuations is a luxury we can no longer afford," concluding that dollarization would "spur growth, reduce inflation, and lower interest rates on government expenses" (quoted in Boardman, 2000). Pro-business politicians, such as Senator Arturo Nava of the National Action Party (PAN) also supported the proposal for dollarization on the grounds that "the Mexican economy has already been dollarized due to the frequent use of the U.S. currency in business transactions" (quoted in Boardman, 2000). Some of the top businessmen, however, such as Carlos Gómez y Gómez, President of the Mexican Bankers Association, did not fully sympathize with the proposal of a rush toward dollarization and recommended instead a gradual approach to its implementation so it could be fully operational in the medium term. Furthermore, though the elite association, the CMHN, supported dollarization, other business associations reached no consensus on the issue with the sectoral interests of different firms explaining differing degrees of support (see Auerbach and Flores-Quiroga, 2003: 276).

The business community's support for dollarization also found some resonance among the general public. Boardman (2000) reports that "a poll by *El Economista* newspaper in May 1999 estimated that 86 percent of Mexicans would like to open up bank accounts in dollars and see dollars move freely in the economy." However, the same poll also revealed that, while wanting greater access to dollars, Mexicans did not want to give up their national currency that they viewed as an important symbol of sovereignty and national identity (ibid.).

President Zedillo, as well as the Finance Minister and the Governor of the Bank of Mexico, rejected the idea of dollarization. They soon issued formal statements backing Mexico's floating exchange-rate regime and saying that there would be no change in this policy in the future. Succinctly, they stated that dollarization was not and would not be implemented in Mexico. The main reason given for this policy stance by Zedillo was that "the free-floating exchange regime has allowed us to buffer the effects of international financial volatility even in the most critical moments, and has allowed us to protect our international reserves" (quoted in Boardman, 2000). An important element to take into account, too, is that a few weeks before—on February 23—Alan Greenspan voiced his frank opposition to a formal dollarization in Mexico. He declared that the United States had no intention or interest whatsoever in having the Federal Reserve become the central bank for the region. Furthermore, he stated that the decisions of the Fed on policy matters were and would be taken with regard to the objectives of the United States and not of other nations. The position of the Fed became a part of the Mexican debate as well. Some influential business, leaders such as billionaire Carlos Slim, chairman of Teléfonos de México, aligned themselves with President Zedillo in opposition to dollarization, notwithstanding the position taken by the CMHN. He argued that "the way you have to stop inflation is by cleaning up your financial house. Besides, the idea that the Federal Reserve would want to take responsibility for our financial system is absurd."

At that time, most private-sector economic analysts and independent consultants in Mexico backed dollarization but only as a long-term policy objective. Among the most well-known Mexican analysts holding this view were Jonathan Heath, Manuel Sánchez González (of GEA consultants), and Enrique Quintana, chief editor of economic affairs of the newspaper *REFORMA*. For example, Quintana (1999) wrote in early 1999 that a common currency for North America was unavoidable in the long run but should be rejected as a short-run course of action. As he claimed, Mexico had institutional weaknesses that needed to be corrected before implementing a formal dollarization program. He identified two main weaknesses: the fragility of its banking system and the inadequacy of the financial regulatory framework. As he said, these weaknesses had been dramatically exposed by the Tequila crisis in 1994–95 that led to the virtual collapse of numerous domestic banks. Some analysts strongly argued for a rejection of dollarization as an alternative for Mexico. As an example, Rogelio Ramírez de la O argued that given the likely asymmetry of oil-related external shocks on Mexico and the U.S. economies, Mexico needed an independent exchange-rate policy. Many of the economists at UNAM and other public universities shared this view.

The international academia was perhaps more evenly split on this issue regarding the Mexican case. Among the international experts who voiced their full support for dollarization in Mexico, not surprisingly, was Steven Hanke. Writing in 1999, he forecast that the benefits of dollarization were so evident and significant that the PRI (then Mexico's ruling party) would implement it in the very near future. He added that—and as a consequence—the PRI would win the presidential elections of July 2, 2000! Both predictions were incorrect. With less optimism than Hanke, other academics of wide international recognition declared their open support for the idea that Mexico should—sooner rather than later—embark on a full dollarization process. The list included, inter alia, Rudiger Dornbush, Ricardo Hausman, and Gary Becker.

A more cautious approach was suggested by others. Albert Fishlow explicitly declared that dollarization should be implemented in Mexico but no sooner than a decade. Robert Mundell rejected the idea that Mexico should dollarize in the short run. He considered instead that Mexico should first adopt a currency board.

Many other international experts were highly critical of dollarization as a policy for Mexico, both in the short and in the long run. For example, Paul Krugman pointed out in 1999 that dollarization could be harmful for Mexico unless the U.S. Fed. also accepted to act as a lender of last resort for Mexico with the full and active participation of Mexico in its decisions. José Antonio Ocampo, at the time ECLAC Executive Secretary, stated that dollarization could perhaps be an alternative for small economies in Central America but not for Mexico. For Jeffrey Sachs and Felipe Larraín, dollarization was applicable only to cases of extreme market instability, but a flexible exchange-rate policy vis-à-vis the U.S. dollar was much more prudent and preferable for the vast majority of developing countries, and certainly for Mexico.

The debate in Mexico did continue for some time up until 2000 but was always met by the strong rejection from President Ernesto Zedillo, from Guillermo Ortiz, Governor of the Central Bank, and from the Finance Minister. In our view, the debate on dollarization in Mexico, rather than being settled by analytical arguments, simply faded away as a consequence of key events in the evolution of the Mexican and the Latin American economies. In fact, during the campaign for the Presidential elections held on July 2, 2000, no candidate included dollarization as an element of their economic programs. Vicente Fox, who won the election and served as Mexico's President from 2000 to 2006, had as a key element of his economic platform the proposal that the government should commit to maintaining a real exchange rate that helped the international competitiveness of Mexican producers in international markets: a position that could not be in more dramatic contrast with dollarization (and, to a large degree, in contrast with the subsequent path actually taken by the peso)! International academic economists, such as the Inter-American Development Bank's Chief Economist Ricardo Hausman, was still publicly advocating dollarization in 2001, even predicting that Mexico, along with Brazil, would soon set up currency boards.[4] However, for all intents and purposes, the debate had fizzled out in Mexico by then, notwithstanding Hanke's (2003) attempt to raise it again.

What are the reasons that the debate on dollarization ended "not with a bang but with a whimper?" First of all, from 1996 up until 2003, there has been a gradual but systematic appreciation of the real exchange rate of the peso vis-à-vis the U.S. dollar. This appreciation toned down the enthusiasm for the supporters of dollarization. Moreover, the voices of pro-dollarization were gradually replaced by complaints, key manufacturing organizations arguing that the real appreciation of the exchange rate had to be reversed soon as it was weakening Mexican producers in the international markets and against imports. This view was strengthened by the increasing concern among policymakers in Mexico and among business and civil society that though Mexico has made substantial progress against inflation, its economic growth performance has been extremely weak. In addition, the support for dollarization of the Association of Mexican Bankers ended as soon as their banks were taken over or bought by foreign banks.

The economic collapse and banking crisis of Argentina was a severe blow to the supporters of dollarization (or of any form of fixed exchange-rate regime) not only in Mexico but all over the continent. And finally, the aftermath of September 11, 2001 brought about a substantial decline in Mexico's place on the United States' political and economic priority list. Given this decline, it has been very difficult for supporters of dollarization to argue that transferring monetary policy authority from the Mexican government to the Federal Reserve would be in the nation's best interests.

In synthesis, and with the benefit of hindsight, it seems fair to say that the debate on dollarization in Mexico never reached a scale of social or political relevance. It remained rather circumscribed to the press and academia. Dollarization was an issue strongly supported by a rather small—though powerful—group of entrepreneurs, and this support lasted for a limited time. The Mexican economy has been marked in the last six years (2000–06) by a combination of single-digit inflation, slow economic growth and widely insufficient employment opportunities, and strictly constrained credit for production and investment purposes. Not surprising, given this context, the attention of political and economic analysts has shifted to other matters far removed from dollarization.

Analyzing the debate

The timing of the Mexican debate was influenced by two key developments elsewhere: the impending birth of the euro and the increasing consideration given to dollarization by Argentina following its (at the time and in its own terms) successful experience with a currency board. The influence of developments elsewhere, external to the dynamics of the Mexican economy itself, were therefore critical in stimulating the debate. The terms of the debate were also influenced by these developments and used as reference points.

The terms of the debate clearly resonate with several of the interpretations of globalization surveyed in Chapter 2. Globalization as a process that strengthens international financial markets and reduces the policy autonomy of nation states was clearly in evidence. Mexico's turbulent experience with exchange-rate crises go back until at least the mid-1970s and includes subsequent crises in 1982, 1986, and 1994. The earlier crises were largely attributed to the influence of external shocks, such as changes in global growth and oil price shocks. As such, they resembled shocks that affected other countries during these time periods (in Latin America and elsewhere as the "sterling crises" demonstrate) and are therefore not closely linked to the more recent phenomenon of "globalization." The 1994 crises, however, has been interpreted in this way. Kessler (2000: 43), for example, argues that "in the wake of the devastating devaluations in several of the world's largest emerging markets, including Russia, South Korea, Indonesia and Brazil, the Mexican experience is now seen as the harbinger of a new economic phenomenon: the volatility of global capital markets."

The 1994–95 Tequila crisis can, therefore, be seen as an episode demonstrating the constraints placed on national policy makers by powerful and volatile global financial markets. These constraints meant that Mexican policy makers were faced with a choice of either adopting super-hard fixes, such as a currency board or dollarization, or abandoning fixed exchange rates and moving to purely floating rates. That is, the Mexican case provides evidence for the bipolar view. The previous financial crises provided cause for both the Mexican public and international investors to have low levels of trust in the credibility of the country's monetary institutions, so dollarization was an option for active consideration. Thus, the credibility arguments for dollarization were plausible for Mexico.

Business support and the evidence from polls among the general public indicate that credibility was a concern and that dollarization in some form was seen as a potential solution to this. However, though these arguments suggested a policy move in favor of a rapid transition to an officially dollarized economy, other business supporters argued for such a transition to be a long-term goal. The difference in the reasoning between the two groups is that a rapid transition arises from viewing the credibility issue as critical whereas the longer transition was premised on the integrationist arguments for the use of a single currency. That is, business support for the adoption of a single currency, the U.S. dollar, was also the result of the increasing levels of economic integration between the two countries as a result of the NAFTA. As the data provided above indicate, NAFTA resulted in a large increase in exports, FDI, and intra-industry trade associated with a relatively small number of MNCs. As such, there was a powerful constituency that might potentially benefit from a reduction in transactions costs. Some in the Mexican business community supported dollarization on these grounds but viewed it as more akin to an EU-type process in which monetary union would be the result of a longer process of economic integration. President Fox, an advocate of a North American Common Market, also viewed the further integration of North America as a step-by-step process with the harmonization of external tariffs the next step, though it did include monetary union as a possible long-term goal.

Evidence on the degree of business cycle synchronization as a result of NAFTA suggests that the case for the use of a single currency on these grounds may not yet have been reached and that the longer-term argument is more appropriate in an integrationist perspective. Kose et al. (2004: 20) find that NAFTA "appears to have been associated with an increased degree of comovement of business cycles of Mexico and its NAFTA partners. The increase in comovement can be seen from the marked increase in cross-country correlations of the major macroeconomic aggregates, including output, consumption, and investment. In particular, the output correlation between Mexico and its NAFTA partners rose from almost zero in the pre-NAFTA period to around 0.75 during the post-crisis period." This appears to be a very strong result and indicates that the economies of Mexico and the United States have moved rapidly from being uncorrelated in their business cycles to now having highly correlated cycles; a result in keeping with Frankel and Rose's (1998) finding and an argument used in favor of the use of common currencies. When analyzing the causes of the variance of output, that is, in examining which factors are causing the business cycles to move together, Kose et al. (2004: 23) find that "regional factors became more important in driving business cycles in

Mexico with the advent of NAFTA. The proportion of output volatility explained by the regional factor in Mexico rose from less than 1 percent in the period 1980–93 to more than 19 percent in the 1994–2002 period." Though this again shows the increasing importance of regional dynamics, it still leaves 81 percent of the variance in output explained by world, country-specific, and idiosyncratic factors (see also Cuevas et al., 2002 for the importance of idiosyncratic factors for Mexico). A regional economy is emerging, but it is not yet clear that the immediate adoption of a common currency is warranted on these grounds.

The relatively large degree of support within the CMHN for dollarization was, therefore, based on two quite distinct lines of reasoning. For those most concerned about the credibility of Mexico's institutions and the ability of global financial markets to inflict damage, an Argentinean quick-fix solution was more appealing. Efficiency arguments garnered support for a longer-term approach. Together, they produced an important political force that sought to push Mexican policy makers in the direction of dollarization as a response to the forces of globalization.

Other interpretations of the 1994–95 Tequila crisis place much less emphasis on the uniqueness of the crisis as a harbinger of a new world of volatile global financial markets. As the arguments presented in Fligstein (2001) and discussed in Chapter 3 indicate, for some it is not international financial markets that should take the blame for the 1994–95 debacle (though they may certainly be partly culpable) but rather the mismanagement by both the Mexican and U.S. governments in propping up the peso for political reasons in the first place and thereby inviting a crisis. A similar account is found in Edwards (1997). He argues that Mexico's trade deficit and overvaluation of the peso in the 1987–93 period were sufficient to suggest that an imminent exchange-rate crisis could be expected. However, members of the international financial institutions and private investment agencies chose to overlook this in favor of "inventing" a Mexican "miracle"—an invention made to support Mexico's path of neoliberal reforms based on optimism over NAFTA entry rather than reflecting Mexico's actual performance. When corrective action was required, Edwards (1997: 3) argues, "Mexico had the opportunity to undertake a number of measures that would have allowed a smooth landing. Political considerations and overoptimism, however, stood in the way of corrective actions." Furthermore, "the US Treasury was fully aware of what was going on."

According to these interpretations, therefore, it is not so much the power of international financial markets as the folly of domestic governments that caused the financial crises. On this reading, the 1994–95 crisis does not necessarily mark the arrival of a new type of financial crisis accompanied by new constraints on government policy; it resembles more a continuation of the old problems associated with policy mismanagement. The implications of this are that pressures for dollarization are more likely the result of "contingent neoliberalism" than globalization imperatives. In support of this position, that is, national rather than global pressures provide the explanation, it should also be noted that, contrary to the assertions of some, Mexico is not by international standards a highly dollarized economy. In fact, unofficial dollarization has been relatively modest. In Mexico, Balino et al. (1999) report an estimate for the ratio of foreign currency deposits to broad money to be 7.2 percent, substantially below the level of other Latin American countries. Estimates computed by Feige et al. (2003) suggest an unofficial dollarization rate of 20 percent, still low compared to other Latin American countries, such as Uruguay, Argentina, Peru, and Bolivia and below the 35 percent that they calculate to be the threshold at which network externalities occur. Furthermore, the structural differences between the Mexican and U.S. economies remain large, the importance of trade integration through NAFTA in synchronizing business cycles discussed above notwithstanding, so that the maintenance of a separate currency to adjust to external shocks remains a powerful argument and, indeed, was the one used by Mexican officials in rejecting the calls for dollarization.

According to a "globalism" interpretation, the interest in dollarization was supported by business as they saw it as a means to cement neoliberal policies in favor of small government; that is, dollarization would play the same "locking-in" role for the monetary sector as NAFTA played in the trade and investment sectors. This is the "ideological dogma" to which Ibarra and Moreno-Brid (2001) refer in the quotation that opens this chapter. In this instance, this refers to the strong anti-government position of the Mexican business community and some academics, a position that regards limitations to state authority and discretionary policies as a key medium-term objective. That is, the continuing neoliberal agenda in Mexico placed dollarization on the policy agenda more firmly than might otherwise have been expected. Thus, Auerbach and Flores-Quiroga (2003: 275) argue that "the demand for dollarization is yet another expression of the private sector's persistent 20-year campaign to impose constraints on the Mexican government's policymaking discretion. Regarding monetary policy, the first step was to take it away from the president's direct control. The last step would be take away that instrument entirely from the Mexican government's hands by adopting another country's currency."

Also, the support for dollarization can be seen as part of the Mexican business community's wider neoliberal agenda to constrain the state. Government leaders and such key institutions as the Bank of Mexico might be expected to resist this pressure, as indeed they did, out of their own institutional interests and desire to retain policy discretion.

However, the debate cannot simply be reduced to institutional interests; it must also be remembered that it was the PRI that initiated the neoliberal reform agenda in Mexico in the mid-1980s and was widely praised by the international financial institutions and in international business circles for its "radical reforms." It was these neoliberal politicians who had deliberately removed their (and subsequent governments') policy discretion in the trade and investment areas when they entered NAFTA. However, now it was these same neoliberal politicians who now explicitly rejected dollarization—as did neoliberal economists both inside and outside Mexico, and as did Mexico's wealthiest businessman, Carlos Slim, as indicated above, who argued that it was necessary for Mexico to put its own financial house in order.

These factors reinforce the point that though institutional interests may play some explanatory role, there is also the wider context of disagreement between neoliberals on appropriate monetary institutions and exchange-rate regimes. Those who rejected the idea of dollarization believed that Mexico was capable of putting its own financial house in order. In early 1994, ironically only months before the financial crisis, the government amended Article 28 of the Constitution to provide greater independence to the Bank of Mexico. Under this amendment, the Governor of the Bank would be appointed for a fixed term, and the terms of other board members would be staggered. The scope for "political interference" in monetary policy was, therefore, reduced. Subsequently, President Zedillo sought to increase the transparency of the financial system "by issuing a weekly report on the level of international reserves and money supply, which is scrutinized carefully by investors trading peso futures at the Chicago Mercantile Exchange" (Boardman, 2000).

However, the move to central bank independence did not reassure international investors sufficiently to prevent the Tequila crisis. And the ability of the Mexican political elite to respect this new independence was still open to question. Thus, at the end of 1997, just as the issue of dollarization was surfacing as an intensely debated topic as a result of developments in Europe and Argentina, further questions were being asked about the management of Mexico's financial system. It was then that President Zedillo appointed his Minister of Finance, Guillermo Ortiz, as the new central bank Governor. This appointment raised a "storm of controversy" (Salinas-León, 1998) because Ortiz was seen as being too close to the government and because his appointment was viewed as owing to the unwillingness of Zedillo to appoint the bank's deputy governor because the latter was seen as being "too independent." Some critics of the appointment went so far as to call Ortiz's appointment another "December mistake" in reference to the mistakes that led to the Tequila crisis in December 1994 (Salinas-León, 1998). As it happens, Ortiz displayed his independence and neoliberal credentials in 1999 when the Bank of Mexico formally adopted inflation targeting as its sole objective.

During the period of the dollarization debate, from 1998–2001, there was room for disagreement as to whether the cause of neoliberalism and constrained government in Mexico would best be served by dollarization that would remove from Mexican authorities the capacity to exercise monetary autonomy or by making changes to the institutional structure and functions of central banking. The business community largely took the first position, as did many neoliberal-oriented economists and policy analysts inside and outside Mexico. The PRI government, some academics, and some businessmen opted for the second route. However, these were debates between neoliberals; which side they were on depended on their assessment of which institutional fixes were most appropriate given the situation (i.e., their neoliberalism was "contingent" on this assessment). Neoliberals in the private sector tended to side with dollarization as the institutional fix to avoid the dirigisme of the past whereas neoliberals in government had more faith in reforming Mexican institutions. The latter group won out in the debate, and the continued stability of the exchange rate and low inflation in subsequent years, and Argentina's failure, have meant that there has been no basis for reopening the debate. The "contingent neoliberalism" approach has considerable traction, therefore, in explaining the Mexican debate.

The imperialism interpretation, however, finds no support. The United States made it explicitly clear that it was not interested in Mexico officially dollarizing. Mexico's state-owned industries and banks were being privatized anyway, many being sold to U.S. interests. There was no added benefit from official dollarization and, indeed, the United States regarded the fragility of the Mexican banking system as constituting considerable potential added costs. There was simply no interest by the United States in extending the official role of the U.S. dollar. Furthermore, the support for dollarization came from the Mexican business elite rather than from U.S. business interests. There were arguments from the political Left in Mexico against dollarization (see Auerbach and Flores-Quiroga, 2003) on the grounds that it would lead to the further subordination of the Mexican economy to the demands of capital accumulation in the United States. However, this is not something that the U.S. state or its corporations actively sought. This does not necessarily rule out U.S. imperial ambitions pointing in this direction. Carchedi (2001: 162), for example, argues that "it is (fractions of) the local bourgeoisies of the dominated countries (especially of Latin America) which push for dollarization. The US need not push. The job is being done for them." Though it is certainly the case that the Mexican bourgeoisie has closely aligned itself to U.S. interests, nevertheless its support for dollarization is better explained by the contingent neoliberal ideological preference of (some of) the Mexican business community. And it should be remembered that no less a figure than Alan Greenspan actively intervened in the debate to say that the United States did not support official dollarization in Mexico. Even if Cypher and Delgado Wise (2007: 28) are correct in arguing that globalization in the form of NAFTA have "had the impact on Mexico of raising its level of dependency on the US industrial system," it is still the case that this dependency has not extended to a push (or even acquiescence) by the U.S. state for dollarization.

The regionalism interpretation has some limited appeal. The regionalization of trade and production networks under NAFTA provided a basis for monetary integration to also be considered. Even so, it was the CMHN rather than United States-based multinationals that were the most vocal supporters of dollarization, suggesting that domestic rather than regional issues were key here. Nevertheless, the European experiment with the euro attracted attention in Mexico and helped to put on the agenda the question of whether this might also be a model for North America. However, it is also clear that regionalism, as a political project, is quite different in North America than in the EU and that the paths being taken in each are quite distinct. There is only a very limited regional political superstructure in NAFTA, so the institutional foundations for a common currency are nonexistent. This was realized in the Mexican debate wherein the only serious discussions were about a currency board or dollarization. And though the U.S. dollar has circulated in Mexico for a long time, there is no evidence that unofficial dollarization has increased with the current phase of regional integration; in fact, in recent years, the dollar's role as a regional currency has been reduced in Mexico. Mexico–U.S. economic integration has gathered pace under NAFTA, but it is a regional project that lacks the necessary political institutions that would be capable of promoting and managing the adoption of a regional currency. In Mexico, regional integration has always placed special emphasis on labor mobility, given the high levels of emigration to the United States. To the extent that a common currency is seen as requiring labor mobility, the post-September 11, 2001 security concerns in the United States and the tightening of the U.S.–Mexico border (with a wall, no less) have further reduced the possibilities for regional monetary unification.

7   Norway

with Ådne Cappelen

> The word "globalization" ("globalisering" in Norwegian) was rarely used in Norway before 1997–8. A few trendy academics and journalists had picked it up from international sources, but it surfaced only occasionally in the mass media, and it did not form part of either political or intellectual controversy.
>
> (Øyvind Osterud, 2004: 40)

> For over thirty years, Norway has hosted an E[uropean] C[ommunity] debate that only surfaced in the Community during the Maastricht treaty ratification process ... What sets Norway apart from all these countries (with the exception of Denmark) is that this debate started so early, has been conducted with such emotion, and has resulted in victory for the opposition to membership.
>
> (Brent Nelsen, 1993: 219–20)

Overview of Norwegian development

In June 2005, Norway celebrated the centenary of the dissolution of the union with Sweden that had been in place since the end of the Napoleonic war. A hundred years ago, Norway was a relatively poor, staple goods-producing economy, highly integrated into the international trading system. At the time of independence, the staple goods were fish, timber, and wood products that between them accounted for two-thirds of commodity exports. In addition to integration through trade, Norway was also integrated into the international markets of the late nineteenth century through labor flows. Norway experienced mass emigration to North America, and Norway and Ireland were the European countries with the largest emigrations measured as a percentage of the resident population.

After World War I, Norway developed a manufacturing industry based on hydroelectricity as an energy source. A significant part of this industry was export-oriented and produced semi-manufactured goods used as inputs in the production process in other countries. The firms in these export industries were mainly owned by foreigners, again an indication of how closely Norway was integrated into the international economy in the early stages of its economic development. The trade: GDP ratio was close to 35 percent in this period.

The 1920s and 1930s saw a shift away from the internationalization of the Norwegian economy. The trade:GDP ratio fell, and gradually a home-market-oriented consumer industry developed. Emigration virtually came to a standstill after 1930, and inflows of capital declined as well. Though Norway was significantly hit by the crisis in the world economy and unemployment was high, the extent of the crisis was nevertheless not as severe as in many other countries. Social conflicts and labor disputes were frequent, but gradually a new social consensus emerged that resulted in the establishment of new corporatist institutions. These institutions have become defining characteristics of the "Scandinavian model of development" and were established in Norway, as in other Scandinavian countries, during the 1920s and 1930s. Corporatist institutions and the consensus approach to politics have played important roles in Norway and continue to do so. Though their significance has been somewhat modified recently by the move toward more market-oriented policies, they remain important especially in comparative international terms.

Though Norway was neutral during World War I, it was occupied by Germany during World War II. The occupation served to consolidate the national consensus view and the corporatist institutions that had been established earlier. There was also strong support for closer political and economic integration with the allied countries in World War II. Though there was opposition from parts of the political Left, both within the Labor Party and of course from the Communist Party, to membership in NATO and to relinquishing some state control of the economy, economic and political integration had widespread support from most parties and the electorate. A gradual liberalization of trade took place in Norway as in other OECD countries in the post-1945 period as Norway became a committed member of the Western alliance. Openness, again defined as the trade:GDP ratio, rose by 10 percentage points between 1939 and the mid-1950s and was fairly constant until the discovery of oil in the 1970s. Labor mobility, on the other hand, remained very low. Capital markets were regulated, and exchange-rate controls in place in line with the Bretton-Woods system (see Fagerberg et al., 1990).

The 1970s represent the beginning of a new era for Norway in some ways but also a strengthening of historical patterns, and much of this has to do with oil. Production of oil started in 1971. Exports of natural gas to Europe started later than those of oil, though they will become more important than oil in the future. The discovery of oil led to a return to relatively more exports of staple goods and a reversal of the trend toward a more diversified industrial structure that had been occurring during the previous decades. For most of the period since 1980, oil exports have accounted for approximately one-third of Norway's exports. More recently, that increased to nearly one-half of total exports, mainly owing to high oil prices. The transition to an oil-export economy also led initially to high capital inflows and to a large role for multinationals in this sector as Norway lacked the skills and technology necessary to develop the oil industry. Both of these features recall the conditions under which the phase of industrialization in the early twentieth century took place. The result was that during the 1970s, the Norwegian economy became even more internationally oriented, especially as oil is a global commodity rather than a regional (i.e., European) one. With natural gas there is more of a regional market, but with the development of an LNG (liquid natural gas) industry, this will change.

The high levels of oil revenue led to the establishment of the Petroleum Fund in the mid-1990s. Through this fund, government oil revenues were invested abroad on international capital markets, and Norway became a large net capital exporter owing to large current account surpluses. This is for Norway a new feature that has made the economy vulnerable to shocks in global financial markets. However, the liberalization of international capital markets in recent decades has benefited Norway by enabling the country to separate exploration of oil from the use of the oil revenues. This has enabled Norway to avoid undesirable changes in industry structure (typically known as the Dutch Disease) whereby the manufactured export sector shrinks as a result of the new oil exports.

Though Norway had a GDP per capita (in purchasing power parity – PPP) that was 10 percent below the OECD average in 1970, by 2003 the level was 30 percent higher. This relative richness, and low unemployment by OECD standards, probably explains why a country with net emigration turned into one of net immigration in the early 1970s. With a liberalized labor market between the Nordic countries dating back to the 1960s and later within the European Area from 1994, the most recent enlargement of the EU has meant that the Norwegian labor market now is open to the 450 million citizens of Europe. As well as increased labor market flows, capital market liberalization has also occurred. Domestic credit markets were liberalized during the 1980s, and the remains of foreign exchange controls were lifted in the early 1990s.

In spite of Norway's historically longstanding integration into the world economy and the more recent further integration in terms of trade, labor mobility, and capital mobility, Norway has twice rejected membership in the European Union in referenda (1972 and 1994). These decisions cannot simply be interpreted as a stance against globalization. Though there is a sizeable right-wing populist party that is vaguely against both immigration and the EU, the majority of parties combine an internationalist orientation with different views about Norwegian EU membership.

Norway has little to gain economically by joining the EU, and the effect is probably negative owing to the size of the membership fee that would have to be paid. It is mainly political issues that are at stake and, in particular, the issue of national independence and control over the natural resources that are vital to the Norwegian economy. The farming community—although no longer large in numbers—is strongly against EU membership as agricultural markets remain to a large extent sheltered from international competition (even more so than EU agricultural markets).[1] These markets are perhaps the last remaining area of the economy that is not heavily exposed to the global economy.

There were debates in the 1970s over excessive internationalization and trade openness. The issue was the vulnerability of an open economy to shocks from international trade both in demand and prices. At the time, the current account recorded large deficits partly due to the huge investments in the oil sector but also partly due to expansionary fiscal and monetary policy combined with an exchange-rate policy that led to a loss of international competitiveness. Openness reduced the room for maneuver in national policies owing to trade leakages, for example. Whether the economy should become more open through joining the EU was therefore an issue. With the more recent huge surpluses on the current account, however, this is hardly an issue anymore. For a small and specialized open economy, there are large benefits of trade and access to global capital markets when investing revenues from oil exports. This is acknowledged by most parties, interest groups, and voters to be vital to avoid Dutch Disease problems. The question with respect to EU membership is now more whether such benefits might be reduced by EU membership.

The consequences of large exchange-rate movements in response to both domestic and global changes in capital markets have become an issue related to the debate on globalization, especially since the introduction of inflation targeting in 2001. We now turn to changes in monetary policies in recent decades.

Brief history of monetary institutions and exchange-rate regimes

The Norges Bank was established in 1816 by an Act of Parliament and assumed many of the functions of a central bank over the course of the next two centuries. Norway was a participant at the international conference on the Gold Standard held in Paris in 1867 and formally joined the Gold Standard in 1874. However, convertibility was often suspended and was finally abandoned in 1931, a week after Britain left the Gold Standard. The krone floated for two years before being fixed against sterling in 1933, and subsequently against the U.S. dollar in 1939.

During the Second World War, the Norwegian government-in-exile set up a new Board of Directors in London, and gold reserves were moved out of Norway. On its return to Norway, the Norges Bank continued to operate as a central bank, but it continued to do so as a limited company with shares still owned by private individuals. This was changed in 1949 when all the private shares were bought by the state funds, but it was not until the Central Bank Act of 1985 that it became a separate legal entity (see www.norgesbank.no).

In the post-1945 period, various forms of fixed-exchange regimes have continued to be dominant. Norway joined the Bretton Woods agreement in September 1946. Norway followed the devaluation of most European currencies against the dollar in 1949 but not the devaluation of sterling in 1967. When the Bretton Woods system ended in August 1971, the Norwegian krone floated for some time but joined the Smithsonian agreement later that year. In May 1972, Norway joined the European "snake" and moved to a fixed rate against other European currencies. When the Smithsonian agreement broke down in March 1973, the U.S. dollar floated against the "snake currencies."

During 1973–78, there were a number of changes of the krone within the European currency cooperation system. In December 1978, Norway left the snake and based the exchange rate on a trade-weighted basket of currencies. A number of currency crises in the late 1970s and 1980s resulted in devaluations. During the first half of the 1980s, several minor devaluations took place to restore competitiveness. This policy was not successful. After the large fall in oil prices during 1985–86, there was a "final" large devaluation, and the new Labor government that came into power tried to gain credibility for a new fixed exchange-rate target by restrictive fiscal and monetary policies.

In October 1990, Norway became the first non-EC country to fix against the ECU (see Nelsen, 1993: 215–16). Norges Bank reached a swap agreement with EU central banks that gave access to short-term credits. Following the exchange-rate crisis in the European Exchange Rate Mechanism (ERM) of 1992, Norway moved to a "managed float" under which exchange rate "stability" was the goal but with no specific target or exchange-rate band announced. Appreciations and depreciations of the krone have been expected to be temporary, and the exchange rate returned to a medium-term "stable value" over time. In May 1994, the government issued new guidelines to Norges Bank stating that monetary policy was to aim at maintaining a stable exchange rate of the krone against European currencies based on the rate since December 1992. No precise margins or obligations to intervene in the foreign exchange-rate market were prescribed, other than the general statement that the Bank should conduct policies to preserve a stable rate. Though some problems, in particular during 1998, occurred within this framework, it lasted until March 2001, when Norway moved to a floating exchange rate and inflation targeting.

The history of exchange-rate policies is summarized in Table 7.1.

The fixed exchange-rate regime maintained during most of the postwar period was adopted not only because it was the international norm but because it was a central component of the corporatist system developed since the 1930s and acted as the inflationary anchor. During the period wherein the system of credit controls was effective, the potential problem of maintaining a fixed exchange rate was relatively easily managed. When the system of credit rationing was gradually dismantled from 1984 onward and became fully liberalized when

Table 7.1 Exchange-rate regimes in Norway, 1946–2007

September 1946–August 1971	Fixed against the U.S. dollar
August 1971–December1971	Float
December 1971–May 1972	Fixed against the U.S. dollar
May 1972–December 1978	Fixed within the European "snake" limits; floating against the U.S. dollar
December 1978–October 1990	Fixed against a trade-weighted basket with devaluations
October 1990–September 1992	Fixed against the ECU
September 1992–March 2001	Managed float with "exchange-rate stability" against other European currencies as the objective
March 2001–2007	Float with some interventions

Source: Compiled from Norges Bank website (http://www.norges-bank.no/english/nb/history.html)

all capital controls were lifted in 1991, the central bank had to rely more on setting interest rates and foreign currency market interventions to defend the external value of the currency. Wage negotiations were focused on maintaining competitiveness in the tradable-goods sector and maintaining a relatively egalitarian wage structure at the industry level. When wage bargaining led to inflation and a loss of too much competitiveness, devaluation was the typical policy response, as was also the case in Sweden. However, in periods of crisis, direct interventions in the bargaining process were also used (in 1978–79 and 1988–89).[2] Within this policy regime, the general aim of fiscal policies was to help maintain full employment.

The traditional division of responsibilities under the corporatist model was, therefore, that interest rate policy would be used by the Norges Bank to stabilize the exchange rate. Based on this exchange rate, the tripartite wage negotiations between employers, labor, and government would establish the conditions for international competitiveness and income equality. Government fiscal policy would aim at promoting full employment (within a context in which inflation would be controlled through the fixed exchange rate and centralized wage negotiations) and the provision of a social wage in return for income wage-restraint by labor.

Summary of recent trends and policies

The Norwegian economy of the early 1990s was characterized by unusually high unemployment and low economic growth, partly owing to the banking crisis following the boom and deregulation of the mid-1980s. The policy issue that dominated the discussion was how to restore full employment.

The European exchange-rate mechanism crisis of 1992 affected Norway through its fixed link with the ECU. A return to the devaluation policy of the previous decade was rejected, and though fiscal policies became more expansionary in line with traditional policy routines, budget deficits quickly became so large (though still small by international standards) that further stimuli were ruled out. Once again, income policy was seen as the main ingredient in a new policy package. The preferred solution was the so-called solidarity alternative, an alternative to neoliberal deflation. This "alternative" relied on the traditional corporatist formula whereby wage restraint would increase profitability in those sectors exposed to foreign competition. That would improve the current account and allow fiscal policy to stimulate job creation while the fixed exchange band would secure an inflation rate in line with ECU countries.

Membership of the EU continued to be an important political issue. Perhaps because the Norwegian economic crisis was not on the scale it was in Sweden, EU membership was more easily rejected in favor of a more independent path. Though many Norwegians believed it was important to join the EU for economic reasons, a balanced analysis showed that this was probably not the case (see Bowitz et al., 1997). Norway rejected EU membership again in the Referendum of 1994. Since then, membership in the EU has really not been an issue. This reflects not only a respect for the decision of the voters but, more important, the divisive nature of the EU issue within the main political parties and between potential coalition partners.

During the second half of the 1990s, the Norwegian economy showed rapid growth and gradually reached "full employment" again. Price inflation was in line with trading partners and, as oil prices increased, surpluses once again appeared on the current account and on government budgets. However, there were setbacks, such as the experience in 1997 and 1998 when the exchange rate appreciated rapidly. Figure 7.1 shows the exchange rate against the U.S. dollar and the ECU/euro. As is apparent, there have been significant changes in the krone–euro exchange rate after 2001 as well. This is not surprising given that the intermediate target of a semi-fixed exchange rate was abandoned in that year in favor of a floating exchange rate. The reasons for this, and wider currency debates, are discussed in the next section.

The contemporary currency debate

On March 29, 2001, Norway, a country with one of the longest postwar commitments to a fixed (or "stable") exchange rate formally abandoned its policy and opted for a floating exchange rate similar to that of Sweden and most Anglo-Saxon countries that initiated this policy during the 1980s and 1990s. Among the Nordic countries, Finland joined the European monetary union, while Norway and Sweden chose to retain their individual currencies, and both have now moved to floating exchange rates. Denmark retained its own currency but fixed it to the euro. In general, this divergence in Nordic policies requires an explanation, but we shall focus on the Norwegian case and return to the more general Nordic case later.

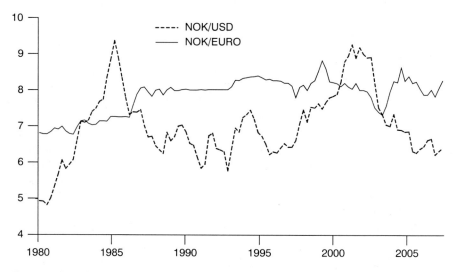

Figure 7.1 Exchange rates (NOK/USD and NOK/EUR) 1980–2006

Though the traditional postwar exchange-rate regime in Norway was one of fixed (nominal) exchange rates, it did not go without challenge during the post-Bretton Woods period. As noted in the section Brief History of Monetary Institutions and Exchange-Rate Regimes, there was certainly a period from around 1977 until 1986 when the exchange rate was changed fairly regularly to improve international competitiveness. This policy ended in 1986 after the oil price collapse and has been regarded as unsuccessful and leading to unwarranted inflation. The return to a fixed exchange rate (against a basket of currencies at that time) coincided with a deregulation of the credit markets, so it could be argued that monetary policy changed from interest-rate control to exchange-rate control, giving monetary policy and the central bank a much more prominent position in the making of economic policy. This was clearly acknowledged and welcomed by the governor of the bank, Mr Skånland, in his annual address in February 1987.[3] When the return to fixed exchange rate occurred in 1986, the general view was that this change was well founded.

The first opposition to a fixed exchange rate came during 1992, when the banking crisis (itself a result of the liberalization of the financial system) hit the Norwegian economy very strongly and the domestic business cycle was clearly out of phase with that of the rest of Europe. The Bundesbank tried to counteract the inflationary effect of German unification by raising interest rates to a very high level. To maintain the exchange rate, Norges Bank had to raise interest rates as well, even though the Norwegian economy was in a poor state at the time. This prolonged the downturn of the economy and deepened the banking crisis. Inflation became very low, lower than in the rest of Europe but at the expense of very high unemployment and low growth by Norwegian standards. The interest rate policy was criticized for being procyclical. The chief economist of the saving banks federation wrote in the main Norwegian newspaper (*Aftenposten*, January 8, 1991) that interest rates should be lowered. When interest rates were increased again in the autumn of 1991 after having been cut during the spring, the central bank was again heavily criticized by economists working in financial institutions. The defense of the high interest rate policy offered by spokespeople from the central bank was the need to support the exchange-rate target.[4]

In the autumn of 1992, the banking crisis in both Sweden and Norway led to a currency crisis as the turmoil in the ERM spread across the region. After raising interest rates to more than 500 percent, Sweden conceded defeat, gave up its fixed exchange rate, and moved to inflation targeting. The Norwegian krone was floated at the time, but there was no clear policy change as in Sweden. There was a more pragmatic approach that aimed at seeing out the crisis, and then the idea was that the krone would gradually be brought back to its "normal" level before the float was adopted on December 10, 1992. This was clearly stated in the government's policy regulation of May 1994. There seems to have been a consensus at the time that an exchange-rate band with fairly narrow limits (± 2 percent) would be acceptable and in line with the so-called "solidarity alternative" that coordinated fiscal policy, monetary policy, and incomes policies. However, there were critical voices, too. The new governor of the central bank, Mr Moland, argued in 1995 that price stability was more important than exchange-rate stability. He was applauded by the chief economist of the employers' federation whereas his counterpart in the trade union movement (the LO) disagreed. Later, several economists from the central bank argued for a move to inflation targeting. However, the Minister of Finance clearly rejected this and argued for a fairly fixed exchange rate (within a band), referring to the need for an incomes policy to be complemented by stable exchange rates. When the upturn in the Norwegian economy continued and there was clearly a need for more restrictive policies, it again turned out that interest rates had to be reduced to support the exchange-rate target whereas the domestic economy "needed" higher interest rates. The need for higher—not lower—interest rates was argued for by one bank economist who also recommended abandoning fixed exchange rates completely.[5]

The problems with the monetary policy regime were clearly the reason why the central bank arranged a seminar on monetary policy (see Christiansen and Qvigstad 1997). And the central bank argued in its Bulletin (no. 4, 1997) that a monetary policy that aimed at low and stable inflation would be a better way of supporting full employment and sustainable economic growth than would the existing policy. When the boom in the Norwegian economy continued during 1997 and 1998 and neither monetary nor fiscal policy were able to counteract the boom, a new exchange-rate crisis occurred in the late summer of 1998, and interest rates had to be raised significantly. Again, a number of economists argued for a regime change. However, the head of the employers' federation was strongly against a move away from the fixed exchange-rate regime.[6]

A new governor of the Norges Bank came into office in January 1999. Many observers argue that his statements and policies indicate that a change in the exchange-rate regime took place at that time and not at the end of March 2001, when it was formally announced. The basis for this interpretation is that on January 4, 1999, the new governor, Mr Gjedrem, stated that the bank had to take two factors into account when deciding on interest rates: first, they needed to keep inflation in line with that of the euro-zone and, second, monetary policies should not contribute to a recession that could weaken the confidence in the exchange rate. One bank economist stated later in 1999 that a regime change had already taken place.[7] In the autumn of 1999, the central bank stated in a letter to the Ministry of Finance that in its policy, the bank aimed at the underlying factors that would sustain a stable exchange rate with the euro and that was to set interest rates so that inflation was in line with that of ECB targets. Though this was not in direct conflict with the policy instruction, it was clearly a different interpretation of the policy mandate given by the government. The Ministry of Finance denied that this was a new policy and so did the vice-governor of Norges Bank. However, when the formal change in regime did take place, the Bank said it would simplify how the Bank would communicate with the markets and that the change, in isolation, would not change how the Bank implemented its policy in any significant way. For many, these statements are interpreted as indications that the real change in regime took place early in 1999 and only formally in March 2001.

However, it is not clear from the path of the euro–krone exchange rate shown in Figure 7.1 that a regime change really took place in 1999. The euro–krone exchange rate stayed more or less constant from 1999 onward, and the krone became clearly floating against the euro only after 2001. Also, the inflation target in the eurozone is less than 2 percent, whereas the inflation target in Norway is 2.5 percent and symmetric. So the policy statement in 2001 clearly meant at least some changes compared to earlier policies.

The change to a floating exchange rate and inflation targeting was accompanied by other changes in government policy. In a government White Paper to the Storting in March 2001,[8] the Ministry of Finance introduced two policy rules. The first and perhaps the most important was a fiscal policy rule that had no predecessor in previous documents. This rule stated that government revenues from petroleum (i.e., the various taxes on petroleum activities and the profits from direct ownership of petroleum resources) should be transferred to a petroleum fund that had been set up some years earlier. This financial fund is allowed to invest its assets only in foreign financial assets (shares and bonds). The expected real rate of return of these assets (estimated to be 4 percent of the domestic value of the fund) is transferred to the annual state budget and can be used to increase government spending or to reduce taxes. The purpose of the rule is to ensure that petroleum wealth is not consumed but transferred to financial wealth. With an aging population, this financial wealth can help to finance a generous welfare state in the future. Another purpose of the rule is to separate current revenues from petroleum production and the spending of these revenues so that domestic spending does not vary with the highly fluctuating oil price. This rule would, at least in the long run, approximate spending the permanent income from petroleum wealth. The idea was also that the rule would contribute to a more stable industrial structure in that the tradable sectors would face more stable market conditions compared to a situation in which domestic spending is determined by current income. The aim was thus to avoid parts of the Dutch Disease problem associated with a booming oil sector. At the time of the introduction of the fiscal rule, actual spending was close to the rule but, according to government calculations, it was expected at the time that fiscal policies in the years to follow would be somewhat more expansionary than earlier expected. Though this allowed the government to stimulate the economy, it could claim that it was doing so in a responsible way that was based on sound long-run policy.

The second policy rule was the explicit inflation target (2.5 percent p.a.) for monetary policy. The Ministry of Finance recognized in the White Paper that Norges Bank already had changed its focus away from short-run exchange-rate targeting in its practical operation of monetary policy. However, the Ministry went on to state that under the present circumstances, it was better to establish a more explicit target or anchor for monetary policy.[9] Nevertheless, according to the Ministry, the new monetary policy should support fiscal policy in stabilizing production and employment. Thus, it was claimed that the actual use of monetary policy instruments should not change even if the formal mandate had changed.

The new mandate for Norges Bank that was given by the government in March 2001 explicitly stated that the Bank should aim at a stable value of the krone both domestically (i.e., low inflation) and in international markets (i.e., the exchange rate). However, the krone should also be floating. How can two targets be achieved using only one policy instrument, the interest rate? According to the Ministry of Finance, this is possible because in a small open economy it is unlikely that one country can maintain an inflation rate similar to that of its main trading partners without a fairly stable exchange rate between these countries. This position is, of course, simply a restatement of the traditional Scandinavian model of inflation that had been the backbone of Norwegian macroeconomic policy analysis since the 1960s (see Aukrust, 1977 for details). Accordingly, the change in monetary policy was not seen by the government as that dramatic but merely as a change to new circumstances wherein strict exchange-rate targeting had become impossible owing to the deregulation of capital markets. Though this reasoning may have been that of the government at the time, it was probably not how Norges Bank interpreted the change. This became clear within a year after the change in its mandate.

During 2002, the positive output gap between Norway and the eurozone was reduced as the Norwegian growth rate fell below trend. The respective output gaps from 1979 to 2004 are shown in Figure 7.2. In 2005 and 2006, the output gap in EMU area has been quite stable while an increasing positive output gap (2 percent in 2006) has emerged in Norway.

Inflation was close to the target in 2002, but wage costs increased more rapidly than was believed to be compatible with the inflation target. Economic growth was slowing down abroad as the United States was in a recession and Europe about to enter one. Interest rates were on their way down both in the United States and in

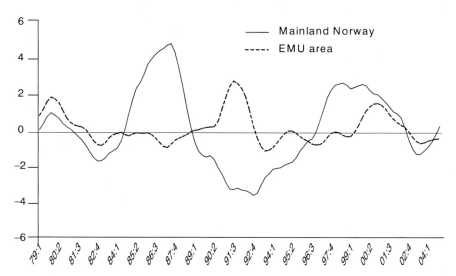

Figure 7.2 GDP gap in Norway and EMU area 1979–2004 (percent) (Source: OECD and Statistics Norway)

the EMU area. Since the summer of 1998, Norway had a large positive interest-rate differential as compared to EMU. The krone–euro rate had returned to normal levels already during 1999 but had slowly appreciated during 2000 and 2001. As global interest rates came down, Norges Bank maintained its high interest rates during 2002 and raised them even further in the spring of 2002 in spite of a strong appreciation of the krone. Norges Bank defended this policy with reference to its new mandate of achieving the inflation target one to two years ahead.[10] Thus, exchange-rate stability seemed to have no place in the policy of the bank in spite of the policy mandate that clearly emphasized a stable external value of the krone in addition to keeping inflation in line with that of trading partners. After the summer of 2002, it was clear that the krone appreciation had a significant effect on the inflation rate that was diving below the target rate. However, the Norges Bank stuck to its policy of high interest rates. This policy error ended in December 2002, and Norges Bank reduced interest rates aggressively during the next five quarters down to levels close to that of the euro rate set by the ECB.[11] Since 2004, Norwegian interest rates have been very close to euro rates, as shown in Figure 7.3. With hardly any interest differential, the krone–euro exchange rate returned to normal levels during 2003 and has remained roughly so thereafter.

In a recent report from an independent review of monetary policy-making in Norway undertaken by academics, the Norges Bank is criticized for having paid too little attention to the exchange rate in its earlier policy (see Dørum et al., 2005). However, the Report notes that the Bank seems to have modified its policy statements recently and is now more concerned with exchange-rate stability. Thus, after an initial trial-and-error period, the krone–euro exchange rate seems to have come more into focus. However, it would be incorrect to claim that this reversal has gone as far as to reinstall the old regime of an exchange-rate target. It is more likely that Norges Bank, as well as other observers of the way the economy

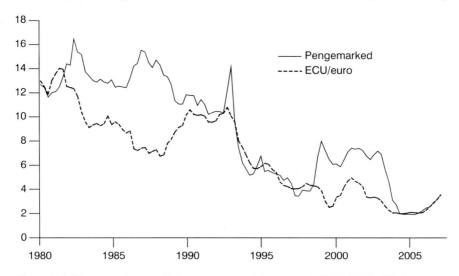

Figure 7.3. Short term (3-month) interest rates in Norway and EMU (1980–2006)

functions, have learned a lesson from the previous three to four years and have modified their views accordingly.

Analyzing the debate

One point to notice immediately is that the debate in Norway over exchange-rate regimes has been carried out within a small circle of economists working in government agencies and economists working in the private sector, for the labor organization or in academia. Though neighboring Sweden had a national debate about whether to join the euro in 2003 (which resulted in a victory for the "No" side), there was hardly any notice taken of the birth of the euro in Norway and no public debate about currency issues. As a researcher with the Bank of Norway observed, "the euro was a non-event in Norway."[12]

The fact that the EU adopted a single currency had no discernible impact on the long-term prospects for the viability of the krone. Indeed, the introduction of the virtual euro as a result of the Economic and Monetary Union was assessed by the Ministry of Finance and Customs (1999: 2) as follows: "On the whole, the direct economic effects of the establishment of the EMU on Norway are expected to be limited." Furthermore, "in the National Budget for 1999, the Government affirmed that monetary policy will remain unchanged after the establishment of EMU and the introduction of the euro" (ibid.).

The "historic event" of the euro had little impact, therefore, on policy makers in Norway. This can be attributed to a number of causes. First, Norway had already signed the European Economic Area Agreement in 1991 committing Norway to implementing most EU regulations with the exception of those related to natural resources. So economic integration with the EU had been occurring on the basis of this agreement for a decade. Two decades earlier, in the aftermath of the first referendum of EU membership in Norway, a separate trade agreement between the EU and Norway had been negotiated. Thus, the separate effects of a single currency were considered "limited." The fact that Norway was a small open economy trading with Europe and the rest of the world did not result in any trend in unofficial euroization or dollarization or any debate about whether such a small country's currency might be eventually eliminated by competition from currencies from larger economic blocs. A Norges Bank official summed up the mood as follows: "There are no concerns about being economically marginalized in an otherwise euroised Europe and no pressures from exporters concerned about transactions costs."[13]

Second, membership of the euro has always been understood as requiring a prior political commitment to join the EU. EU membership and euro membership have been subject to referenda throughout Europe, so the question of adopting a single currency is regarded as a political choice rather than a historic inevitability. Norwegians are aware that they can say no to Europe; of the four occasions on which they applied to join the EC-EU, they have withdrawn their applications twice and voted against membership on the other two occasions. The divisive nature of the EU within the main political parties resulted in the absence of any attempts to put the issue back onto the political agenda; the birth of the euro was not used to start a new debate about the merits and course of European integration. Norway essentially chose to ignore the creation of the euro as a topic requiring attention or as having significant implications.

Consideration of currency debates during this period, therefore, did not appeal to and were not influenced by wider concerns about the pressures of globalization leading to a reduction in the number of viable currencies. If the euro and "globalization" have not led to any trends in, or debates about, the ability to maintain a separate currency, the question of why Norway changed its long-held policy of exchange-rate fixity remains. Here, the impact of globalization may be relevant if it can be shown that the bipolar view is correct. That is, given that Norway had not joined the EU and did not have an irrevocably fixed exchange rate against the euro, its quest for "stability" through an intermediate "managed float" exchange-rate regime may have been unsustainable.

The argument that an intermediate regime per se was impossible to sustain is not plausible in the Norwegian case. The upward pressure on the krone was certainly substantial as a result of rising oil prices and growing revenues during the late 1990s, but the central bank was prepared to allow this with the aim of using interest policy to eventually bring the exchange rate back into a "stable" range. Though speculators played a role in the krone's instability, there was no exchange-rate "crisis" comparable to that in 1992 and 1998, which dictated an immediate change of policy at the time when Norway (formally) moved to inflation targeting in March 2001. Furthermore, the fact that Denmark had been able to maintain a fixed exchange rate with the euro without problems in this period also adds doubt to the view that anything other than a super-hard fix or a free float are viable options. It is certainly true that financial market liberalization has made exchange-rate targeting more difficult, but it is not the case that this was the overwhelming reason for moving to a floating rate in 2001.

More plausible is the view that Norway's oil endowments make its business cycles different from—indeed, often opposite to—those of the rest of Europe for whom increasing oil prices represent a deflationary threat. This has typically been met by lower interest rates in Europe. In Norway, this has led to problems when the aim of interest rate policy has been to target the level of the exchange rate. As oil prices rise, the Norwegian economy expands, and the krone has a tendency to appreciate. However, to prevent this, the Norges Bank is required to keep interest rates low—as low as in the rest of Europe facing deflationary tendencies—with the result that inflationary pressures are increased in Norway, placing strains on the corporatist framework designed to check inflationary pressures through wage bargaining. Thus, Norway's resource endowment means that its business cycles are opposite those of other European countries, and fixing to, or "stabilizing" against, the ECU as Norway did during the 1990s results in a counter-cyclical monetary policy. There is no doubt that this caused problems for macroeconomic management in Norway during the 1990s.

The decoupling of the business cycle in Norway from the European cycle is illustrated in Figure 7.2. The cycles are quite correlated in the late 1970s and early

1980s but are uncorrelated from the mid-1980s and until quite recently, when the degree of correlation has increased again. Note in particular the recession in Norway in the early 1990s at a time when German unification boom affected the euro area markedly.

Norway entered a major boom from 1997, whereas the upswing in EMU countries did not start until 1999. From 1999 onward, the cycles have again become quite similar. Low interest rates in the EMU area forced the Norges Bank to keep interest rates low in 1996 and 1997 in spite of the upturn and rapid growth in consumer spending. Also, high growth in petroleum investments during 1997 and 1998 spurred further growth in the Norwegian economy, with monetary policies unable to counteract this development because of the policy of targeting the euro–krone exchange rate.

As argued in the section Brief History of Monetary Institutions and Exchange-Rate Regimes, a fixed exchange-rate regime was a central part of the corporatist institutional framework and, as such, had operated for decades. The fact that Norway was not an optimal currency area with Europe, and hence was not ideally suited to a fixed exchange-rate regime, had been true at least since the breakdown of the Bretton Woods system in 1971. The importance of oil in the national economy dates back to the early 1970s, and the non-synchronicity of European and Norwegian business cycles was clearly evident by the mid-1980s. However, in 1986, Norway chose to make its exchange-rate regime *more* rigid, and the decision to move to floating rates did not occur until thirty years after the discovery of oil. Optimal currency area arguments may be valid in pointing to the difficulties of maintaining a fixed exchange rate in the face of differing resource endowments and business cycles, but it is hardly able to explain why it took so long for this to be reflected in policy terms. So, though Norway may be a distinct national economy, it is necessary to look for other reasons why the floating rate with inflation targeting was introduced.

The change in the role of the central bank, the Norges Bank, from using monetary policy to target the exchange rate to introducing an inflation target with a flexible exchange rate is a change that the central bank itself did much to bring about. The repositioning of the central bank as operating under an inflation target was accompanied by an increase in its autonomy. The groundwork for this change had been undertaken in the mid–late 1990s as bank staff and researchers sought to borrow from abroad "best practice" in the institutional design of central banks (see Christiansen and Qvigstad, 1997). This was also recognized in the 2001 government White Paper. The move toward central bank independence and inflation targeting has been a global trend. The expansion of international financial markets has given credence to the idea of the need for "credible" central banks, as indicated in Chapter 3, and the trend can be seen in part as a response to this. However, central bank independence—better termed *autonomy*—with an inflation target can also be seen as part of a broader neoliberal agenda aimed at privileging inflation control as the key macroeconomic policy goal. Objectives such as full employment and equity have taken a secondary role in this general policy framework (see Bowles and White, 1994).

Should the change in the role of the central bank and the exchange-rate regime, therefore, be seen as a part of a broader pattern of neoliberal reform in Norway? That is, does the neoliberal globalism interpretation offer insights into the Norwegian case? The challenge of globalization and neoliberalism for the Nordic corporatist model has been a topic of considerable debate over the last decade. In Norway, the influence of neoliberalism can be seen in the drive toward, and debates over, outsourcing and the introduction of the "new public management" in the public sector. More broadly, the share of government spending in GDP has fallen slightly in recent years because the center-right coalition has favored tax cuts rather than the supply of government services.[14] The shift toward neoliberalism can be traced back to the mid-1980s with the "modernizers" in the ruling Labor Party (DNA) under Gro Harlem Bruntland. Geyer (2000: 183) describes the shift as follows:

> In the early 1980s Bruntland quickly moved the party to the right, accepting a growing role for the market, lower taxation of the wealthy, the reduction of credit controls, and the importance of inflation control and international competitiveness. In the mid-1980s, Bruntland initiated the 'freedom campaign' debate within the DNA. During this debate, Bruntland emphasized that the party was no longer socialist, but social democratic, was non-class-oriented, pragmatic and electorally oriented, less reliant on the links to trade unions, and had to accept the importance of the market, international constraints and limitations of the public sector. By the mid-1980s, Bruntland and the modernizers had pushed the DNA substantially to the right and cut off the rise of the Conservative Party. By 1986, the party was back in power as a minority government.

Subsequently, accession to the European Economic Area was achieved, and integration into the EC was advanced, albeit without political representation through formal membership.

There has, therefore, been a discernible shift to the right in Norwegian party politics and the legitimation and implementation of neoliberal policies. However, the extent of this shift is still modest in international comparative context, and it would be premature to claim that Norwegian social democracy and corporatism have "collapsed." Notermans (2000: 23–4), for example, argues that "maintaining full employment is the cornerstone of any successful social democratic strategy … The only country to have successfully pursued full-employment policies in the 1990s is the only country not to have joined the EU, namely Norway." More recent developments in labor market outcomes in the United Kingdom, Denmark, Sweden, and the Netherlands extending beyond the 1990s suggest that Norway's uniqueness in achieving full employment is in need of revision but that it still is valid for Norway in the 1990s, and the policy commitment in the 2000s has remained.

The extent to which neoliberalism has taken control of the Norwegian body politic is, therefore, open to debate. A senior researcher at the Norwegian Confederation of Trade Unions argued that "neoliberalism hasn't taken root and is without strong appeal."[15] Whether the increased power and autonomy of the central bank and its move to inflation targeting with a flexible exchange rate arises from a shift away from corporatism and toward a neoliberal model is again debatable. Certainly, the move was in the institutional interests of the Norges Bank, raising its profile and reducing that of the Ministry of Finance, and can be explained within a traditional model of bureaucratic rivalry. However, this is in itself an insufficient explanation, as the change in policy still had to be approved by the government of the day. It was, in fact, a Labor government that implemented the change of policy with the support of the peak labor organization, the LO, and over the objections of the employers' federation, which wished to retain the traditional corporatist institutional structure with a fixed exchange rate.

The change of policy relied on a fortuitous coincidence of interests, the groundwork having been done by the central bank and a government in a pre-election period seeking to enhance its electoral appeal by spending some of the accumulated oil revenues. In 2001, the government adopted the policy rule of spending 4 percent of the oil revenue, as explained above. This expansionary fiscal policy would have put pressure on the "stability" of the exchange rate, and it was decided to relieve the Norges Bank of this responsibility. The Bank was supportive, as was the LO, because the program was expansionary, the government saw political capital in the move, and only the employers' federation opposed it. Thus, domestic political considerations within the context of a "globally available" model of central banking, explain much of the policy shift.

However, more broadly, the new institutional arrangement can also be seen as an evolution of the social-democratic corporatist model in the face of wider regional (European) and global institutional changes. Just as we may speak of a "contingent neoliberalism," it may also be appropriate to speak of a "contingent corporatism" with respect to exchange-rate policies. Traditionally, a fixed exchange rate has been an integral part of the corporatist system designed, as explained above, to deliver low inflation whereas wage bargaining was designed to provide full employment, international competitiveness, and a high degree of income equality. This traditional assignment of responsibilities has, however, been challenged by the more complex regional and international institutional changes. In the Nordic countries, as noted above, while Finland has joined the euro, Denmark has retained a fixed exchange rate but has opted not to join the euro and, therefore, to leave open the possibility of future devaluations while Sweden and Norway have moved to floating exchange rates. However, these different outcomes cannot simply be translated as a decisive shift toward neoliberalism.

In Sweden, the case could be made that corporatist institutions have been undergoing a systematic weakening over the last two decades. Much of this has to do with the power of the business class that, with the investment opportunities offered by liberalization, has taken advantage of this and has had less commitment to—and need for—the domestic corporatist institutions. Coates (2000: 100–1), for example, argues that the removal of capital controls in Sweden in 1985 led to a large export of capital by Swedish firms. The result was a sharp reduction in "the willingness of Swedish capital to tolerate the costs and constraints imposed upon it hitherto by the power of Swedish labour." The weakening of corporatism in Sweden can also be seen in the way in which wage negotiations changed. From 1945 until the mid–late 1980s, wage settlements were highly influenced by agreements at the national level between the trade unions (LO and PTK) and the employers federation (SAF). Thereafter wage bargaining took place at the sectoral level. However, an early indication of the breakdown of the central system came in 1983 with the agreement between the metal workers union and their counterpart within the SAF. The "Swedish model" had, therefore, been in decline for a considerable period before Sweden abandoned its fixed exchange-rate regime as part of the fallout from the 1992 ERM crisis, and the change of exchange-rate regime was not explicitly linked to any broader changes away from the corporatist model. And, of course, joining the euro was defeated in a referendum.

Furthermore, there have been more recent indications that corporatism is back on the agenda in Sweden as a viable institutional system, a system that includes maintaining the flexible exchange rate. For example, in 1997 a national wage agreement was signed by a number of unions and employers federations in the industrial sector. This agreement included statements regarding the economy-wide preconditions for wage negotiations. This agreement was later followed by similar agreements in other sectors of the economy. The government responded by appointing a commission that analyzed wage formation in the economy. On the basis of proposals from this commission, the Riksdagen (the Swedish parliament) decided on new laws and institutions that should support wage negotiations. Among these was the National Mediation Office (Medlingsinstitutet) that was set up in the autumn of 2000. The return to a more centralized form of corporatism in Sweden has occurred without any discussion of the need to change the exchange-rate regime to facilitate it. Corporatist institutions are compatible with a variety of exchange-rate regimes.

This conclusion is also applicable to Norway. Though there has been an important policy change in moving to a flexible exchange-rate regime, so far this has not been accompanied by any change in the commitment to corporatist institutions. In fact, the "solidarity alternative" adopted in 1992, although modified as time passed, has been restated in government policy documents again and again and has also been supported by many academics who have taken part in independent policy evaluations more recently.[16]

The question remains, however, of whether the change in the monetary policy regime in 2001 and the move to inflation targeting will, in the longer run, undermine corporatist institutions related to wage bargaining. Too little time has elapsed since 2001 to give a definitive answer, but a partial answer may be possible based on recent events. First of all, it remains a consensus view that income policies and corporatism in Norway have contributed greatly to the low unemployment rate. Wage bargaining in Norway takes place both at a national level (or at least for wide industry groups) and locally at the firm level. Out of total wage growth in the economy, roughly half is due to local bargaining, but this share varies a lot within the two-year bargaining cycle. Nationwide wage bargaining has also contributed to a small dispersion in wages so that the large increase in wage inequality seen in many countries during the last two or three decades is hardly evident in Norway. Even the center-right coalition (2001–2005) took steps to strengthen the corporatist institutions related to wage bargaining in spite of the fact that the principal view of industry (as represented by the employers' federation NHO) is that bargaining should take place only at the firm level and not at the industry or national level. New corporatist institutions have been set up to deal with various labor market issues.[17]

The degree of unionization has been stable over the last two decades, and data up to the end of 2005 show little tendency for unionization to decrease; if anything, the trend is upward. Also, there has been a concentration of membership in the large unions that support collective bargaining.[18] On the employers' side, the degree of organization seems to be more or less stable. The wage bargains apply to a wider set of employees than those who are members of unions, as collective agreements are used as the basis for wage settlements outside of the unionized areas or for employees who are not members of unions in areas where wages are negotiated by unions on behalf of all employees and not only union members. Roughly three-fourths of all employees, therefore, have their wages based on wage bargains whereas the formal degree of unionization is just above 50 percent.

A reasonable prediction is that unionization will decline in the future as those sectors in which unionization is very high, such as the public sector, may decline relative to the private service sector, where the degree of unionization is usually lower. The privatization that recently has taken place also in Norway, though on a very modest scale, points in this direction. However, there is no automatic effect here, as traditional unions may increase their efforts to recruit more members in these sectors.

Perhaps more important for the future of the corporatist system in Norway is the liberalization of labor markets with the enlargement of the EU and the increasing role of the internal labor market within the European Economic Area that also includes Norway. Since May 2004, when this enlargement took place, Norway has experienced a large inflow of workers from Eastern Europe who work for foreign companies for wages unheard of in the Norwegian labor market. Interestingly enough, there seems to be an interest among Norwegian employers to demand that these firms should pay workers according to the minimum wages that are part of the standard bargaining system in Norway. So even among the employers, there are many who support the existing system because competitiveness is eroded by foreign firms entering Norwegian markets. At present, this takes place in the building sector in particular. Also, many workers who move with their families to Norway join the unions, so more labor mobility may not change labor market institutions that much. However, on this matter it is too early to conclude.

At the empirical level, therefore, there is no evidence of any change in the commitment to corporatism since the change in exchange-rate regime. Rather, there has been a change in the responsibilities of the various agents for securing desirable economic outcomes. Now, the Norges Bank has assumed more responsibility for inflation control whereas the wage bargaining system and government fiscal policy are primarily designed to deliver full employment. International competitiveness and inflation are now more closely linked to the behavior of the exchange rate. There has, therefore, been a change in the assignment of responsibilities but not in the commitment to the corporatist institutional framework. In this sense, the exchange-rate regime is again "contingent," and different exchange-rate regimes can be used to support corporatist objectives; the wider policy environment, of which the exchange-rate regime is just one component, is again critical to an understanding of the role that it plays.

Even though there is no empirical evidence that the change in exchange-rate regime has had negative implications for the corporatist system and that this new form of "contingent corporatism" is working, potential problems still remain if economic circumstances change. These relate mainly to the tradable-goods sector and the implications of this for wage bargaining.

It can be argued that the change to more active interest rate policy based on inflation targeting leads to a more volatile nominal exchange rate and a more stable business cycle (less variation in the GDP gap) than has been experienced since, say, 1980. These two assumptions certainly are supported empirically and can be seen from the data presented in Figures 7.1 and 7.2, where the exchange rate and business cycle trends show different patterns after 2001. One consequence of the more stable business cycle is that there is less inflationary pressure in the labor market. Thus, the income policy and wage coordination related to wage bargaining will face fewer challenges than earlier. The negotiations will take place in a more stable nominal environment from the trade unions' point of view.

From the view of the tradable-goods sector of the economy, however, there is more uncertainty with regard to their competitive situation, owing to uncertain exchange rates. Though wage costs and domestic costs in general will change in a more stable way, import prices will fluctuate more and export prices in domestic currency likewise. This will affect profitability in the export-oriented sectors perhaps just as much, or even more, as compared to the old exchange-rate-targeting regime. However, fluctuating prices in world markets are not new to these sectors, and they also have the possibility to insure themselves to some extent against currency fluctuations through hedging. Yet, all in all, it is not surprising that many observers, both before inflation targeting was introduced and afterward, have pointed to the problems facing the tradable sector of the economy under the present regime.[19]

If, on the other hand, a country-specific demand shock should affect the Norwegian economy, such as much higher oil investments, and fiscal policy does not become more restrictive, the interest rate will be increased to keep inflation within the target range. Then, both tighter labor markets, which will lead to rapid wage increases and higher interest rates, which will lead to an appreciation of the krone, will affect the competitive position of the tradable sector in a very negative way. This is what happened in 2002. The problem here is simply that though the political authorities have views about the industry structure (i.e., the traditional tradable sector should not become too small), this is not part of the monetary policy objectives.

Thus, the future of the corporatist system may depend on wage bargaining changing so that it becomes more in tune with monetary policy making. If inflation targeting is based on inflation forecasting within a one- to three-year horizon, this could require longer wage contracts to simplify inflation forecasting. Thus, tying oneself to the mast, unions can make life easier for the central bank by making domestic inflation components easier to forecast. However, this would come at a cost for the unions in that it is not clear what the gains for them would be unless it could be claimed that this would lead to more stable employment. However, stability may be different for unions in different sectors. Those who mainly organize workers in the tradable sector face a different kind of instability as compared to those in the sheltered sectors. One way out of this dilemma for the unions would be to try to merge unions even more than is the case already in Norway so that they cover workers across the tradable- and non-tradable-goods sectors. This has, in fact, taken place already, and though some attempts have not succeeded yet, they are an indication of the forces at work. Mergers are also taking place, or at least being discussed, between employer federations. So there has been a tendency for mergers of institutions on both sides of the labor market that could be interpreted as changes that will support the corporatist model, at least in the short and medium run.

To sum up this argument, the change to a flexible exchange-rate regime was the result of domestic political forces rather than the response to external pressures generated by the forces of globalization. This change in regime does not seem to have led to any movement away from a corporatist system that had previously relied on the fixed exchange rate as a central component of this system. Rather, the assignment of responsibilities for macroeconomic performance has been changed, and agents appear to be adapting to these new responsibilities. It is clear that Norwegian corporatism is in this respect undergoing change and adaptation, and though this is still very much a work in progress, there is little evidence to support the view that this has led (or will lead) to the necessary demise of corporatism and the shift toward a more neoliberal-oriented model. Of course, there are neoliberal pressures in Norway, though they are modest by international standards. However, it is not clear that the change in exchange-rate regime constitutes a part of those pressures and is best described as a "contingent corporatism."

The change in exchange-rate regime in Norway has been remarkably free from any pressures of "regionalism." We have already seen that the emergence of the world's premier regional currency, the euro, had little impact on Norway in terms of generating either official or unofficial pressures for joining this regional currency bloc. In fact, Norway has moved away from it by abandoning the link with the euro. One additional reason for the lack of influence of regionalism may be that though trade with European countries is more much important for Norway than trade with the United States, this trade pattern is not similar to the settlement currencies used in foreign trade. Table 7.2 illustrates the various weights of trade, and settlement.

The U.S. dollar is more important for Norway as a settlement currency in international trade than is the euro. There are two reasons for this. First, oil exports

Table 7.2 Trade weights and settlement currencies. Norway 2003 (percent)

	Currency	Imports	Exports
US dollars	34	8	10
Euro	25	48	48
Sterling	5	7	10
Swedish krone	4	16	10
Others	7	21	22

are paid in U.S. dollars and, second, most trade with Asian countries uses the U.S. dollar as the settlement currency.[20] One-fourth of Norwegian foreign trade uses the Norwegian krone as settlement currency (and is why the foreign currency settlements in Table 7.2 sum to only 75 percent). Thus, the share of the Norwegian krone as a settlement currency is similar to that of the euro. As long as trade takes place in so many different currencies and no single currency is dominant, it is perhaps not surprising that euroization or dollarization has not really become an issue; there is no evidence of Norway's long outward-oriented business class pushing the issue either. One might even claim that the globalization of trade, and the increasing trade with Asia in particular, have prevented the euro from becoming so dominant and that therefore, from the Norwegian viewpoint, the importance of the euro as a regional currency has been limited.

Table 7.2 shows the importance of the U.S. dollar as a settlement currency, an importance derived to a significant extent because of the pricing of oil in U.S. dollars. It is the dollar's role as an international currency that has been argued to have played a role in supporting U.S. power and imperial ambitions in the post-1945 period, as indicated in the imperialism interpretation. Though some countries have defiantly switched to the pricing of oil in euros (Iraq under Saddam and Venezuela under Chavez) as part of an "anti-imperialism" program, there have also been more general discussions about the operations of the oil market by Middle East oil producers. The planned opening of an oil market by Iran to compete with London and New York is one important example. The Iranian bourse would also price oil in euros. This reflects a wider discussion within OPEC about the pricing of oil and about the possibility of switching from the dollar to the euro, a move that would have significant implications for the relative role of the two currencies in the international monetary system and the power that their issuers derive from this.

The possibilities of this switch taking place depend on a large number of factors, both political and economic. Clark (2005) documents that

> During an important speech in April 2002, Mr. Javad Yarjani, an OPEC executive, described three pivotal events that would facilitate an OPEC transition to euros. He stated this would be based on (1) if and when Norway's Brent crude is re-dominated in euros, (2) if and when the U.K. adopts the euro, and (3) whether or not the Euro gains parity valuation relative to the

dollar, and the EU's proposed expansion plans were successful. Notably, both of the later two criteria have transpired: the euro's valuation has been above the dollar since late 2002, and the euro-based E.U. enlarged in May 2004 from 12 to 22 countries. Despite recent 'no' votes by French and Dutch voters regarding a common EU constitution, from a macroeconomic perspective, these domestic disagreements do not reduce the euro currency's trajectory in the global financial markets—and from Russia and OPEC's perspective—do not adversely impact momentum towards a petroeuro. In the meantime, the U.K. remains uncomfortably juxtaposed between the financial interests of the U.S. banking nexus (New York/Washington) and the E.U. financial centers (Paris/Frankfurt).

From the perspective of this chapter, what is interesting is the identification of Norway's pricing strategy as a key element in the wider debate over the roles of the euro and the dollar. Despite this, Norway has stood on the sidelines of this discussion and shown little interest in it. As a major oil producer, Norway has undoubted interests and has on some occasions acted in concert with OPEC to restrict the supply of oil. Furthermore, the Norwegian and Saudi oil ministers are in regular contact to exchange views on the market outlook for oil. Nevertheless, Norway has not been a participant in the discussion of the pricing of oil. Norway's commitment to the Western alliance includes accepting U.S. leadership of the international economy, and Norwegian "internationalism" has not questioned the role of the dollar as the international reserve currency or led to any assessment of the pricing of its key commodity export. Norway has, therefore, been a contributor to the "dollar bloc" in this way.

In the future, natural gas exports will exceed those of oil, and the international market prices for natural gas are set in both dollars and euros. Thus, Norway is integrally linked to the wider structures of international commodity markets, to the use of particular currencies as international currencies, and to the potential rivalry between the U.S. dollar and the euro for dominance as an international currency. Despite Norway's importance in determining the future use of the dollar and the euro within the international monetary system, this issue has played no role in Norwegian political or economic debate. And it has been of no significance in discussions of exchange-rate regimes and the future of the krone either.

Part III
Conclusion

8 Comparative conclusions

"Contingent neoliberalism" and the limits of globalism

Are systemically significant national currencies being threatened with extinction by the forces of "globalization?" The short answer to this question, based on the four case studies presented here, is a decisive no. That said, two of the currencies in our case studies have been threatened, and could be again, by a contingent neoliberalism. Of the interpretations of globalization identified in Chapter 3, it is *globalism*, or more accurately *neoliberal globalism*, that has posed the greatest threat.

Certainly, the last three decades have seen a substantial change in the operations of international financial markets; they are now much larger—"exploding" in Rogoff's (2007) assessment—and currencies flow much more freely across national borders. However, for all that, in all four of the countries analyzed here, there is no compelling evidence that the currencies' existence is being threatened by the inexorable technologically driven forces of *globalization* that are alleged to be weakening nation-states and all things national in their wake. Despite the claims made by advocates of common currencies or dollarization (or both) in both Canada and Mexico that "inevitable" processes are at work, the evidence for these claims is weak. In Australia and Norway, despite the proximity of the latter to the newly created euro area, such claims were not even made. Though Canadian academics debated whether the Canadian dollar could survive in a world of fewer currencies with the creation of the euro, Australian commentators celebrated the Australian dollar's rise in comparative importance with the disappearance of European currencies.

In terms of arguments for supranational currencies based on *integrationist* arguments, trade and investment integration with the United States is important for both Canada and Mexico, though it should be noted that the most oft-used measures, trade:GDP ratios, overstate the level of trade integration. This arises because of the way in which cross-border trade in inputs enter into trade data as their full price whereas only the value-added component enters in the GDP figures. There is little compelling empirical evidence that Canada–United States, Mexico–United States, or North America as a whole have become optimal currency areas (as reviewed in Chapters 5 and 6). Neither are business pressures uniformly pushing for supranational currencies. In Mexico, the elite Mexican Council of Businessmen pushed for dollarization, but other business associations did not have a common position; neither did those in Canada. The level of the exchange rate seems to have been a greater concern than the exchange-rate regime itself, especially in Canada. In Norway, the oil economy determines that it is not part of any optimal currency area in Europe, though the euro is also widely thought not to be such an area itself in any case.

If the integrationist arguments for moving to common currencies are not compelling, a case might also be made on *credibility* grounds, that is, that the power of international financial markets increases the appeal of the hard-fix option. Otherwise, countries must accept freely floating exchange rates and all of the instability that this entails in a world of volatile international financial markets. This is the bipolar view. This argument has little relevance to Norway. Here, Norway was the first non-EU country to link to the ECU and continued its fix to the euro until 2001. A fixed exchange rate proved sustainable; it did not, however, prove desirable given the different business cycles of Norway and the eurozone and this, together with a reconfiguration of the corporatist social pact, best explains Norway's move to floating rates rather because of the bipolar view. The example of Norway, and other countries such as Denmark, makes the claims made by Australian commentators (such as Bryan and Rafferty, 1999) that since 1983 it has been impossible to contemplate a fixed exchange rate for Australia because of the global nature of the Australian dollar, difficult to accept. Furthermore, supporters of a common currency in Canada also argued that a traditional fixed exchange rate would be perfectly workable in Canada. For Australia, Canada, and Norway, the bipolar view is unconvincing and, as it falls, so does one argument for a move toward common currencies on credibility grounds.

That said, the credibility argument does have some relevance for Mexico. It also played some role, though in a somewhat different way, in the Canadian debate as well. With respect to the latter, the fall in the value of the Canadian dollar caused widespread concern among the general population; the evidence from surveys of business leaders also indicated that the support for a common currency varied inversely with the value of the dollar. The decline in the value of the dollar did not lead to an abandonment of the currency and to a rise in unofficial dollarization, but perhaps the potential was there if the currency fell further. What requires explanation, however, is why similar sentiments were not found in Australia despite the strikingly similar behavior of the two currencies on international markets. As the Australian dollar fell to new lows, this did not lead to any concern about the viability of the currency or the appropriateness of the floating exchange-rate regime. The dominant view taken by business leaders and policy makers was that the depreciation of the dollar was exactly what was supposed to happen following an external shock such as the Asian crisis.

For Mexico, the successive exchange-rate crises of 1976, 1982, 1986, and 1994 did much to alter perceptions of the credibility of the currency after twenty years of a stable exchange rate. After each of the first three crises, Mexico sought to return to a fixed exchange rate only for it to unravel again. After the 1994 Tequila crisis, it might well be argued that by that time Mexico had lost the credibility necessary to return to a fixed exchange rate for a fourth time and that it was faced with a bipolar choice: either a hard fix such as a currency board or a floating exchange rate. However, there is room for debate about whether this was due to the new power of international financial markets, with the 1994 crisis marking the start of a new type of crisis reflecting this, or was the result of the culmination of four crises caused by domestic mismanagement. If the latter, the decision to float was not so much a reflection of the new power of international financial as of their exhaustion with Mexican domestic policies. Though the credibility argument has some resonance in the Mexican case, in general the threat posed to the four national currencies analyzed here by the forces of *globalization* and interpreted as a process that weakens the nation-state and strengthens markets is only a weak one.

In terms of the *imperialism* interpretation, it is clear that the use of the U.S. dollar and the euro as international currencies provides the United States and the EU with considerable economic and political advantages. It is no surprise that the United States, for example, wishes to maintain this role for the dollar and uses its influence to achieve this end. However, it is not the case that any of the countries under consideration here experienced any pressure to either adopt the U.S. dollar or the euro; in fact, quite the opposite. In both Canada and Mexico, the impetus for the discussion of dollarization came from domestic, not U.S., sources. The latter, through Alan Greenspan, publicly argued that dollarization in Mexico was not in the interests of the United States, whereas the Canadian debate was met with indifference to the point where no response to the Canadian debate was forthcoming at all.

The pressure for dollarization came from academics in Canada and from academics and business leaders in Mexico. It might be argued that they are not "domestic" sources but rather a part of a transnational capitalist class. In such a case, the solidarity of this class was sorely lacking in the dollarization debate, and it was not joined by the members of the "transnational class" based in the United States. True, the Mack Committee considered the issue and various high-profile individuals (see Summers, 1999) spoke in favor of dollarization. However, no official position was taken, no clandestine operations put in place to promote it, and no pressure placed on the United States' two contiguous geographical neighbors to move in the direction of dollarization.

The EU did exclude Norway from membership of the eurozone banking settlement mechanisms, a move that increased the costs of Norwegian non-participation in the EU and the euro and, as such, could be interpreted as an incentive for Norway to reconsider its position. Even if one were to accept this interpretation, it is only a small incentive and, unaccompanied by other evidence, would be insufficient to carry the weight of an imperial-pressure argument. Norway, as a major oil producer—and this argument extends to Mexico as well, though Mexico is not nearly as important an oil producer as Norway—plays an important role in sustaining the role of the dollar as an international currency by continuing to price its oil in dollars. In important ways, Norway occupies a pivotal space in rivalries between the dollar and the euro—a potential switch from pricing its oil in dollars to euros is argued by some (including in OPEC) to be of particular significance for the wider oil-producing community, and the pricing of its future gas exports in euros may also have important implications for the relative roles of the two international currencies. Despite the significance of Norway as a player in this global currency rivalry, there is no evidence that Norway has experienced any particular pressure from either camp in this regard, or indeed that this has been an issue in policy-making circles in Norway at all. This may be the result of Norway's not challenging the status quo in terms of pricing its oil in dollars and its gas exports being primarily an issue for the future. Nevertheless, the absence of any sign of pressures in this regard from either the United States or the EU does weaken the case for viewing the rivalry between the dollar and the euro as international currencies as being best described as reflecting inter-imperialist rivalries.

The use of the Australian dollar in some of the micro-states of the Pacific region relates both to the economic and political importance of Australia; certainly Australia's role in the region is capable of being interpreted as imperialistic with respect to these territories. However, in the debate that was initiated by New Zealand, Australia offered to allow New Zealand to adopt the Australian dollar if it wished, much as the Australian constitution still allows New Zealand to join if it wishes. The prospect of a common currency was engaged by the Australian political elite but with little profile and certainly no urgency. It stayed on the periphery of the policy agenda and subsequently slipped off altogether.

In all four countries, therefore, the imperialism argument provides little evidence that national currencies are threatened. This does not necessarily imply that the U.S. dollar does not provide the United States with "empire-like" advantages, to use Wade's words, or that wider imperial structures are not evident. What is does mean, however, is that countries whose currencies are systemically significant have not been subject to imperial pressures to adopt "imperial currencies" and retain considerable autonomy in their choice to retain their national currencies.

The argument that *regionalism* in the form of the emergence of regional monies is threatening the continued existence of national currencies is also unpersuasive for the four countries considered here. While the U.S. dollar is obviously widely used in the Americas, it does not directly threaten the continued existence of the Canadian dollar or the Mexican peso because of a market-led regionalization or a politically driven regionalism. The market-led integration that has taken place under the auspices of the NAFTA has not led to widespread unofficial dollarization in either country or to the formation of a strong business constituency across the region in favor of a common currency or dollarization. As a political project, regionalism in the Americas has not included a currency dimension. Post-September 11, 2001 plans at further integration have conspicuously omitted monetary integration as a goal, and the importance of North American (or wider hemispheric) integration has slipped down the U.S.'s policy agenda as its foreign policy has become more focused on other parts of the world.

As for Asia, the emerging regionalism may cover monetary cooperation and trade liberalization, but the prospects for an Asian common currency, the efforts of the ADB notwithstanding, are decidedly weak over the medium term. Even if it were to emerge, it is not at all clear that it would represent any kind of threat to the continued existence of the Australian dollar. As argued in Chapter 4, Australia has a politically ambiguous relationship with Asia and has shifted its focus toward the United States (including a Free Trade Agreement). Indeed, the regional context indicates that the Australian dollar might best be thought of as a regional currency itself, with no obvious other currency partners. This argument has some weight given its use in other micro-states and its use by international investors as a vehicle for diversifying currency holdings, a role that the Australian dollar plays at least in part because it is in a separate geographical region. This view has some plausibility, but it is not clear that the Australian dollar is likely to play an expanded role in this regard, even with respect to New Zealand, let alone further afield.

Thus, despite a plethora of academic treatises on the implications of the euro for North America and East Asia, perhaps the real lesson is that of European exceptionalism: the euro arose as a result of a specific politically driven regional project that has no close parallel elsewhere in the world. This can also be inferred from the Norwegian case and helps to explain why the advent of the euro sparked debates in other continents but had no such effect in Norway. To put it bluntly, the Norwegians had a better understanding that the euro was the culmination of a political process that had to be analyzed in these terms rather than as an economic innovation that might have relevance elsewhere. Norway had rejected EU membership twice and, having done so, the euro had no special significance. Adoption of the new regional currency would, for Norway, require the prior decision to join the political project that is the EU. Standing outside of this political project, the euro was not seen as a signal for the demise of the krone as the national currency.

The conclusion to this point can be summed up as follows. It is certainly the case that the currency landscape has changed over the last three decades. International financial markets are far larger today than they were at the end of the Bretton Woods period, and with the end of exchange controls, currencies circulate much more easily and widely throughout the world than they used to. The euro has been created; however, this does not mean that other systemically significant currencies are in danger of disappearing. Based on an examination of debates and evidence from four countries presented here, the threat is minimal, whether globalization is viewed as a technologically driven process integrating markets around the world or as a byword for imperialism. The conclusion is also warranted if regionalism is seen as the more important dynamic underway in the contemporary period.

The most significant challenge to national currencies comes not from a technologically driven globalization, from imperialism, or from regionalism but from *globalism* in the form of a more domestically rooted "contingent neoliberalism." Even here, it is not all national currencies that are endangered but only those in countries where neoliberalism takes a particular form. Thus, contingent neoliberalism was a significant force supporting a common currency or dollarization (or both) in Canada and Mexico but not in Australia. In Mexico, there has been a twenty-year program of constraining the power of the state, advocated by business leaders and implemented by successive government, first by the PRI and then by the PAN, which represented a radical change in direction from the development strategy that Mexico pursued from 1940 to 1982. Following the oil price shock and debt crisis of 1982, Mexico changed direction and followed the neoliberal policies of the "Washington Consensus." This culminated in Mexico's entry into the NAFTA in 1994, an international agreement that led to an economic restructuring and a deliberate political "lock-in" of neoliberal policies. The debate over dollarization at the end of the 1990s can be seen as a debate about whether to extend this political lock-in to the monetary sphere. Some parts of the business community, as well as academics and policy institutes, argued that the power of the state should be further constrained by taking monetary sovereignty away from Mexican institutions. Other parts of the business community, as well as the politicians who were responsible for implementing other parts of the neoliberal agenda, argued that a floating exchange rate should be retained and that monetary discipline could be restored by domestic institutional reform, such as granting the Bank of Mexico greater formal independence. Though the institutional interests of government ministries may provide a part of the rationale for this response, it is also plausible to view the differences between the pro- and anti-dollarization camps as ones of strategy rather than of ideology. Prominent members on both sides of the debate can be considered as neoliberal in ideological orientation, and both wanted to constrain government discretionary power. One side sought to do this through the external constraint of dollarization while the other was willing to rely on domestic institutional reform. That is, their positions, though both neoliberal, were contingent on their assessments of the relative chances of success of the two strategies.

The Canadian debate can be analyzed in much the same way. Here the debate was also predominantly between neoliberal economists. On one side were those who regarded Canada's adoption of a flexible exchange-rate regime and the depreciation of the dollar as reasons why Canada's productivity growth rate was low and why the welfarist bent of the Canadian state (to both firms and labor) had been allowed to continue. In their view, adoption of a common currency would force corrective (neoliberal) action to be taken. In contrast, other neoliberal economists in academia and in government institutions argued that the trade and investment liberalization under NAFTA together with the monetary and fiscal discipline adopted by the deficit-cutting Federal Liberal government in 1995 constituted real progress; the monetary order had been restored, and a change of exchange-rate regime was not required. A flexible exchange rate had other advantages, such as allowing adjustment to external shocks, and should be preserved because disciplinary neoliberalism had been restored to government. Again, many participants in the debate shared a common ideology but differed on strategy. Of course, there were others outside the neoliberal camp who (mostly) opposed any proposals for a common currency, or more likely dollarization, with the United States. However, they were mainly reacting to the debate initiated by the neoliberals.

In both cases, therefore, the main thrust for the abolition of national currencies came from neoliberalism, but it was a contingent neoliberalism, a neoliberalism based on an assessment of the particular context of the two countries and an assessment with which other neoliberals might disagree. In both cases, the neoliberals supporting the status quo (of national currencies) won, and the pro-common currency–dollarization camp could not muster sufficient political support to lead to a change in policy. National currencies survived because one set of neoliberal arguments defeated another set, but the challenge to national currencies was there, albeit more strongly in Mexico than in Canada.

In Australia, there was a strong neoliberal consensus in favor of maintaining flexible exchange rates and an independent currency. Here, the switch to a flexible exchange-rate regime in 1983 was associated with the wider rejection of the "Australian settlement" and an acceptance of the need for neoliberal restructuring. As such, the flexible exchange rate had become an icon of the commitment to neoliberalism—an indicator of the willingness of the government to submit to market forces. For this reason, the debate over exchange-rate regimes and the future of the Australian dollar has been much more muted than in either Canada or Mexico.

This is despite the fact that Australia and Canada in particular share many commonalities in terms of economic structure and exchange-rate trends over the last twenty years (see Bowles 2006). The way in which the exchange-rate regime has been uncontested in Australia but a subject of debate in Canada has also been reflected in the interpretation given of other similar trends. For example, in the Canadian debate, attention was focused on the "puzzle" of the relatively poor productivity performance in manufacturing industry and links with the exchange-rate regime hypothesized. In Australia, academics and government agencies puzzled over the existence and causes of Australia's productivity "miracle" of the 1990s. The irony is that productivity performance in both countries has actually been quite similar. For example, the Australian Productivity Commission's Dean Parham (2002), in a paper entitled "Productivity Growth in Australia: Are We Enjoying a Miracle?" reproduced an OECD figure (shown below as Figure 8.1) as illustrating the "miracle" in need of examination.

Australia has certainly performed well on this measure, but so has Canada; the "productivity miracle" on this measure is applicable to both Canada and Australia. Furthermore, in both countries, manufacturing productivity has lagged behind this aggregate measure. In Australia, the sectors in which productivity growth have been the highest are the wholesale trade, construction, and finance and insurance. There has been no "miracle" in manufacturing; indeed, Productivity Commissioner Gary Banks conceded that manufacturing's contribution to overall productivity growth in the 1990s "slumped" (see Banks, 2003). The "productivity puzzle"— why trade liberalization has not spurred productivity growth in manufacturing—is applicable to both Australia and to Canada.

However, in Australia, the focus of attention has been on understanding the causes of the good overall productivity record, with the most common explanation being the importance of microeconomic and regulatory reforms. In Canada, the

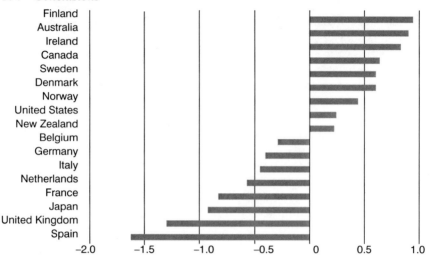

Figure 8.1 Trends in multifactor productivity growth (annual percentage change 1980–90
to 1990–99) (Source: Parham (2002: 6))

focus has been on Canada's relatively poor productivity record in manufacturing despite the good overall productivity performance. The impact of a macroeconomic variable, the exchange rate, on productivity has been a significant area of debate as a result of the "lazy manufacturers" hypothesis noted in Chapter 5.

The contingent neoliberal explanation suggests that the Canadian dollar was (and may again be) threatened by a contingent neoliberalism whereas the Australian dollar, despite the similarities in many areas between the Canadian and Australian economies, is not. In Australia, the policy consensus is that there has been a decisive shift in favor of neoliberalism and that the move to a flexible exchange-rate regime is an important part of this. In Canada, there has been no such neoliberal consensus. Some neoliberals continue to doubt whether Canada is neoliberal enough, whereas others are willing to accept that monetary and fiscal disciplines have been restored and a change in the exchange-rate regime is not required as part of the policy package needed to achieve this.

The importance for national context in understanding exchange-rate regime choices is also supported by examination of the Norwegian case. Norway operated with a fixed exchange-rate regime but switched in 2001 to a flexible regime. However, this decision was taken within the context of an ongoing consensus among business, labor, and the main political parties of the need for a corporatist framework. This framework, which supported the so-called Solidarity Alternative, is seen as a mechanism to avoid the neoliberal path that most other countries have followed. The language of neoliberalism and globalization is to be found in Norwegian policy debates but is much less prevalent and does not constitute the starting point as it does in many other country contexts. The change in the exchange-rate regime in 2001 is best interpreted as a reformulation of the corporatist framework designed to continue the search for the best way of meeting the objectives of macroeconomic stability and a viable manufacturing sector in an oil-rich country. In this way, the change in exchange-rate regime can be seen as constituting a "contingent corporatism." Though this did include a long period with a fixed exchange rate, a common currency was not part of the discussion.

The answer to the question of whether national currencies are endangered species in the four countries analyzed is, therefore, and on balance, no. And where pressures are present, they come mainly from contingent neoliberalism.

Table 8.1 summarizes the explanatory power of the four interpretations of globalization for currency trends and debates in each of the four countries. This Table highlights some of the more important aspects of the discussion and indicates which of these factors support the interpretation of globalization (+) and which do not (–).

The summary information provided in Table 8.1 illustrates the conclusion from the foregoing discussion. That is, the arguments derived from the globalism interpretation have the greatest explanatory power for explaining currency trends and debates in the four countries. Thus, we conclude that of the four approaches presented in Chapter 2, that which views globalization as *globalism*, a neoliberal ideology, is the most persuasive. The twist in the argument as applied to the case of national currencies is that this is a contingent neoliberalism. To put the conclusion in a different form, the reconfiguration of the powers of the state and market, the two "authoritative domains" (Cohen, 1998) of money during the last three decades has not been sufficient to shift the balance of power decidedly in favor of markets.

In reaching this conclusion, it is also evident that conjunctural factors were critical in determining the timing of debates. In Canada, the temporal spur for the debate over a North American common currency or dollarization (or both) was the birth of the euro, which offered a model of a new monetary arrangement just at the time that the Canadian dollar was falling to historic lows in the wake of the Asian financial crisis. These events were seized on by some as a spark that could ignite a debate about Canada's monetary order. The discussions of dollarization elsewhere in the Americas also played a role in stimulating debate in Canada.

Debates elsewhere in the Americas, and the Argentinean experience in particular, played a large role in stimulating Mexico's debate. Argentina's newfound monetary stability, based on the adoption of a currency board in 1994, contrasted with Mexico's peso crisis later in that same year. In the late 1990s, Argentina considered moving to full dollarization, and the euro was about to appear in virtual form. These events coincided with the Mexican presidential election cycle, a time when the currency typically came under pressure. This conjuncture led to a brief, but intense, debate about dollarization as an option for Mexico.

In Australia, it was the role of international speculators in the Asian financial crisis that provided the spur for the 1999 inquiry by the House of Representatives Standing Committee on the Economy, Finance, and Public Administration into "International Financial Markets: Friends or Foes?" In this context, other exchange-rate regimes and currency choices were briefly considered even though there was widespread consensus that the flexible rate should be maintained.

Table 8.1 Four interpretations of globalization and their applicability to currency trends and debates in Australia, Canada, Mexico and Norway: summary

	Globalization	Globalism	Imperialism	Regionalism
Australia	The Australian dollar has become an internationally traded currency, playing a larger role in global currency markets than the Australian economy does in global trade (+)	Neoliberal consensus in support of the flexible exchange-rate regime following policy shift in 1983; explains limited debate in Australia (+)	Role of the Australian dollar in Pacific micro-states (+)	Absence of an obvious regional partner and complex relations with Asia (–) Discussion of ANZAC dollar with New Zealand (+)
Canada	Relatively low level of unofficial dollarization (–) Not an OCA with the U.S. (–)	No neoliberal consensus with some arguing for the need for neoliberal discipline through a fixed (hard or conventional) exchange-rate regime; other neoliberals view monetary order as having been restored (+)	No interest in Canadian debate in the U.S. (–)	Proximity to U.S. spurred debate (+) Regionalization not at the point where a common currency is necessary (–) Regionalism does not include a currency dimension (-)
Mexico	Credibility of the fixed exchange-rate regime undermined by a series of currency crises (+) Low to medium level of unofficial dollarization (–) Not an OCA with the U.S. (–)	No neoliberal consensus with some, especially the most powerful business association arguing for the need for neoliberal discipline through dollarization; other neoliberals support domestic institutional reform (+)	U.S. made clear it had no interest in extending Federal Reserve Bank's mandate to accommodate dollarized countries (–)	Proximity to U.S. spurred debate (+) Regionalism does not include a currency dimension (–)
Norway	Change to flexible exchange-rate regime in 2001 explained by contingent corporatism (+)		No discussions of the international pricing of oil and gas exports (–)	Euro seen as the outcome of a politically-driven regional project which Norway has rejected (–)

Debates emanating from New Zealand, in large part triggered by the birth of the euro, also contributed to raising the currency issue.

In Norway, there was no debate when the euro came into being. The change in exchange-rate regime to a flexible rate occurred as a result of a coincidence of the political interests of the government, the preferences of the peak labor organization, and the institutional interests of the central bank. The global trend toward inflation-targeting central banks and the prevalence of flexible exchange-rate regimes elsewhere undoubtedly made the Norwegian switch easier to make.

Just as conjunctural factors were important in determining the timing of currency debates, so they were important in those debates fizzling out. In the two countries where the debate was most prominent, Mexico and Canada, the debate had ended by around 2002 even though there were sporadic interventions thereafter. For Mexico, the collapse of the Argentinean currency board at the end of 2001 combined with the peso's relatively stability over the period took the wind from dollarization's sails. In Canada, the dramatic rebound in the value of the dollar against the U.S. dollar during 2003 removed the Canadian dollar as an issue of public concern. The debate, already very muted in Australia, disappeared as the Australian dollar also rose.

Conjunctural factors were, therefore, important in providing the opening for neoliberal debate on exchange-rate regimes and currency issues in the late 1990s in Australia, Canada, and Mexico, though it was only in the latter two that a debate arising from disagreements between neoliberals was really in evidence. Conjunctural factors were also important in closing the debate rather than a decisive intellectual victory for either side. Thus, when Bogetic (2000) asked whether dollarization was a "fad or the future," conjunctural factors point to its being very much a fad.

Though conjunctural factors are, therefore, important, the conclusion that it is globalization as *globalism*, that has been the main driving force in the debates, also raises the relationship between the currency debates and the broad interpretations of globalization with which this book started. That is, a number of authors have recently argued that globalism has effectively peaked and is now in decline. The question arises, therefore, of whether the emergence and subsequent trailing off of currency debates in the four countries are part of this wider phenomenon.

Saul (2005: 133) has argued that globalism peaked in 1995 with the establishment of the WTO and the initiation of talks by the OECD countries on the Multilateral Agreement on Investment (MAI), the completion of which would herald a new era of neoliberal globalism. Similar analysis is found in Gill (2003). Saul documents how this project unraveled as a variety of events, including the Asian financial crisis, the failure of the MAI, widening income gaps, the "Battle of Seattle," September 11, the Argentine collapse, and Enron, sucked the lifeblood from the globalist project, concluding that we find ourselves in a "new vacuum" (ibid.: 217).

Bello (2006: 1348) has argued that "the globalist project" was driven by the Clinton Administration wherein "the dominant position of the USA allowed the liberal faction of the US capitalist class to act as a leading edge of a transnational ruling elite in the process of formation—a transnational elite alliance that could act to promote the comprehensive interest of the capitalist class" with its "crowning achievement the founding of the WTO in 1995" (ibid.: 1349). It was this body that was to permit "institutionalizing the emerging neoliberal global order" (ibid. 1349). However, just as in Saul's account, this has failed to pass the test of time and, for Bello, "at the structural level the much-vaunted relocation of industrial facilities, outsourcing of services and decline in trade barriers have not resulted in a functionally integrated global economy where nation-states and their institutions are ceasing to be central determinants of economic affairs" (ibid.: 1364–5).

The argument advanced by both Saul and Bello is that the globalism, as a neoliberal ideology seeking to reduce the power of nation-states and lock them into neoliberal global economic "constitutions," held sway in the mid–late 1990s but has subsequently declined. For Saul, this is because the promises made by advocates of this approach have not materialized and there has, therefore, been a reaction to and resistance against it. This has resulted in a "resurgence of [the] theoretically old-fashioned institution" (2005: 232) of the state in the West and elsewhere as the emergence of China, India, and Brazil testify. For Bello, China's integration into the world economy has produced a persistent tendency to overaccumulation, with the "global economy being held hostage by geopolitics on the part of two political leaderships [in China and the US] that value the accumulation of strategic power above all" (2006: 1365), a far cry from the globalist vision.

The conjunctural factors that led to the emergence of currency debates in the late 1990s, therefore, also coincided with a period in which globalism had wider appeal, a period in which supranational currencies could be envisaged as part of wider supranational neoliberal institutions and structures. However, globalism has been shown to have had its limits, and as globalism has waned so has the possibility of arguing for supranational currencies as part of new global economic structures. The disappearance of currency debates after the early 2000s can, therefore, be seen as part of a larger disillusionment with globalism in general. The view that the state is or should be weakened in the face of "inevitable" global forces no longer holds such sway. If the mid–late 1990s does indeed turn out to represent the historical "moment of neoliberal globalism," then the disappearance in the early 2000s of the idea that countries are inevitably destined to give up their currencies could last a long time.

This study has also shown that the same exchange-rate regime and currency arrangements can be used to support a variety of objectives; the flexible exchange-rate regimes in Australia and Norway, for example, have been shown to be consistent with quite different institutional frameworks and policy environments. As a result, it is possible to find globalization enthusiast Martin Wolf (2004) arguing for a global currency on the grounds that "if the global market economy is to thrive over the decades ahead, a global currency seems the logical concomitant. In its absence, the world of free capital flows will never work as well as it might." Exactly two years later, globalization sceptic Robert Wade (2006) argued for a global currency on the grounds that "for the United States to become a more responsible country, the world economy needs to move from the current U.S.

dollar standard to a global currency." Currencies, national or global, must be analyzed within the wider institutional contexts in which they will be used. The threat to national currencies from contingent neoliberalism may have abated with the waning of globalism more generally. However, this does not mean that debates over the desirability and future of national currencies will not reappear as the context changes. It has hoped that this book, by analyzing the debates of the recent past, will also prove useful as a guide to those of the future.

Notes

1 Introduction

1 Slovenia joined the original 12 members of the eurozone on January 1, 2007. Lithuania, which was also to join on this date, has delayed its entry.
2 See also the collection of essays in Gilbert and Helleiner (1999).
3 Although I am more skeptical of his prediction that "the global population of currencies is set to expand greatly" (2004: xiii).
4 Eichengreen and Razo-Garcia (2006: 396) attribute this observation to Branson.
5 See McKinnon (2005) for a ranking of major currencies according to these different measures.
6 Thus, the G17 SSCs is not defined in terms of governance structures, as is the economic counterpart of systemically important economies discussed above, but in terms of their importance in the ranking of national currencies.

2 The economic and political dynamics of globalization

1 Of course, "globalization" has many other dimensions—cultural, social, and environmental—to name three. Although "money" plays cultural and social roles—particularly in the construction of "identity"—the emphasis here is on the political and economic dimensions of globalization.
2 www.globalpolicy.org, accessed November 2, 2004.
3 The importance of technological factors also finds expression in the A.T. Kearney–Foreign Policy Globalization Index that tracks and assesses changes in four key components of global integration and incorporates such measures as trade and financial flows, the movement of people across borders, international telephone traffic, Internet usage, and participation in international treaties and peacekeeping operations. See the Foreign Policy web site, www.foreignpolicy.com.
4 Still other analyses, such as Rycroft (2002), stress the importance of technological change but argue that technology has "coevolved" with globalization rather than positing a direct causal relationship.
5 See also Bryan (1995), who provides a novel approach in analyzing capital's "chase across the globe" for profit. He argues (1995: 8), using a Marxist framework, that there is a "contradiction between the internationality of capital accumulation and the nationality of the state."
6 See, however, Greenspan (2004), who states that "the correlation coefficient between paired domestic saving and domestic investment, a conventional measure of the propensity to invest at home for OECD countries constituting four-fifths of world GDP, fell from 0.96 in 1992 to less than 0.8 in 2002."
7 According to Veseth, Nike would satisfy the global firm definition, but even such large firms as Boeing and Microsoft would not.

8 See also Guillén (2003: xi), whose book seeks to "shatter the notion that globalization encourages convergence to a single organizational form."

9 See Veseth (2005) for the origins of the term *globaloney*.

10 The term *neoliberalism* has gained wide usage most often by its critics. Neoliberalism here is taken to be a general belief in the efficacy of markets and the desirability of a limited role for the state. See Bowles (2005) for further discussion. Neoliberalism is similar to what Helleiner (1999) has termed "economic liberalism." Neither "neo-liberalism" nor "economic liberalism" includes the "embedded liberalism" of Ruggie (1983), that is, "the more interventionist forms of liberalism that became popular in the Keynesian age" (Helleiner, 1999: 155n1). In fact, neoliberalism represents a reaction to that and can be dated as starting in the late 1970s with the demise of post-war Keynesianism.

11 See also Johnson (2000) for a non-Marxist interpretation of current U.S. policy as one of imperialism.

12 For analysis of the impact of China's rise on regional trade flows, see Gaulier et al. (2006).

13 For an early view on this see UNCTC (1991). See Poon et al. (2000) for a critique of the Triad notion as it applies to foreign direct investment.

14 Available at the UNCTAD web site www.unctad.org [accessed April 4, 2007].

15 The G-6 countries used in the Goldman Sachs (2003) report are the G-7 countries minus Canada.

3 The implications of the four interpretations of globalization for national currencies

1 See also Bonpasse (2006) for the case for a Global Central Bank based on extensive historical and contemporary arguments and proposals.

2 See, for example, the Canadian debate discussed below in Chapter 5.

3 For the East Timor case, see United Nations Temporary Administration in East Timor, Regulation no. 2000/7, *On the Establishment of Legal Tender for East Timor.*

4 Of course, for some, intermediate regimes never went out of fashion. See, for example, Williamson (2000).

5 For review, see Obstfeldt et al. (2005).

6 Regionalism is another example. Some neoliberals (such as Bhagwati) are generally skeptical about the ability of regional trade agreements to lead to global free trade; others (such as Richard Lipsey) are much more favorably inclined to regional free trade agreements as being consistent with the goal of global trade liberalization.

7 Thus, while Hayek (1976) wrote of the need for competition between note-issuing banks, Issing (2000) argued the case for a European central bank. Both arguments were made in publications of the neoliberal Institute for Economic Affairs.

8 See, for example, their debate in Mundell and Friedman (2001).

9 See Arestis and Basu (2003) for arguments in favor of a single world currency. See Arestis and Sawyer (2003) for a critique of the workings of the euro project. There is no inconsistency here once it is recognized that context is critical.

10 Though complexly so, with some colonies adopting the imperial currency and others not. For an analysis of these complexities, see Helleiner (2003).

11 I focus here on these three main regions. Of course, there are significant monetary developments in other regions as well. See, for example, Masson and Pattillo (2004) for the case of Africa.

12 The emphasis is on the political and economic dynamics. For wider aspects of the euro's creation, see Fishman and Messina (2006).

13 This discussion draws on Bowles et al. (2003). Though a joint paper, the European section and analysis was primarily provided by Croci. I am grateful to him for allowing me to reproduce it here.

14 The role of serendipity, as it were, is recognized by one of the participants in the process: "Even those of us who laboured to complement the single market with a monetary union and to embody such a transformation into a treaty held only that such a transformation was desirable and feasible, not that it was probable, or much less, inevitable. ... Thus we might speak of a benevolent historical conspiracy, but certainly not of inevitability" (Padoa-Schioppa, 1994: 9).

4   Australia

1 Rosewarne (1999: 129), for example, in reviewing a left history, writes that "the critical role of the state is argued to have been one of the distinctive features of Australian capitalism." In this interpretation, it is the state's role in supporting the hegemony of capitalism that receives the most attention.
2 This term comes from Kelly (1992).
3 The Australian dollar was introduced on February 14, 1966. As Schedvin (1992: 412) notes, "symbolically the introduction of decimal currency represented a further erosion of the imperial connection and acceptance of the country's growing role in the Pacific rim and the involvement with the United States' dollar system." The government's preferred name for the new currency, the "Royal," was eventually withdrawn as public opinion was firmly in favor of the "dollar" (ibid.: 414–15).
4 Personal communication March 4, 2003.
5 For an account of media reports about the declining dollar, see Greenfield and Williams (2000).
6 Approximately 50 percent of Australia's exports are priced in U.S. dollars.
7 See, for example, the set of papers in "The Falling Australian Dollar: A Forum," *Journal of Australian Political Economy*, no. 46, 2000.
8 In subsequent years, both the Treasury and Reserve Bank of New Zealand published a number of studies that investigated the case for a currency union, an investigation that continued into 2004 with no apparent loss of interest. See also Haug (2001) for an academic study that concludes, on traditional OCA grounds, that New Zealand should not enter into a currency union with Australia, Japan, the United States, or the eurozone.
9 Even so, adoption of the U.S. dollar was advocated by an editorial in the Asian *Wall Street Journal* and by New Zealand National Party leader Bill English. See "Anzac Finance Union wins Support," *New Zealand Herald*, September 15, 2000, and Neill (2001).
10 Coleman (2001). He provides an overview of some costs and benefits of monetary union (defined as New Zealand adopting the Australian dollar) but does not reach a firm conclusion. See also Crosby and Otto (2000: 1), who argue that "Australia and New Zealand do not appear to be the best candidates for one currency."
11 Presumably this prediction was based on Britain's joining the euro.
12 This reading of Australia's political history dates the emergence of neoliberalism with the Hawke-Keating governments of the 1980s. See, for example, Beeson and Firth (1998) for this interpretation. However, for a different interpretation which sees the Hawke–Keating era as "New Labor" rather than "neoliberal," see Pierson (2002).
13 See Kelly (1992: 84).
14 Celebrating two decades of reforming government, *The Australian*, Tuesday March 4, 2003.
15 Ranking of countries depends on the data source and international conversion methods. These rankings are based on OECD statistics. They are consistent with those reported in Emy (1993: 44).
16 As reported in Harvey (2003).
17 This is the conclusion also favored by Cohen (2004: 168).

18 At the ASEAN meeting held in Thailand in October 2000, a recommendation to move forward on an AFTA-CER agreement was rejected. See Chong (2001). Since then, an AFTA-CER Closer Economic Partnership has been agreed and, in 2005, there was agreement to begin negotiating an FTA covering ASEAN, Australia and New Zealand.

19 See Department of Foreign Affairs and Trade, Summary of Australia's Trade, Monthly Trade Data, May 2007.

5 Canada

1 Chinese and Japanese immigration into Western Canada, initially the result of the 1850s gold rush and continued to support the building of the transcontinental railway, was first controlled and then reduced to very low numbers as governments were pressured to restrict non-Caucasian immigration.

2 Pomfret (1993: 83) notes "the significance of foreign investment in Canadian [Gross Domestic Capital Formation] from an early date", being as much as 50 percent of total investment in the immediate pre-World War I years. See also McBride (2005).

3 Bordo (2000: 7) argues that the float was "relatively 'clean'" with only occasional interventions.

4 See, however, Bordo (2000), who argues that Canada's exchange-rate regime from 1820 until 1970 followed "the gold convertibility contingent rule in various guises" with the "contingency or 'escape clause' exercised only briefly." For him, therefore, Canada's exchange-rate regime has been characterized by greater commitment to a fixed regime than is suggested by Helleiner's analysis.

5 In 1975, the Bank adopted an "avowed monetarist approach" (Norrie and Owram, 2002: 403).

6 For a recent discussion of trends, see Pilat (2005). For a collection of papers that generally take the productivity gap between Canada and the United States as large and requiring government action, see Rao and Sharpe (2002). For a more skeptical view of the gap, see Keay (2000).

7 The export:GDP ratio had fallen back to 38.0 percent by 2003.

8 There had been a debate in the early 1990s over the Canadian dollar as well, though it was less high profile than the one at the end of the decade analyzed here. See Helleiner (2006) on previous debates. This section draws on material presented in Bowles (2004, 2006) and Bowles et al. (2003, 2004).

9 The federalist party is the Bloc Quebecois, whereas at the provincial level it is the Parti Quebecois.

10 Beine and Coulombe (2003) argued that Ontario and Quebec shared the same business cycles as the United States and might benefit from dollarization, whereas the other provinces (which they term the "peripheral regions") benefit from the flexible exchange rate. Alberta, one of the "peripheral regions," instigated its own examination of the common currency issue. It was, however, the heartland of the conservative Reform Party that showed the most interest among the Anglophone parties in the issue (see Henton, 1999). The Alberta Treasurer at the time, Stockwell Day, went on to become leader of the Canadian Alliance (which resulted from the merger of the Reform and Conservative Parties).

11 This point was refuted by Canadian Auto Workers economist Jim Stanford (1999), who drew attention to the rise in U.S. interest rates in the United States on June 30 not being matched by changes in Canada. By performing these types of actions, the Bank of Canada was demonstrating that "little acts of independence, repeated over time and across circumstances, add up to real sovereignty" (1999: 15).

12 The argument was further refined in Harris (2001a) in which he argued that the United States was benefiting for its adoption of general purpose technology but that Canada was hampered from doing so by the flexible exchange rate. The conclusion remained

the same—Canada remained wedded to the "old economy" and was missing out on the "new economy."

13 In the 1980 sovereignty referendum, the question included the provision for a sovereign Quebec to continue using the Canadian dollar.

14 *The Globe and Mail*, January 26, 2002.

15 This is likely to remain the case, though Guy Legault, President of the Certified General Accountants Association of Canada, also argued that Canada should not harmonize its accounting standards with those of the United States as it increases the chances of an Enron-style debacle happening in Canada. See, "Quit Trying to Harmonize Accounting with US," *Financial Post*, May 4, 2002: FP7.

16 See Murray et al. (2002) for tests of the asymmetric responses by Canada, the United States, and Mexico to exogenous shocks. See also Crowley (2001) and Carr and Floyd (2001).

17 The two sectors were "industrial machinery and equipment" and "electronic and other electronic equipment." See also McCallum (1999).

18 On the question of institutional structure, see also Buiter (1999) and Crowley and Rowley (2002).

19 The Senate Standing Committee on Foreign Affairs (1998: 61) argued that "the Canadian dollar … has perhaps been the real victim of the deepening Asian financial and economic crisis." The Canadian dollar continued to depreciate for several years after the Asian crisis. See Figure 5.1 above.

20 Personal interview with the Canadian Association of Manufacturers and Exporters, 250402. Survey research by the Bank of Canada in the post-2002 exchange-rate appreciation period found that 50 percent of firms reported that they were hurt by the rising Canadian dollar, 25 percent were helped by it, and 25 percent were unaffected. See Mair (2005).

21 See, for example, Mundell (2000).

22 See "Medium of Exchange was the Message in 2003: C$ Rise Rated Top News Story," *The National Post*, December 31, 2003.

23 Centre for Research and Information on Canada, "Many Canadians Want Closer Ties to US but a Majority Oppose a Common Currency," Press Release, October 28, 2003.

24 See "High Loonie is Mixed Blessing for REITs," *Financial Post*, December 23, 2004.

25 This Task Force is sponsored by the Council on Foreign Relations, the Canadian Council of Chief Executives, and the Consejo Mexicano de Asuntos Internacionales.

26 McCallum later argued that he had conceded too much in this respect.

27 Different multinationals have different arrangements for dealing with exchanges between their affiliates operating in different countries. For example, Ford Canada has been arguing for a higher value for the Canadian dollar as it is adversely affected by a low dollar increasing its input costs and reducing its revenues in U.S. dollar terms in its trade with Ford U.S. GM in Canada has expressed no such concerns as its accounting practices operate on a continental basis. Personal interview, 250402.

28 In reaching this conclusion, Weir (2007) adjusts export data to reflect value-added exports rather than total exports. This reduces Canada's exports to the United States from approximately 44 percent of GDP to 27 percent. He also includes service exports and exports of goods; a higher percentage of the latter are traded with the United States than the former.

29 Helleiner (2004c) makes a similar point in disputing "the arguments that Canadian participation in NAMU is 'inevitable' and that the loonie is 'doomed' to extinction."

30 Certainly some pro-dollarization business commentators have drawn parallels with the free trade debate. For example, Sherry Cooper has argued that if arguments for monetary integration with the United States and Mexico sound far-fetched, "so did the idea of a free-trade deal in 1980," a view recently also expressed by Ted Carmichael,

chief Canadian economist at the U.S. investment bank, J. P. Morgan, who argues that "in the medium term ... a common currency has the potential to make the transition from political issue to policy reality in much the same way as Canada-U.S. free trade did in the 1980s."

31 This coincided with the emergence of a public perception in Canada that the United States was once again home to a highly dynamic economy. From the mid-1990s, when the Federal Reserve Board under Alan Greenspan decided to put to the test the hypothesis that the U.S. unemployment rate could not be allowed to fall below 6 percent or so without triggering a surge in the inflation rate, and until 2000, the United States enjoyed exceptionally rapid growth in employment, productivity, and output (Baker, 2000). The economic dynamism that the United States exhibited in the late 1990s, and the way in which rapid U.S. economic growth translated into rapid expansion of Canada's net exports to the United States during the same period, added appeal to claims that Canada should strive to be "competitive" with the United States and that the two countries should become more highly integrated. Toward the end of the 1990s, greater integration with the United States sounded much more attractive to the Canadian public than it did as late as 1993 when the United States was seen as experiencing a "jobless recovery" or since 2003 when the United States' economic problems under George W. Bush have become more evident and when tying to the U.S. dollar is problematic given the twin U.S. deficits. I am grateful to Brian MacLean for this point.

32 Personal interview 270901.

33 The Watkins Report (Canada, Privy Council Office 1968: 21) argued that "foreign investment ... has been one aspect of a process operative for a century, which has increasingly bound Canada to a North American economy. The tendency inherent in direct investment to shift decision-making power in the private sector outside Canada has, on occasion, posed serious problems for those responsible for formulating Canadian policy, and has created widespread unease among Canadians as to the continuing viability of Canada as an independent nation-state."

6 Mexico

1 Data from the Bank of Mexico.

2 This section draws on Moreno-Brid, Santamaria, and Rivas (2005) and Moreno-Brid, Ruiz, and Rivas (2005). Data are from these sources unless otherwise indicated.

3 The membership has now been reduced to only thirty members.

4 See *La Nación*, April 6, 2001. See also Starr (2002) for analysis of the debate.

7 Norway

1 Though Norway has a strong internationalist orientation and commits approximately 1 percent of its GDP to foreign aid each year, it also has protectionist trade policies for agricultural products that harm developing country exporters among others. This is highlighted in the Centre for Global Development/Foreign Policy Commitment to Development Index, which shows Norway's trade commitment, uniquely among the major aid donors, to be negative. For more details, see www.cgdev.org. Recently, Norway has opened its market completely for imports from the least developed countries.

2 This kind of direct income policy has really never been used in Sweden. It was proposed by the Minister of Finance, Feldt, during the Swedish crisis in 1990–91 but was turned down, and Feldt resigned.

3 See Bulletin of Norges Bank, no.1, 1987.

4 See, for example, the debate in *Dagens næringsliv*, September 20, 1991.

5 See articles by Dr A. Mork in the newspaper *Dagbladet* in 1992.

6 Both in an article in *Aftenposten* in 1997 and an interview in the same newspaper in 1998.
7 This is also discussed in his later article; I. Furre, Inflasjonsmål I pengepolitikken— omleggingen sett fra et markedssynspunkt, Økonomisk forum nr. 7, 2001, 6–11.
8 St. meld. nr. 29 (2000–01) Retningslinjer for den økonomiske politikken (Guidelines for economic policy).
9 Ibid.: 10.
10 In 2004, this was modified to three years ahead.
11 One of the consequences of the appreciation of the krone during 2002 was that imported inflation was considerably reduced and inflation dropped well below the inflation target and even below the inflation band (2.5 percent ± 1 percent), remaining below 1 percent for two years.
12 Personal interview 1505021. This point was reinforced by a senior researcher at the Confederation of Norwegian Business and Industry (NHO), who noted that "there is no sense of inevitability about using the euro" (personal interview 160502).
13 Personal interview 1505022.
14 It is misleading to take the decline in government expenditures as share of GDP as an indication of "outsourcing" in Norway owing to the large impact of oil on the GDP level. With high oil revenues, almost "everything" will fall as a share of GDP in Norway. It is more useful to look at the share of, say, government expenditures in non-oil GDP. This share has not changed much except for cyclical reasons.
15 Personal interview 1505025. He continued that although the Conservative Party wanted a slimmer state, all parties, with the exception of the radical right party, shared a consensus framework.
16 The team that reexamined the situation of the corporatist model after the first two years of inflation targeting was headed by a professor of economics specializing in macroeconomics.
17 Cf. NOU 2003: 13, Konkurranseevne, lønnsdannelse og kronekurs, Finansdept. Oslo 2003: 88–9.
18 In 2005, the loosely organized union of academics who are against centralized bargaining even lost some of its smaller member unions owing to its attitude toward centralized bargaining. The wage round in spring 2005 gave wage increases only according to centrally negotiated wages and left little room for local bargaining.
19 See the discussion in Christiansen and Qvigstad (1997) op. cit. and NOU 2003: 13, Ch. 7.6. on this issue.
20 Norway's trade with China exceeds that with the United States.

References

ADB (Asian Development Bank) (2004) "East Asia Should Start Addressing Challenges of Adopting a Single Currency, Seminar Told," available at http: //www.adb.org/ annualmeeting/2004/Media/single_currency_news.html, accessed June 20, 2005.

Alesina, A., and Barro, R. (2001) "Dollarisation," *American Economic Review, Papers and Proceedings*, 91(2), May: 381–5.

Ali, T. (2006) *Pirates of the Caribbean: Axis of Hope*, London: Verso.

Anderson, K. (1987) in Maddock, R., and McLean, I., "Tariffs and the Manufacturing Sector," *The Australian Economy in the Long Run*, Cambridge: Cambridge University Press, 165–94.

Andrews, D. (ed.) (2006) *International Monetary Power*, Ithaca: Cornell University Press.

Antweiler, W. (2002) "Is the Canadian Dollar in Secular Decline?" Mimeograph, April.

Arestis, P., and Basu, S. (2003) "Financial Globalization: Some Conceptual Issues," *Eastern Economic Journal* 29(2): 183–9.

Arestis, P., and Sawyer, M. (2003) "Macroeconomic Policies of the Economic Monetary Union: Theoretical Underpinnings and Challenges," *Economics Working Paper 385*, The Levy Institute.

Arrighi, G. (2005) "Hegemony Unravelling—I," *New Left Review*, 32, March–April.

Aubry, Jack (1999) "MPs Incensed as Senate Opts to Study Common Currency," *Vancouver Sun*, March 25: A6.

Auerbach, N., and Flores-Quiroga, A. (2003) "The Political Economy of Dollarization in Mexico," in Salvatore, D., Dean, J., and Willett, T. (eds) *The Dollarization Debate*, Oxford: Oxford University Press, 266–82.

Aukrust, O. (1977) "Inflation in the Open Economy: A Norwegian Model," in Krause, L., and Salant, W. (eds) *Worldwide Inflation: Theory and Recent Evidence*, Washington, DC: The Brookings Institution, 107–66.

Australian Stock Exchange (ASX) (1999) Submission to the Standing Committee on Economics, Finance and Public Administration Inquiry into the International Financial Market Effects on Government Policy (May).

Bach, D. (2005) "Regionalism as Fragmentation," *International Studies Review* 7: 98– 100.

Bailliu, J., and King, M (2005) "What Drives Movements in Exchange Rates?" *Bank of Canada Review*, Autumn.

Bairoch, P. (1996) "Globalization Myths and Realities: One Century of External Trade and Foreign Investment," in Boyer, R., and Drache, D. (eds) *States Against Markets: The Limits of Globalization*, London: Routledge, 173–92.

Baker, D. (2000) "NAIRU: Dangerous Dogma at the Fed," *Financial Markets and Society*, Financial Markets Center (December): 1–16.

Balino, T., Bennett, A., and Borensztein, E. (1999) *Monetary Policy in Dollarized Economies*, Washington, DC: International Monetary Fund.

Ball, R. (1999) "The Institutional Foundations of Monetary Commitment: A Comparative Analysis," *World Development* October 27: 20.

Banks, G. (2003) "Australia's Economic 'Miracle,'" speech to the *Forum on Postgraduate Economics* held at Australian National University, Canberra, August 1.

Bazant, J. (1991) "From Independence to the Liberal Republic, 1821–1867," in Bethell, L. (ed.) *Mexico Since Independence*, Cambridge: Cambridge University Press, 1–48.

Beddoes, Z. (1999) "From EMU to AMU? The Case for Regional Currencies," *Foreign Affairs* July–August, 78(4): 8–13.

Beeson, M. (2001) "Australia and Asia: The Years of Living Aimlessly," *Southeast Asian Affairs*, 44–55.

Beeson, M. and Firth, A. (1998) "Neoliberalism as a Political Rationality: Australian Public Policy Since the 1980s," *Journal of Sociology* 34(3): 215–31.

Beine, M., and Coulumbe, S. (2003) "Regional Perspectives on Dollarization in Canada," *Journal of Regional Science* 43: 541–70.

Belkar, R., Cockerell, L., and Kent, C. (2007) "Current Account Deficits: The Australian Debate," Reserve Bank of Australia, *Research Discussion Paper RDP2007–2*, March.

Bell, S. (1997) *Ungoverning the Economy: The Political Economy of Australian Economic Policy*, Melbourne: Oxford University Press.

Bell, S. (2004) *Australia's Money Mandarins: The Reserve Bank and the Politics of Money*, Cambridge: Cambridge University Press.Bellavance, J.-D. (1999) "Common Currency Motion Quashed by Liberals, NDP," *National Post*, March 16, p. A7.

Bello, W. (2006) "The Capitalist Conjuncture: Over-accumulation, Financial Crises, and the Retreat from Globalization," *Third World Quarterly* 27(8): 1345–67.

Bergsten, F. (2000) "The New Asian Challenge," Institute for International Economics, *Working Paper 00–4*, March, available at http: //www.iie.com/CATALOG/WP/2000/00–4.html

Bienefeld, M. (1996) "Is a Strong National Economy a Utopian Goal at the End of the Twentieth Century?" in Boyer, R., and Drache, D. (eds) *States Against Markets: The Limits of Globalization*, London: Routledge, pp. 415–40.

BIS (Bank of International Settlements) (2005) *Triennial Central Bank Survey of Foreign Exchange and Derivatives Market Activity 2004—Final Results*, Basel: BIS.

Blainey, G. (1967) *The Tyranny of Distance: How Distance Shaped Australia's History*, Melbourne: Macmillan.

Blecker, R. (1999) *Taming Global Finance*, Washington, DC: European Policy Institute.

Boardman, M. (2000) "The Elusive Free Trade of the Americas Agreement (FTAA): Political and Economic Roadblocks to Hemispheric Economic Integration in 2005," *Mexico and the World, Web Journal* Spring, 5: 2, available at http://www.isop.ucla.edu/profmex/webjournal.htm.

Bogetic, Z. (2000) "Full Dollarization: Fad or Future?" *Challenge* 43: 2.

Bonpasse, M. (2006) *The Single Global Currency: Common Cents for the World*, Newcastle, ME: Single Global Currency Association.

Bordo, M. (2000) "Alternative Exchange Rate Regimes: The Canadian Experience1820–2000," Remarks prepared for the Bank of Canada conference "Revisiting the Case for Flexible Exchange Rates," November 1–3, Ottawa.

Bordo, M., and Helbling, T. (2003) "Have National Business Cycles Become More Synchronized?" *NBER Working Paper 10130*, December.

Bordo, M., and Redish, A. (1987) "Why Did the Bank of Canada Emerge in 1935?" *Journal of Economic History* 47(2): 405–17.

Bowitz, E., Fæhn, T., Grünfeldt, L., and Moum, K. (1997) "Can a Wealthy Economy Gain from an EU Membership? Adjustment Costs and Long Term Welfare Gains of Full Integration. The Norwegian Case," *Open Economy Review* 8: 211–31.

Bowles, P. (1997) "ASEAN, AFTA, and the 'New Regionalism,'" *Pacific Affairs* Summer 70(2): 219–33.

Bowles, P. (2002) "Asia's Post-Crisis Regionalism: Bringing the State Back In, Keeping the (United) States Out, *Review of International Political Economy* May 9(2): 230–56.

Bowles, P. (2004) "Money on the (Continental) Margins: Dollarization Pressures in Canada and Mexico," in Cohen, M., and Clarkson, S. (eds) *Governing Under Stress: Middle Powers and the Challenge of Globalization*, London: Zed Books, 197–217.

Bowles, P. (2005) "Globalization and Neoliberalism: A Taxonomy and Some Implications for Anti-globalization," *Canadian Journal of Development Studies* XXVI(1): 67–87.

Bowles, P. (2006) "The 'Tyranny of Geography' and 'Contingent Neoliberalism': Canada's Currency Debate in Comparative Context," *Current Politics and Economics of Europe* 17(2): 263–88.

Bowles, P., and Wang, B. (2006) "'Flowers and Criticism': The Political Economy of the Renminbi Debate," *Review of International Political Economy* May, 13(2): 234–58.

Bowles, P., and White, G. (1994) "Central Bank Independence: A Political Economy Approach," *Journal of Development Studies*, December, 31(2): 235–64.

Bowles, P., Croci. O., and MacLean, B. (2003) "Globalisation and Currency Convergence: What Do the Regions Tell Us?" in Busumtwi-Sam, J., and Dobuzinskis, L. (eds) *Turbulence and New Directions in Global Political Economy*, London: Palgrave, 165–98.

Bowles, P., Croci, O., and MacLean, B. (2004) "The Uses and Abuses of the Euro in Canadian Currency Debates," in Crowley, P. (ed.) *Crossing the Atlantic: Comparing the European Union and Canada*, Aldershot: Ashgate, 135–52.

Brockett, M. (2000) "Clark cuddles up to Aussie dollar," *The Dominion* (Wellington) September, 9: 1.

Broomhill, R. (2007) "The Political Economy of Australian Development in Long-run Perspective," in Bowles, P., Broomhill, R., Gutierrez-Haces, T., and McBride, S. (eds) *International Trade and Neoliberal Globalism: Towards Re-peripheralisation in Australia, Canada and Mexico?*, London: Routledge (forthcoming).

Bryan, D. (1995) *The Chase Across the Globe: International Accumulation and the Contradictions for Nation States*, Boulder, CO: Westview Press.

Bryan, D. (2002) "Bridging Differences: Value Theory, International Finance and the Construction of Global Capitalism," Paper presented at the Australian Society for Heterodox Economics conference, Sydney, December.

Bryan, D. (2004) "Australia: Asian Outpost or Big Time Financial Dealer?" in Cohen, M., and Clarkson, S. (eds) *Governing Under Stress: Middle Powers and the Challenge of Globalization*, London: Zed Books, 110–31.

Bryan, D., and Rafferty, M. (1999) *The Global Economy in Australia: Global Integration and National Economic Policy*, St. Leonards, NSW: Allen and Unwin.

Bryan, D., and Rafferty, M. (2000) "Globalization as Discipline: The Case of Australia and International Finance," in McBride, S., and Wiseman, J. (eds) *Globalization and Its Discontents*, New York: St. Martin's Press, 41–54.

Buiter, W. (1999) "The EMU and the NAMU: What is the Case for North American Monetary Union?" *Canadian Public Policy/Analyse de Politiques* September, 25(3): 285–305.

Burgess, J., Campbell, I., and May, R. (2006) "Pathways from Casual Employment to Economic Security: The Australian Experience," Mimeograph, September.

Calvo, G., and Reinhart, C. (2002) "Fear of Floating," *Quarterly Journal of Economics* 17: 379–408.

Canada Privy Council Office (1968) *Foreign Ownership and the Structure of Canadian Industry. Report of the Task Force on the Structure of Canadian Industry* (Watkins Report), Ottawa: Privy Council Office.

Carchedi, G. (2001) "Imperialism, Dollarization and the Euro," in Panitch, L., and Leys, C. (eds) *Socialist Register 2002: A World of Contradictions*, London: Merlin Press.

Carr, Jack, and Floyd, John (2001) "Real and Monetary Shocks to the Canadian Dollar: Do Canada and the U.S. Form an Optimal Currency Area?" Toronto: Department of Economics, University of Toronto, *Working Paper, UT-ECIPA-Floyd-01–02.*

Cecchini, P. (1988) *The European Challenge 1992: The Benefits of a Single Market*, Aldershot: Wildwood House.

CEESP (1998) *Propuesta de Adopción en México de un Nuevo Régimen Monetario*, Mexico City: CEESP.

Cerny, P. (2000) "Globalization and the Restructuring of the Political Arena: Paradoxes of the Competition State," in Germain, R. (ed.) *Globalization and Its Critics*, London: Palgrave Macmillan

Chapa, G., and Angel, M. (1999) "Plaza Pública/Dolarización," *Reforma*, March 15.

Chen, Yu-chin, and Rogoff, K. (2002) "Commodity Currencies and Empirical Exchange Rate Puzzles," *DNB Staff Reports No 76/2002.*

Chong, F. (2001) "Tightening Trade Ties," *The Australian*, February 6, 28.

Chortareas, G., and Pelagides, T. (2004) "Trade Flows: A Facet of Regionalism or Globalization?" *Cambridge Journal of Economics* March, 28(2): 253–72.

Christiansen, A., and Qvigstad, J. (eds) (1997) *Choosing a Monetary Policy Target*, Oslo: Scandinavian University Press

Clark, W. (2005) "Petrodollar Warfare and The Iranian Oil Bourse," Mimeograph, August 8, accessed at www.petrodollarwarfare.com/PDFs/PetrodollarWarfareAndTheIranian OilBourseWebsite.pdf, August 23, 2005.

Clarkson, S. (2002) *Uncle Sam and Us: Globalization, Neoconservatism and the Canadian State*, Toronto: University of Toronto Press.

Coates, D. (2000) *Models of Capitalism: Growth and Stagnation in the Modern Era*, Malden, MA: Polity Press.

Cobb, C. (2004) *Ego and Ink: The Inside Story of Canada's National Newspaper War*, Toronto: McClelland and Stewart.

Cohen, B. J. (1977) *Organizing the World's Money: The Political Economy of International Monetary Relations*, New York: Basic Books.

Cohen, B. (1993) "The Triad and the Unholy Trinity: Lessons for the Pacific Region," in Higgott, R., Leaver, R., and Ravenhill, J. (eds) *Pacific Economic Relations in the 1990s: Conflict or Cooperation?*, Sydney: Allen and Unwin and Boulder, CO: Lynne Rienner.

Cohen, B. (1998) *The Geography of Money*, Ithaca and London: Cornell University Press, 1998.

Cohen, B. (2004) *The Future of Money*, Princeton: Princeton University Press.

Coleman, A. (1999) "Economic Integration and Monetary Union," New Zealand Treasury, *Working Paper 99/6.*

Coleman, A. (2001) "Three Perspectives on an Australasian Monetary Union," in *Future Directions for Monetary Policy in East Asia*, Canberra: Reserve Bank of Australia.

Commission of the European Communities (1992) *From the Single Market to European Union*, Luxembourg: Office for Official Publications of the European Communities.

Commission of the European Communities (1996) *First Report on the Consideration of Cultural Aspects in European Community Action*, Brussels: European Commission.

Cooper, R. (2000) "Toward a Common Currency?" Mimeograph.

Cooper, R. (2006) "What About a World Currency? Proposals for a Common Currency Among Rich Democracies," *Bank of Greece Working Paper 44*, June.

Cooper, S. (2002) "Common Currency is a tough-love that will force us to truly compete," *Edmonton Journal*, Sunday, 3 February.

Cooper, S. (2003) "Dollarization not yet dead," *National Post*, p. FP15.

Corcoran, T. (2003) "Dollarization, anyone?" *National Post*, May 3, p. FP11.

Corcoran, T. (2005) "A Common Currency: Maybe now's the Time," *National Post*, September 29, p. FP19.

Courchene, T., and Harris, R. (1999) "From Fixing to Monetary Union: Options for North American Currency Integration," *C.D. Howe Institute Commentary 127*.

Croci, O., and Picci, L. (2002) "European Monetary Integration and Integration Theory: Insights from the Italian Case," in Verdun, A. (ed.) *The Euro: European Integration Theory and Economic and Monetary Union*, Lanham, MD: Rowman & Littlefield, 215–40.

Crosby, M., and Otto, G. (2000) "An Australia New Zealand Currency Union?" Paper presented at the Financial Markets and Policies in East Conference, Australian National University, September 4–5.

Crowley, P. (2001) "Is NAFTA an OCA?" Paper presented at the Western Economics Association meetings, Vancouver, British Columbia, Canada, July.

Crowley, P., and Rowley, J. (2002) "Exchange-rate arrangements for NAFTA: Should We Mimic the EU?" *The International Trade Journal* November, 16(4): 413–51.

Cuevas, A., Nessmacher, M., and Werner, A. (2002) "Macroeconomic Synchronization between Mexico and its NAFTA partners," World Bank, Mimeograph.

Cypher, J., and Delgado Wise, R. (2007) "Subordinate Economic Integration through the Labour-Export Model: A Perspective from Mexico," in Bowles, P., et al. (eds) *National Perspectives on Globalization: A Critical Reader*, London: Palgrave Macmillan, 27–43.

Das, D. (2004) "Structured Regionalism in the Asia-Pacific: Slow but Sure Progress," *Asia Pacific Viewpoint* 45(2): 217–33.

De Brouwer, G. (2000) "Should Pacific Island Nations Adopt the Australian Dollar?" *Pacific Economic Bulletin* 15(2): 161–9.

Dean, J. (2000) "De-facto dollarisation," Paper prepared for the North–South Institute Conference, To Dollarize or Not to Dollarize: Exchange Rate Choices for the Western Hemisphere," Ottawa, October 4–5.

Dean, J. (2001) "Should Latin America's Common Law Marriages to the US Dollar be Legalized? Should Canada's?" *Journal of Policy Modeling* 23: 291–300.

Desai, M. (2004) *Marx's Revenge: The Resurgence of Capitalism and the Death of Statist Socialism*, London: Verso.

Dieter, H. (2000) "Asia's Monetary Regionalism," *Far Eastern Economic Review* July 6: 30.

Ditchburn, J. (1998) "Bloc Mulls Over Possibility of US Dollar as Common Currency," *Canadian Press Newswire*, December 9.

Dore, C. (2000) "Clark backflip on Anzac dollar," *The Weekend Australian*, September 9: p. 4.

Dørum, Ø., Holden, S., and Isachsen, A. (2005) *Norges Bank Watch*, Oslo: Centre for Monetary Economics, BI Norwegian School of Management.

Dowd, K. (1996) "The Case for Financial Laissez-Faire," *Economic Journal* 106: 679– 87.

Duceppe, G. (2006) "Duceppe on Currency," *Globe and Mail*, August 29.

Dyson, K., and Featherstone, K. (1999) *The Road to Maastricht: Negotiating Economic and Monetary Union in Europe*, Oxford: Oxford University Press.

Dyster, B., and Meredith, D. (1997) *Australia in the International Economy in the Twentieth Century*, Cambridge University Press.

Edey, M. (2007) Assistant Governor, Economic, Reserve Bank of Australia, Address to the Australian Industry Group, Economy 2007, delivered in Sydney, March 7.

Edwards, J. (1998) "The Fifth Global Currency," *HSBC Economics and Investment Strategy*, November.

Edwards, S. (1997) "The Mexican Peso Crisis: How Much Did We Know? When Did We Know It?" *NBER Working Paper 6334*, December.

Eichengreen, B. (1997) *European Monetary Unification: Theory, Practice, and Analysis*, Cambridge, MA: MIT Press.

Eichengreen, B. (2001) "What Problems Can Dollarisation Solve?" Paper presented at the ASSA Meetings, New Orleans, January.

Eichengreen, B. (2006) "China, Asia, and the World Economy: The Implications of an Emerging Asian Core and Periphery," *China and the World Economy* 14(3): 1–18.

Eichengreen, B., and Razo-Garcia, R. (2006) "The International Monetary System in the Last and the Next 20 Years," *Economic Policy*, 395–442.

Emerson, M. (1992) *One Market, One Money: An Evaluation of the Potential Benefits and Costs of Forming an Economic and Monetary Union*, Oxford: Oxford University Press.

Emy, H.V. (1993) *Remaking Australia: The State, the Market and Australia's Future*, St Leonards, NSW: Allen and Unwin.

Fabro, Allesandra (2003) "Costello Notes Push for Trans-Tasman Currenc,y" *Australian Financial Review*, February 21.

Fagerberg, J., Cappelen, Å., Mjøset, L., and Skarstein, R. (1990). "The Decline of Social-Democratic State Capitalism in Norway," *New Left Review* 181: 60–94.

Feldstein, M., and Horioka, C. (1980) "Domestic Savings and International Capital Flows," *Economic Journal* June: 314–29.

Ferguson, N. (2001) "Globalization in Historical Perspective: The Political Dimension," Contribution to Panel Discussion, NBER Conference on "Globalization in Historical Perspective," May 4–5, California, Mimeograph.

Fiege, E., Socic, V., Fauleld, M., and Sonje, V. (2003) "Unofficial Dollarization in Latin America: Currency Substitution, Network Externalities and Irreversibility," in Salvatore, D., Dean, J., and Willett, T. (eds) *The Dollarization Debate*, Oxford: Oxford University Press.

Fieldhouse, D. (1981) *Colonialism 1870–1945: An Introduction*, London: Weidenfeld and Nicolson.

Fiess, N. (2004) "Business Cycle Synchronization and Regional Integration: A Case Study for Central America," World Bank, Mimeograph.

Fisher, R.. (2006) "A Perspective on Mexico," Remarks for the José Cuervo Tequila Talk, Institute of the Americas, La Jolla, California, April 5.

Fishman, R., and Messina, A. (eds) (2006) *The Year of the Euro: The Cultural, Social and Political Import of Europe's Common Currency*, Notre Dame, IN: University of Notre Dame Press.

Fligstein, Neil (2001) *The Architecture of Markets: An Economic Sociology of Twenty-first Century Capitalist Societies*, Princeton: Princeton University Press.

Forder, J. (2000) "Central Bank Independence and Credibility: Is There a Shred of Evidence?" *International Finance* 3(1): 167–85.

Frankel, J. (1991) "Is Japan creating a yen bloc in East Asia and the Pacific?" Paper presented to the NBER conference on "Japan and the U.S. in Pacific Asia," Del Mar, CA, April 3–5.

Frankel, J. (ed.) (1998) *The Regionalization of the World Economy*, Chicago: University of Chicago Press.

Frankel, J., and Rose, A. (1998) "The Endogenity of the Optimum Currency Area Criteria," *Economic Journal* 108(449): 1009–25.

Frankel, J., and Rose, A. (2000) "An Estimate of the Effect of Currency Unions on Trade and Growth," *NBER Working Paper 7857*.

Frankel, J., and Roubini, N. (2001). "The Role of Industrial Country Policies in Emerging Market Crises," *NBER Working Paper 8634*, December.

Frankel, J., and Wei, Shang-Jin (1998) "Open Regionalism in a World of Continental Trading Blocs," *NBER Working Paper 5272.*

Frankman, M. (2002) "Beyond the Tobin Tax: Global Democracy and a Global Currency," *Annals of the American Academy of Political and Social Science* 581(1): 62–73.

Frieden, J. (1994) "Exchange Rate Politics: Contemporary Lessons from American History," *Review of International Political Economy* 1(1): 81–103.

Friedland, J. (1998) "Mexicans Quietly Mull Tying Peso To Dollar," *Wall Street Journal*, September 28.

Friedman, M. (1953) "The Case for Flexible Exchange Rates," in *Essays in Positive Economics*, Chicago: University of Chicago Press.

Friedman, T. (2005) *The World is Flat: A Brief History of the Twenty-First Century*, New York: Farrar, Straus and Giroux.

Gallagher, J., and Robinson, R. (1953) "The Imperialism of Free Trade," *Economic History Review* 6(1): 1–15.

Garnaut, R. (2000) "One System, Two Countries: Australia and New Zealand in the International Community," Paper presented at the Conference of the New Zealand Institute of International Affairs, Wellington, July 5.

Garnaut, R. (2003) "Buoyant through the bad times," *The Australian*, December 9.

Gaulier, G., Lemoine, F., and Unal-Kesenci, D. (2006) "China's Reemergence and the Reorganization of Trade Flows in Asia," *CEPII Working Paper No. 2006–05*, March.

Geyer, R. (2000) "Just Say No! Norwegian Social Democrats and the European Union," in Geyer, R., Ingebritsen, C., and Moses, J. (eds) *Globalization, Europeanization and the End of Scandinavian Social Democracy?*, London: Macmillan, 179–97.

Giavazzi, F., and Giovannini, A. (1989) *Limiting Exchange Rate Flexibility: The European Monetary System*, Cambridge, MA: MIT Press.

Gilbert, E., and Helleiner, E. (eds) (1999) *Nation States and Money: The Past, Present and Future of National Currencies*, London: Routledge.

Gill, S. (2003) *Power and Resistance in the New World Order*, Basingstoke: Palgrave Macmillan.

Glick, R., and Rose, A. (1999) "Contagion and Trade: Why Are Currency Crises Regional?" *Journal of International Money and Finance* 18(4): 603–17.

Goldman Sachs (2003) "Dreaming with BRICs—The Path to 2050," *Global Economics Papers*, No. 99.

Government of Australia, Department of Foreign Affairs and Trade (2007) Monthly Trade Data, avalailable at www.dfat.gov.au/publications/stats.html.

Gratton, M. (1994) "The Float: An Economic and Political Discipline," *Economic Papers* 13: 41–5.

Greenfield, C. and Williams, P. (2000) "Media Rhetoric on the Dollar: The Battles of 'Our Dollar,'" *Journal of Australian Political Economy* 46: 22–30.

Greenspan, A. (2004) Remarks on "Globalization and Innovation," at the Conference on Bank Structure and Competition, sponsored by the Federal Reserve Bank of Chicago, Chicago, IL, May 6.

Grimes, A., and Holmes, F., with Bowden, R. (2000) *An ANZAC Dollar? Currency Union and Business Development*, Wellington: Institute of Policy Studies.

Grubel, H. (1999) "The Case for the Amero: The Economics and Politics of a North American Monetary Union," *Critical Issues Bulletin*, Vancouver: The Fraser Institute, September.

Gruen, D., and Stevens, G. (2000) "Australia's Macroeconomic Performance and Politics in the 1990s," in *The Australian Economy in the 1990s*, Canberra: Reserve Bank of Australia.

Guillén, A. (2004) *México: Régimen cambiario e integración en el marco del Tratado de libre comercio de América del Norte* Mexico City: UAMI, Área de Economía Política.

Guillén, M. F. (2003) *The Limits of Convergence: Globalization and Organizational Change in Argentina, South Korea and Spain*, Princeton: Princeton University Press.

Hanke, S. (2003) "It's Time for Mexico to Dollarize," *Wall Street Journal*, May 30 (Internet edition).

Harris, N. (1993) "Mexican Trade and Mexico–US Economic Relations," in Harvey, N. (ed.) *Mexico: Dilemmas of Transition*, New York: St Martin's, 151–72.

Harris, R. (2001a) "Is There a Case for Exchange-Rate-Induced Productivity Changes?" in *Revisiting the Case for Flexible Exchange Rates*, Proceedings of a conference held at the Bank of Canada, November 2000: 277–309.

Harris, R. (2001b) "Mundell and Friedman: Four Key Disagreements," *Policy Options/ Options Politiques*, May.

Harvey, C. (2003) "US Free Trade Deal 'Has Downside,'" *The Weekend Australian*, March 15: 34.

Harvey, D. (2003) *The New Imperialism*, Oxford: Oxford University Press.

Haug, A. (2001) "Co-Movement Towards A Currency of Monetary Union? An Empirical Study for New Zealand," *Australian Economic Papers*, September 307–15.

Hawkins, J., and Masson, P. (2003) "Economic Aspects of Regional Currency Areas and the Use of Foreign Currency," *BIS Papers No. 17*.

Hayek, F. von (1976) "Choice in Currency: A Way to Stop Inflation," *IEA Occasional Paper 48*.

He, B. (2004) "East Asian Ideas of Regionalism: A Normative Critique," *Australian Journal of International Affairs* 58(1): 105–25.

Held, D., McGrew, A., Goldblatt, D. and Perraton, J. (eds) (1999) *Global Transformations: Politics, Economics and Culture*, Stanford: Stanford University Press.

Helleiner, E. (1994) *States and the Re-emergence of Global Finance: From Bretton Woods to the 1990s*, Ithaca: Cornell University Press.

Helleiner, E. (1999) "Denationalising Money? Economic Liberalism and the 'National Question' in Currency Affairs," in Gilbert, E., and Helleiner, E. (eds) *Nation States and Money: The Past, Present and Future of National Currencies*, London: Routledge, 139–58.

Helleiner, E. (2003) *The Making of National Money: Territorial Currencies in Historical Perspective*, Ithaca: Cornell University Press.

Helleiner, E. (2004a) "Canada as a 13th Reserve District? Federalism and the Governance of North American Monetary Union," *Canadian Foreign Policy* 11(2): 91–109.

Helleiner, E. (2004b) "Why Would Nationalists Not Want a National Currency? The Case of Quebec," in Helleiner, E., and Pickel, A (eds) *Economic Nationalism in a Globalizing World*, Ithaca: Cornell University Press, 270–99.

Helleiner, E. (2004c) "The Strange Politics of Canada's NAMU Debate," *Studies in Political Economy* 71(2): 67–99.

Helleiner, E. (2005a) "The Fixation with Floating: The Politics of Canada's Exchange Rate Regime," *Canadian Journal of Political Science* 38(1): 1–22.

Helleiner, E. (2005b) "The Strange Story of Bush and the Argentine Debt Crisis," *Third World Quarterly* 26: 5.

Helleiner, E. (2006) *Towards North American Monetary Union: A Political History of Canada's Exchange Rate Regime*, Montreal: McGill-Queen's University Press.

Helliwell, J. (1998) *How Much Do National Borders Matter?* Washington, DC: Brookings Institution.

Hensmann, R., and Correggia, M. (2005) "US Dollar Hegemony: The Soft Underbelly of Empire," *Economic and Political Weekly*, March 19.

Henton, D. (1999) "Alberta Treasury Examining Effects of Common Currency," *Calgary Herald*, June 24: A12.

Hirst, P., and Thompson, G. (1996) *Globalization in Question: The International Economy and the Possibilities of Governance,* Cambridge: Polity Press.

Hobson, J., and Ramesh, M. (2002) "Globalization Makes of States What States Make of It: Between Agency and Structure in the State/Globalization Debate," *New Political Economy* 7(1): 5–22.

Hosking, R. (2002) "Anzac Dollar Dies," *The National Business Review* (New Zealand) November 29: 1.

House of Representatives Standing Committee on Economics, Finance and Public Administration (2001) *International Financial Markets—Friends or Foes?* Canberra: The Parliament of the Commonwealth of Australia, March.

Hunter, J. (2001) "US dollar would lift our economy 37%," *National Post*, May 19.

Ibarra, D., and Moreno-Brid, J. (2001) "Currency Boards and Monetary Unions: The Road Ahead or a Cul De Sac for Mexico's Exchange Rate Policy?" in Puchet-Anyul, M., and Punzo, L. (eds) *Mexico Beyond NAFTA: Perspectives for the European Debate*, London: Routledge, 16–7.

IMF (2000) Symposium on "One World, One Currency: Destination or Delusion?" November 8, available at http://www.imf.org/external/np/tr/2000/tr001108.htm.

Independent Task Force (2005) *Building a North American Community: Report of the Independent Task Force on the Future of North America*, May.

Issing, O. (2000) "Hayek, Currency Competition and European Monetary Union," *IEA Occasional Paper 111*, London: Institute of Ecnonomic Affairs.

Jacques, M. (2004) "Face it: no one cares," *The Guardian*, July 29 (Internet edition).

Johnson, C. (2000) *Blowback: The Costs and Consequences of American Empire*, New York: Metropolitan Books.

Katz, F. (1991) "The Liberal Republic and the Porfiriato, 1867–1910," in Bethell, L. (ed.) *Mexico Since Independence*, Cambridge: Cambridge University Press, 49–124.

Katzenstein, P. (2005) *A World of Regions: Asia and Europe in the American Imperium*, Ithaca: Cornell University Press.

Kearney, C. (1997) "International Finance and Exchange Rate Policy," in Kriesler, P. (ed.) *The Australian Economy*, St. Leonards, NSW: Allen and Unwin.

Keay, I. (2000) "Canadian Manufacturers' Relative Productivity Performance 1907– 1990," *Canadian Journal of Economics* 33(4): 1049–68.

Kelly, P. (1992) *The End of Certainty: The Story of the 1980s*, St. Leonards, NSW: Allen and Unwin.

Kessler, T. (2000) "The Mexican Peso Crash: Causes, Consequences and Comeback," in Wise, C., and Roett, R. (eds) *Exchange Rate Politics in Latin America*, Washington, DC: Brookings Institution Press.

Kiernan, V. (2005) *America: The New Imperialism*, London: Verso.

Kindleberger, C. (1986) *The World in Depression 1929–39*, Berkeley: University of California Press.

King, D. (2003) "Call for a Single Anzac Currency," *The Dominion Post* (Wellington, New Zealand), April 30: 3.

Knight, A. (1991) "The Rise and Fall of Cardenismo c.1930–c.1946," in Bethell, L. (ed.) *Mexico Since Independence*, Cambridge: Cambridge University Press, 241–320.

Kose, M., Meredith, G., and Towe, C. (2004) "How Has NAFTA Affected the Mexican Economy? Review and Evidence," *IMF Working Paper, WP/04/59*, April.

Krishna, P. (2005) *Trade Blocs: Economics and Politics*, Cambridge: Cambridge University Press.

Krueger, A. (1999) "Are Preferential Trade Agreements Trade Liberalizing or Protecting?" *Journal of Economic Perspectives* 13(4): 105–24.

Kruse, D. (1980) *Monetary Integration in Western Europe: EMU, EMS and Beyond*, London: Butterworth.

Laidler, D. (1999) "What Do the Fixers Want to Fix? The Debate About Canada's Exchange Rate Regime," *C.D. Howe Institute Commentary* 131 (December).

Larrain, F., and Tavares, J. (2003) "Regional Currencies versus Dollarization: Options for Asia and the Americas," *Journal of Policy Reform* 6(1): 35–49.

Le, A., and Miller, P. (2000) "Australia's Unemployment Problem," *The Economic Record* March, 767(232): 74–104.

Leaver, R. (2001) "Australia in Asia," Paper presented at the workshop Regional Integration in the Pacific Rim: Global and Domestic Trajectories, held at the University of Technology Sydney, July.

Linklater, J. (1992) *Inside the Bank: The Role of the Reserve Board of Australia in the Economic, Banking and Financial Systems*, St. Leonards NSW: Allen and Unwin.

Lipsey, R., Blomstrom, M., and Ramstetter, E. (1995) "International Production in World Output," *NBER Working Paper No. 5385*.

Lucas, R. (2000) "Some Macroeconomics for the 21st Century," *Journal of Economic Perspectives*, Winter, 14(1): 159–68.

Ludlow, P. (1982) *The Making of the European Monetary System: A Case Study of the Politics of the European Community*, London: Butterworth.

McBride, S. (2005) *Paradigm Shift: Globalization and the Canadian State*, 2nd edition, Halifax: Fernwood Press.

McCallum, J. (1999) "Seven Issues in the Choice of Exchange Rate Regime for Canada," *Current Analysis*, Royal Bank of Canada, February: 1–10.

McCallum, J. (2000) "Engaging the Debate: Costs and Benefits of a North American Common Currency," *Current Analysis*, Royal Bank of Canada, April: 1–9.

MacFarlane, I. (1999) "Australian Monetary Policy in the Last Quarter of the Twentieth Century," *The Economic Record*, September, 75(230): 213–24.

McGrew, T. (2001) "Review of 'Globalization: A Critical Introduction' by Jan Aart Scholte," *New Political Economy* 6(2): 293–301.

McKinnon, R. (2005) "The World Dollar Standard and Globalization: New Rules for the Game?" Mimeograph, September. Revised version.

Macklem, K. (2002) "Stocks: Had 'X' Today?" *Maclean's Magazine*, May 6.

MacLean, B., and Osberg, L. (eds) (1996) *The Unemployment Crisis: All For Nought?* Montreal-Kingston: McGill-Queen's University Press.

McNamara, K. (1998) *The Currency of Ideas: Monetary Politics in the European Union*, Ithaca: Cornell University Press.

McQuaig, L. (1998) *The Cult of Impotence: Selling the Myth of Powerlessness in the Global Economy*, Toronto: Viking.

McQueen, H. (2001) *The Essence of Capitalism: The Origins of Our Future*, Sydney: Hodder Headline.

Maddock, R. and McLean, I. (1987) "The Australian Economy in the Very Long Run" in Maddock, R. and McLean, I. (eds) *The Australian Economy in the Very Long Run*, Cambridge: Cambridge University Press, 5–32.

Magdoff, H. (2003) *Imperialism Without Colonies*, New York: Monthly Review Press.

Mair, J. (2005) "How the Appreciation of the Canadian Dollar Has Affected Canadian Firms, Evidence from the Bank of Canada Business Outlook Survey," *Bank of Canada Review*, Autumn: 19–25.

Marr, G. (2003) "CEOs certain loonie will hit US71cents," *Financial Post*, March 3.

Masson, P., and Pattillo, C. (2004) *The Monetary Geography of Africa*, Washington, DC: Brookings Institution.

Meltzer, A. (1998) "Asian Problems and the IMF," *Cato Journal* 17: 3.

Menon, J. (1994) "Exchange Rate Pass-Through in the 1980s: The Case of Australian Manufactured Exports" in Johnson, M., Kriesler, P., and Owen, A. (eds) *Issues in Australian Economics*, St. Leonards: Allen and Unwin, 40–56.

Meredith, D., and Dyster, B. (1999) *Australia in the Global Economy: Continuity and Change*, Cambridge: Cambridge University Press.

Meyer, J. (1991) "Revolution and Reconstruction in the 1920s," in Bethell, L. (ed.) *Mexico Since Independence*, Cambridge: Cambridge University Press, 201–40.

Ministry of Finance and Customs (Norway) (1999) "EMU—Implications for Norway," Oslo: Ministry of Finance and Customs.

Mitchell, W., and Carlson, E. (eds) (2001) *Unemployment: The Tip of the Iceberg*, Sydney: CAER/UNSW Press.

Mittelman, J. (2000) *The Globalization Syndrome: Transformation and Resistance*, Princeton: Princeton University Press.

Monbiot, G. (2003) "The Bottom Dollar," *The Guardian*, April 22.

Moreno-Brid, J.C., and Ros, J. (2004) "Mexico's Market Reforms in Historical Perspective," Working Papers on Latin America, Paper No. 04/05–1 Cambridge, MA: The David Rockefeller Center for Latin American Studies.

Moreno Brid, J.C. and Rozo, C. (2000) "Teoría y Condiciones de la Dolarización en México," *Comercio Exterior*, October, 50: 10.

Moreno-Brid, J.C., Ruiz, P., and Rivas, J.C. (2005) "NAFTA and the Mexican Economy: A Look Back on a Ten-year Relationship," *North Carolina Journal of International Law and Commercial Regulation* 30(4): 997–1024.

Moreno-Brid, J.C., Santamaria, J., and Rivas, J.C. (2005) "Industrialization and Economic Growth in Mexico after NAFTA: The Road Traveled," *Development and Change* 36(6): 1095–119.

Mundell, R. (1961) "A Theory of Optimum Currency Areas," *The American Economic Review*, September, 51(4): 657–65.

Mundell, R. (2000) "One World Currency," *National Post*, April 10.

Mundell, R. (2003) "Currency Areas, Exchange Rate Systems, and International Monetary Reform," in Salvatore, D., Dean, J., and Willett, T. (eds) *The Dollarization Debate*, Oxford: Oxford University Press, 17–45.

Mundell, R., and Friedman M. (2001) "One World, One Money? Symposium," *Policy Options/Options Politiques*, May: 10–30.

Murray, J. (2000) "Why Canada Needs a Flexible Exchange Rate," *North American Journal of Economics and Finance* 11: 41–60.

Murray, J., and Powell, J. (2002) "Dollarization in Canada (The Buck Stops There)," Mimeograph, April.

Murray, J., Schembri, L., and St-Amant, P. (2002) "Revisiting the Case for Flexible Exchange Rates in North America," Paper presented at conference on Exchange Rates, Economic Integration and the International Economy, Ryerson University, Toronto, May 17–19.

Nasution, A. (2005) "Regional Financial Arrangements in East Asia," Paper presented at UNU-WIDER conference on the Future of Development Economics, Helsinki.

Naughton, B. (ed.) (1997) *The China Circle: Economics and Technology in the PRC, Taiwan and Hong Kong*, Washington, DC: Brookings Institution Press.

Navarro, V., Schmitt, J., and Astudillo, J. (2004) "Is Globalization Undermining the Welfare State?" *Cambridge Journal of Economics* 28(1): 133–52.

Neill, B. (2001) "Peso Shows Value of Keeping Dollar," *The Christchurch Press*, November 17: 2.

Nelsen, B. (1993) "Norway, the European Community, and the Integration Process," in Nelsen, B. (ed.) *Norway and the European Community: The Political Economy of Integration*, Westport, CT: Praeger.

Newhouse, J. (1997) "Europe's Rising Regionalism," *Foreign Affairs*, January– February.

Norrie, K., and Owram, D. (2002) *A History of the Canadian Economy*, Toronto: Thomson Nelson.

Notermans, T. (2000) "Europeanization and the Crisis of Scandinavian Social Democracy," in Geyer, R., Ingebritsen, C., and Moses, J. (eds) *Globalization, Europeanization and the End of Scandinavian Social Democracy?* London: Macmillan, 23–44.

Oatley, T. (1997) *Monetary Politics: Exchange Rate Cooperation in the European Union*, Ann Arbor: University of Michigan Press.

Obstfeld, M., and Rogoff, K. (2000) "The Six Major Puzzles in International Macroeconomics: Is There a Common Cause?" *NBER Working Paper 7777*, July.

Obstfeldt, M., Shambaugh, J., and Taylor, A. (2005) "The Trilemma in History: Tradeoffs Among Exchange Rates, Monetary Policy and Capital Mobility," *Review of Economics and Statistics*, August 87(3): 423–38.

Ohmae, K. (1990) *The Borderless World*, London: Collins.

Østerud, O. (2004) "Globalization in Norwegian: Peculiarities at the European Fringe" in Cohen, M., and Clarkson, S. (eds) *Governing Under Stress: Middle Powers and the Challenge of Globalization*, London: Zed Books, 33–50.

O'Sullivan, F. (2007) "Clark Warning over Anzac Dollar Support," *New Zealand Herald*, April 23, internet edition [accessed May 10, 2007].

Padoa-Schioppa, T. (1994) *The Road to Monetary Union in Europe: The Emperor, the Kings, and the Genies*, Oxford: Clarendon Press.

Panitch, L. and Gindin, S. (2004) "Global Capitalism and American Empire," in *The New Imperial Challenge, Socialist Register 2004*, New York: Monthly Review Press.

Panitch, L., and Gindin, S. (2005) "Finance and American Empire," in *The Empire Reloaded, Socialist Register 2005*, 46–82.

Parham, D. (2002) "Productivity Growth in Australia: Are We Enjoying a Miracle?" *Staff Working Paper*, Canberra: Productivity Commission.

Parham, D. (2003) "Australia's 1990s Productivity Surge and its Determinants," Mimeograph.

Parizeau, J. (1999) "Globalization and National Interests: The Adventure of Liberalization," in MacLean, B. (ed.) *Out of Control: Canada in an Unstable Financial World*, Toronto: James Lorimer and CCPA, 3–15.

Perkens, T. (2007) "Euro's success raises currency debate; Economist says 'now is the time' to discuss North American dollar," *Toronto Star*, January 3: F1.

Petras, J., and Veltmeyer, H. (2001) *Globalization Unmasked: Imperialism in the 21st Century*, London: Zed Books

Petras, J., Veltmeyer, H., Vasapollo, L., and Casadio, M. (2006) *Empire with Imperialism*, London: Zed Books.

Pierson, C. (2002) "'Social Democracy on the Back Foot': The ALP and the 'New' Australian Model," *New Political Economy* 7(2): 179–97.

Pilat, D. (2005) "Canada's Productivity Performance in International Perspective," *International Productivity Monitor* 10: 24–44.

Pomfret, R. (1993) *The Economic Development of Canada*, 2nd edition, Scarborough, Ontario: Nelson.

Pomfret, R. (2002) "Monetary Integration in East Asia: Lessons from Europe," Paper presented at the 8th Convention of the East Asian Economic association, Kuala Lumpur, November 4–5.

Poon, J.P.H., Thompson E.R., and Kelly P.F. (2000) "Myth of the triad? The geography of trade and investment 'blocs,'" *Transactions of the Institute of British Geographers* 25(4): 427–44.

Pope, D. (1987) "Population and Australian Economic Development 1900–1930," in Maddock, R., and McLean, I. (eds) *The Australian Economy in the Very Long Run*, Cambridge: Cambridge University Press, 33–60.

Porter, T. (2005) *Globalization and Finance*, Cambridge: Polity Press.

Powell, J. (1999) *A History of the Canadian Dollar*, Ottawa: Bank of Canada.

Productivity Commission (1999) *Microeconomic Reforms and Australian Productivity: Exploring the Links,* Commission Research Paper, Canberra: Productivity Commission.

Pusey, M. (1991) *Economic Rationalism in Canberra: A Nation-building State Changes Its Mind*, Melbourne: Cambridge University Press.

Quintana, E. (1999) Coordenadas/Más allá de la dolarización, *Reforma*, February 23.

Radice, H. (2000) "Globalization and National Capitalisms: Theorising Convergence and Differentiation," *Review of International Political Economy* 7(4): 719–42.

Ranald, P. (2007) "The Australia–US Free Trade Agreement (AUSTFA): Reinforcing Reperipheralisation," in Bowles, P., Broomhill, R., Gutierrez-Haces, T., and McBride, S. (eds) *International Trade and Neoliberal Globalism: Towards Re-peripheralisation in Australia, Canada and Mexico?* London: Routledge.

Rao, S., and Sharpe, A. (2002) *Productivity Issues in Canada*, Industry Canada Research Series volume 10, Calgary: University of Calgary Press.

Rogoff, K. (2001) "Why Not A Single World Currency?" *American Economic Review Papers and Proceedings* May, 91(2): 243–6.

Rogoff, K. (2007) "The Way Forward for Global Financial Policy," *Project Syndicate*, April 13.

Rose, A. (2000) "One Money, One Market: Estimating the Effect of Common Currency on Trade," *Economic Policy*, April: 7–46.

Rose, A., and Stanley, T. (2005) "A Meta-Analysis of the Effects of Common Currencies on International Trade," *Journal of Economic Surveys*, July, 19(3): 347–65.

Rose, A., and van Wincoop, E. (2001) "National Money as a Barrier to International Trade: The Real Case for Currency Union," *American Economic Review* 91: 386–90.

Rosewarne, S. (1999) "Review Article: False Paradise," *Journal of Australian Political Economy* 43: 124–35.

Rowbotham, M. (2000) *Globalization, Debt and the Dollar Empire*, London: Jon Carpenter Publishing.

Rubin, S. (2001) "Loonie Gone Within Five Years, says CIBC's Rubin," *National Post*, July 28.

Ruggie, J. (1983) "International Regimes, Transactions and Change," *International Organization* 36(2): 379–405.

Rugman, A. (2000) *The End of Globalization*, London: Random House Business Books.

Rycroft, R. (2002) "Technology-Based Globalization Indicators: The Centrality of Innovation Network Data," *GW Center for the Study of Globalization Occasional Paper, CSGOP-02-09*, October.

Salinas-León, R. (1998) "Mexico Opts for 'So-So' Monetary Independence," *Cato Institute Daily*, January 30.

Saul, J. R. (2005) *The Collapse of Globalism and the Reinvention of the World*, Toronto: Viking Canada.

Saxena, S. (2004) "The Changing Nature of Currency Crises," *Journal of Economic Surveys* 18(3)32–50.

Schedvin, C.B. (1992) *In Reserve: Central Banking in Australia 1945–1975*, St. Leonards, NSW: Allen and Unwin.

Schiff, M., and Winters, L. (2003) *Regional Integration and Development*, Washington, DC: World Bank.

Scholte, J. (2000) *Globalization: A Critical Introduction*, New York: St. Martin's Press.

Scott, A. (2005) *Regions and the World Economy: The Coming Shape of Global Production, Competition and Political Order*, Oxford: Oxford University Press.

Seccareccia, M. (2002) "North American Monetary Integration: Should Canada Join the Dollarization Bandwagon?" Mimeograph, February.

Shore, C. (2000) *Building Europe: The Cultural Politics of European Integration*, London: Routledge.

Siddiqi, M. (2000) "A Single Currency for W Africa?" *African Business* September, 257: 16–7.

Smith, P. (1991) "Mexico Since 1946: Dynamics of an Authoritarian Regime," in Bethell, L. (ed.) *Mexico Since Independence*, Cambridge: Cambridge University Press, 321–96.

Spiro, D. (1999) *The Hidden Hand of American Hegemony: Petrodollar Recycling and International Markets*, Ithaca: Cornell University Press.

Standing Senate Committee on Foreign Affairs (Canada) (1998) "Crisis in Asia: Implications for the Region, Canada, and the World," Ottawa: The Senate.

Stanford, J. (1999) "Waving the Flag for the Loonie," *Canadian Dimension*, Fall, 33(4–5): 14–15.

Starr, P. (2002) "Dollarization in Mexico: Does It Make Sense and Is It Likely?" in Cira, C., and Gallo, E. (eds) *Dollarization and Latin America: Quick Cure or Bad Medicine?* Miami: Latin American and Caribbean Center, International University.

Storper, M. (2005) *The Regional World: Territorial Development in a Global Economy*, New York: The Guilford Press.

Strange, S. (1997) *The Retreat of the State*, Cambridge: Cambridge University Press.

Stubbs, R. (1995) "Asia-Pacific Regionalization and The Global Economy: A Third Form of Capitalism?" *Asian Survey*, September, XXXV: 9.

Stymiest, B. (2002) "Corporate Myths," *Financial Post*, May 10.

Sultan, R. (1999) "The Case for Dollarization," *National Post*, May 17: C5.

Summers, L. (1999) Testimony to The Senate Banking Committee Subcommittee on Economic Policy and Subcommittee on International Trade and Finance, April 22, see http://wwww.ustreas.gov/press/releases/pr3098.htm.

Tavlas, G. (1994) " The Theory of Monetary Integration," *Open Economies Review* 5(2): 211–30.

Taylor, A. (2000) "Dollarisation as a Technology Import," *Federal Reserve Bank of San Francisco Economic Letter*, May 19. Available at http://www.frbsf.org/econrsrch/wklyltr/2000/el2000-16.html.

Taylor, K. (2004) "Anzac dollar splits firms," *New Zealand Herald*, May 15.

Teeple, G. (2000) "What is Globalization?" in McBride, S., and Wiseman, J. (eds) *Globalization and its Discontents*, Basingstoke: Macmillan, 9–23.

Temperton, P. (ed.) (1998) *The Euro*, Chichester: J. Wiley.

The Economist (1995) "The Myth of the Powerless State," October 7.

Trigger, B. (1985) *Natives and Newcomers: Canada's "Heroic Age" Reconsidered*, Montreal: McGill-Queens University Press.

Tsoukalis, L. (1977) *The Politics and Economics of European Monetary Integration*, London: George Allen and Unwin.

UNCTC (1991) *The Triad in Foreign Investment*, New York: United Nations.

UNCTC (1999) World Investment Report, New York: United Nations.

UNCTC (2006) World Investment Report, New York: United Nations.

van Beynen, M. (2000) "Australia Dismissive of PM's Joint Dollar," *The Press* (Christchurch) September 14: 3.

van Ham, P. (2001) "The Rise of the Brand State," *Foreign Affairs*, September–October, 80(5): 2–7.

Verdun, A. (1999) "The Role of the Delors Committee in the Creation of EMU: An Epistemic Community?" *Journal of European Public Policy* 6(2): 308–28.

Vertora, G. (2006) Introduction: "Reinventing Space," in Vertora, G. (ed.) *The Changing Economic Geography of Globalization*, London: Routledge.

Veseth, M. (1998) *Selling Globalization: The Myth of the Global Economy*, Boulder, CO: Lynne Rienner Publishers.

Veseth, M. (2005) *Globaloney: Unravelling the Myths of Globalization*, Lanham, MD: Rowman and Littlefield.

Villareal, R. (1981) *El desequilibrio externo en la industrialización de México (1929–1975)*, Mexico City: Fondo de Cultura Económica.

Wade, R. (1996) "Globalization and its Limits: Reports of the Death of the National Economy are Greatly Exaggerated," in Berger, A., and Dore, R. (eds) *National Diversity and Global Capitalism*, Ithaca: Cornell University Press.

Wade, R. (2003) "The Invisible Hand of the American Empire," *Ethics and International Affairs* 17(2): 77–88.

Wade, R. (2006) "The Case for a Global Currency," *International Herald Tribune*, August 5.

Walter, A. (1991) *World Power and World Money*, Cambridge: Cambridge University Press.

Watkins, M. (1967) "A Staple Theory of Economic Growth," in Easterbrooke, W., and Watkins, M. (eds) *Approaches to Canadian Economic History*, Toronto: McClelland and Stewart, 47–74.

Weir, E. (2007) "The Canada–US Free Trade Agreement and NAFTA," in Bowles, P., Broomhill, R., Gutierrez-Haces, T., and McBride, S. (eds) *International Trade and Neoliberal Globalism: Towards Re-peripheralisation in Australia, Canada and Mexico?* London: Routledge (forthcoming).

Weiss, L. (1998) *The Myth of the Powerless State*, Ithaca, NY: Cornell University Press.

Willett, T. (2003) "The OCA Approach to Exchange Rate Regimes: A Perspective on Recent Developments," in Salvatore, D., Dean, J., and Willett, T. (eds) *The Dollarization Debate*, Oxford: Oxford University Press, 154–71.

Williamson, J. (2000) *Exchange Rate Regimes for Emerging Markets: Reviving the Intermediate Option*, Policy Analyses in International Economics 60, September.

Wolf, M. (2004) "We Need a Global Currency," *Financial Times*, August 3.

Womack, J. (1991) "The Mexican Revolution, 1910–1920," in Bethell, L. (ed.) *Mexico Since Independence*, Cambridge: Cambridge University Press, 125–200.

World Bank (2002) *World Bank Indicators*, New York: Oxford University Press.

World Bank (2004) *World Bank Indicators*, New York: Oxford University Press.

World Commission on the Social Dimensions of Globalization (2004) *A Fair Globalization?* February, available at: http://www.ilo.org/public/english/fairglobalization/report/index.htm.

Yarborough, B., and Yarborough, R. (1994) "Regionalism and Layered Governance: The Choice of Trade Institutions," *Journal of International Affairs*, Summer, 48: 1.

Yue, Chia Siow (1997) "Regionalism and Subregions in ASEAN: The Tree Trade Agreement and Growth Triangle Models," in Takatoshi, I., and Krueger, A. (eds) *Regional Versus Multilateral Trade Arrangements*, Chicago: University of Chicago Press

Zevin, R. (1992) "Are World Financial Markets More Open? If So, Why and With What Effects?" in Banuri, T., and Schor, J. (eds) *Financial Openness and National Autonomy: Opportunities and Constraint*, Oxford: Clarendon Press, 43–84.

Zhang, Y. (2005) "Emerging New East Asian Regionalism," *Asia Pacific Review* 12(1): 55–63.

Index